ALEXANDER HAMILTON

Ambivalent Anglophile

LAWRENCE S. KAPLAN

IN AMERICAN FOREIGN POLICY

Number 9

SR BOOKS

A Scholarly Resources Inc. Imprint
Wilmington, Delaware

© 2002 by Scholarly Resources Inc.
All rights reserved
First published 2002
Printed and bound in the United States of America

Scholarly Resources Inc.
104 Greenhill Avenue
Wilmington, DE 19805-1897
www.scholarly.com

Library of Congress Cataloging-in-Publication Data

Kaplan, Lawrence S.
Alexander Hamilton : ambivalent Anglophile / Lawrence S.
  Kaplan.
       p. cm. — (Biographies in American foreign policy ; no. 9)
    Includes bibliographical references and index.
    ISBN 0-8420-2877-3 (alk. paper) — ISBN 0-8420-2878-1 (pbk. :
alk. paper)
       1. Hamilton, Alexander, 1757–1804. 2. Statesmen—United
States—Biography. 3. United States—Foreign relations—1775–
1783. 4. United States—Foreign relations—1783–1815. 5. United
States—Foreign relations—Great Britain. 6. Great Britain—
Foreign relations—United States. I. Title. II. Series.

E302.6.H2 K37 2002
973.4'092—dc21
[B]   2002022530

∞ The paper used in this publication meets the minimum requirements of the American National Standard for permanence of paper
for printed library materials, Z39.48, 1984.

In memory of Scott L. Bills

1948–2001

About the Author

Lawrence S. Kaplan (Ph.D., Yale, 1951) is University Professor Emeritus at Kent State University and Adjunct Professor of History at Georgetown University. His studies in the Jeffersonian era include *Jefferson and France* (reprint ed., 1980); *Colonies into Nation: American Diplomacy, 1763–1917* (1972); *Entangling Alliances with None: American Foreign Policy in the Age of Jefferson* (1987); and *Thomas Jefferson: Westward the Course of Empire* (1999).

Contents

Preface

Upon completing my dissertation on Thomas Jefferson and France in 1951, I briefly considered a counterpart study of Alexander Hamilton and Britain. I abandoned the idea at that time. Almost two generations later, Andy Fry, general editor of this biography series, and Rick Hopper at Scholarly Resources accepted my proposal to follow up my 1999 Jefferson volume with a comparable biography of Hamilton. I appreciate their support of this project. If my interpretation of Jefferson depicted him as an ambivalent Francophile, I believe that Hamilton's Anglophilia was similarly ambivalent. In brief, the distance between the two statesmen's conceptions of America's place in the world was narrower than most scholars have identified.

This study builds on the many insightful Hamilton biographies written in the twentieth century, and even a few from the nineteenth century. The twenty-seven volumes of *The Papers of Alexander Hamilton*, edited by Harold E. Syrett and Jacob E. Cooke, were indispensable for the writing of this book. Cooke's biography, published twenty years ago, comes closest to my views on Hamilton's approach to foreign relations, even though this facet was not the central theme of his book. Bradford Perkins's first volume of his magisterial trilogy, *The First Rapprochement: England and the United States, 1795–1805*, written over a half-century ago, was especially helpful in my evaluations of Hamilton's last years in power. I continue to appreciate the approach of Samuel F. Bemis to the role of Hamilton in the early Republic, even if I have strayed from his judgments. Four friends—Peter P. Hill of George Washington University, Wayne S. Cole of the University of Maryland, Stanley Bober of the Cato Institute, and Steven L. Rearden of the Joint Chiefs' Historical Office—generously agreed to read the manuscript. I am grateful for their constructive criticisms, coming as they do from perspectives somewhat different from my own. I also owe a special debt to Cristina Steele for facilitating the writing of this manuscript by her mastery of computer technology. Although my wife has reservations about my choice of subtitle in this, as in other, books, I want to thank her for the many valuable comments that she made throughout the course of its production.

Chronology

1755

Born in Nevis, British West Indies

1772

Apprenticed to Nicholas Cruger's countinghouse in Christiansted, St. Croix; dispatched to New York for further education by the Rev. Hugh Knox

1773

Attends preparatory school in Elizabethtown, New Jersey

1774

Stirs audience with speech denouncing Intolerable Acts against Boston

1775

Enrolls at King's College (now Columbia University); publishes first pamphlet, *A Full Vindication*, in response to the Rev. Samuel Seabury, and then *The Farmer Refuted*

1776

Accepts commission as captain of artillery company raised for defense of New York

1777

Appointed aide-de-camp to George Washington

1777–78

With Continental Army at Brandywine, Germantown, Valley Forge, and Monmouth

1780

Marries Elizabeth Schuyler, member of prominent New York family; shocked by Benedict Arnold's treason

1781

Breaks with General Washington over incident of Hamilton's apparent rudeness; publishes "Continentalist" pamphlets; rejoins army in time for attack on Yorktown

1782

Birth of Philip, first of eight children; without prospects for advancement, resigns from army; comments on New York State constitution; serves as receiver of taxes for state; admitted to state bar; represents state at Confederation Congress in Philadelphia

1783

Moves from Albany (home of father-in-law) to New York; opens law office

1784

Publishes "Letters from Phocion"; leads organization of Bank of New York

1785

Co-sponsors New York Society for the Manumission of Slaves

1786

Elected to New York Assembly; serves as delegate to Annapolis Convention on interstate commerce

1787

Appointed as delegate to Constitutional Convention in Philadelphia; advocates national government "able to support itself without the interference of the state governments"

1787–1789

Collaborates with John Jay and James Madison on *Federalist Papers* under pseudonym of "Publius"

1788

Argues Federalist position before Constitution's ratifying convention in Poughkeepsie; presses General Washington to accept office of president

1789

Appointed secretary of the treasury

1790

Moves to Philadelphia; talks with British agent regarding Nootka Sound dispute

1790–91

Issues reports on public credit, central bank, and manufactures

1791

Begins liaison with Maria Reynolds

1792

Answers charges against him of misdirecting public funds to pay blackmail over relationship with Mrs. Reynolds

1793

Takes advantage of Genet affair to warn of threat to U.S. neutrality; falls ill during yellow fever epidemic

1794

Treasury Department investigated by Congress for depositing proceeds of European loans in Bank of the United States; urges embargo on exports in protest against British seizure of American ships in West Indian trade; supports Jay's Treaty

1795

Resigns from Treasury; leaves Philadelphia for New York; serves as "gray eminence" to Federalist Party; publishes first "Camillus" essay

1796

Asked by President Washington to draft Farewell Address; favors Thomas Pinckney as Washington's successor

1797

Promotes sending peace commission to Paris; publishes pamphlet on liaison with Mrs. Reynolds

1798

XYZ affair; Alien and Sedition Acts; quasi-war with France at sea; appointed major general and inspector general

1799

Dispatches troops to quell tax resisters led by John Fries

1800

Works against John Adams's bid for presidency

1801

Son Philip killed in duel; co-founds anti-Jefferson *New-York Evening Examiner*

1802

Moves to "The Grange," his newly built house in upper Manhattan

1803

Comments on implications of Louisiana Purchase

1804

Warns New York Federalists not to support Aaron Burr for governor; killed by Burr in duel (July 12); buried in Trinity churchyard, lower Manhattan

1

The Rise of a Wunderkind

Of all the Founding Fathers of the American Republic none, with the possible exception of Thomas Jefferson, has evoked more passions and aroused more controversy than Alexander Hamilton. As with Jefferson, they originated in the political wars of the Federalist decade and still resonate two centuries later. The seemingly permanent friction between Hamiltonians and Jeffersonians, replicated in every generation, might inspire a historian to emulate the heroic effort of Merrill Peterson two decades ago to interpret the course of the nation's history from the ways in which contemporaries treated Thomas Jefferson. In the Jefferson–Jackson era, Hamilton's persona as an elitist urban aristocrat condemned him as an enemy of an expanding democratic America—an Anglophile at a time when Great Britain was the nation's major adversary, a defender of the central national bank when political pressures for decentralization doomed both the First and Second National Banks of the United States, and a spokesman for an Eastern oligarchy at a time when the westward movement assured the expansion of political rights. Such was his reputation as an enemy of the common man that his deep-seated opposition to the institution of slavery won little recognition even among northern abolitionists.

By contrast, historians after the Civil War, when America was increasingly urbanized under administrations sympathetic to the new industrial trusts, rated Hamilton as a more authentic inspiration to the Republican Party than Abraham Lincoln. Only Hamilton's aloof personality and his widely known moral lapses prever.ted him from being deified in the manner of Lincoln. But there was no doubt among leaders of the Gilded Age that

Hamilton laid out the blueprints for their America. And while the cult of Jefferson was revived under the Democratic presidencies of the twentieth century, Hamilton's aura was only slightly less bright than that of his rival. It was Franklin D. Roosevelt who fused the two traditions by consciously exploiting Hamiltonian means—a strong central government—to achieve Jeffersonian ends—the advancement of the individual's freedom of opportunity in America.

The intention of this study is not to join either the Hamiltonian or Jeffersonian camp, or to celebrate the fusion of two apparently antagonistic interpretations of American history. Rather, it is to examine Hamilton's conception of America's role in the world and the foreign policies that followed from his vision. How he acted upon his views on the course of American foreign relations is the major theme of this volume. In examining Hamilton's years as a public man, particularly in the Federalist decade of the 1790s, it should be possible to identify similarities as well as differences between Hamiltonians and Jeffersonians, and to judge just how significant both were in the formative years of the new nation.

From Nevis to New York, 1755–1772

Although Jefferson's critics have delved into every aspect of his character and career, frequently with conflicting results, there have been few questions regarding his birth and youth. Such is not the case with Hamilton. That he was illegitimate is one of the few issues about which there is consensus, although John Adams's angry description of a "bastard brat of a Scotch pedlar"[1] raises questions about the occupation of Hamilton's father. James Hamilton, the younger son of a Scottish aristocrat, was a ne'er-do-well on the British island of Nevis in the West Indies where Alexander Hamilton was born, but the label of "peddler" hardly fits. The name of his mother, Rachel Fawcett, was spelled in a variety of ways, a problem familiar to French Huguenots in English lands, and similarly, for her husband, Johan Michael Lavien, a Danish or German merchant in Danish St. Croix. Biographer Broadus Mitchell has suggested that Lavien's background was German–Jewish, based on the possibility that the name was originally Lewine or Levine, of Jewish origin.[2] But there is no doubt that James Hamilton was his father and that his mother was an adulteress, forbidden by Danish law to remarry after Lavien divorced her in 1758. Although his father paid little attention to his famous son, that son did later provide money to his improvident parent, arguably because of the distinction of the family name. Hamilton made a point of saying that his "blood is as good as that of those who plume themselves upon their ancestry."[3]

Of all the uncertainties of his early years, the date of his birth is the most prominent. Hamilton listed 1757, a claim uncontested in his lifetime when the West Indies were far from New York or Philadelphia. Given the circumstances, it is hardly surprising that Hamiltonian admirers would have no trouble accepting the date as January 11, 1757. There is better evidence, however, that he was born in 1755 rather than in 1757. In his carefully researched biography, Broadus Mitchell cited the same day, but two years earlier, as the probable date, taken from probate court records in St. Croix. The discrepancy may be dismissed, as Forrest McDonald does, as "inconsequential," except for the role it may have played in Hamilton's self-image.[4]

It would be understandable if the young immigrant cramming to complete his studies as rapidly as possible at a preparatory school in Elizabethtown, New Jersey, in 1773 should have wanted to shave off two years to minimize the age difference between him and his younger classmates It would be equally understandable if the articulate and ambitious young undergraduate at King's College in 1775 was aware of the impact his broadsides against British behavior in the colonies had upon his audience. How much more impressive it would be for him to be a Wunderkind of eighteen instead of a precocious twenty-year-old. Whether or not this consideration influenced the young immigrant has to be speculative. But the controversy provided an occasion for the Jeffersonian-inclined journal, *The William and Mary Quarterly*, to upstage the Hamiltonians by dedicating an issue to the bicentennial of his birth—in 1955. For the most part, the Spring issue of the journal was respectful in its approach, but the editors had to be aware that Hamilton's alma mater, Columbia University, formerly King's College, was preparing a bicentennial celebration for 1957.

Hamilton's family history in the West Indies placed a premium on the support of powerful patrons as well as on the spur of ambition. There was little else to count on. His father abandoned the family—Rachel and their two sons (Alexander's older brother was born in 1753)—in 1766, and his mother struggled to survive by operating a modest general store in Christiansted on St. Croix. Even this source of security was lost when Rachel died in 1768 after a brief illness. Nothing was left to her sons at her death. Johan Lavien had finally divorced her in 1759, but the terms of the divorce forbade remarriage and specifically labeled her sons as illegitimate. Aside from some thirty-four books, her meager estate was seized by her legitimate son, Peter Lavien. Small wonder that Hamilton had little to say about his mother beyond passing references in two letters. If he had more to say about his father, who lived on to 1799, it was only because of the social standing his family enjoyed in Scotland.

There is a serious disjunction between the material circumstances of an impecunious youth, with apparently just an elementary education cut short not only by his mother's death but also because of his apprenticeship to a merchant trader, and the intellectual sophistication that was evident even in his earliest writings. He seemed to have steeped himself in classical literature, gleaned perhaps from his mother's small library. He was equally adept in the intricacies of bookkeeping and trade by the age of fifteen, presumably through his association with the David Beekman & Nicholas Cruger firm, an import–export business established by two New Yorkers in Christiansted. Hamilton's precocity was of such an order that he rose quickly from a lowly apprenticeship to managing the business in the temporary absence of Nicholas Cruger.

It was not simply that he learned how to keep books or to read the poetry of Alexander Pope and the histories of Plutarch based on what appeared to be only rudimentary schooling. Rather, the remarkable elements in his early youth were his ability to write poetry with the intention of having his poems published and to engage in business correspondence as if he were the proprietor of the establishment. These accomplishments were driven by an ambition he openly proclaimed. Writing to a boyhood friend then in New York in 1769, at the age of fourteen he confessed that his ambition was such that "I contemn the grov'ling condition of a Clerk or the like, to which my Fortune &c. condemns me and would willingly risk my life tho' not my Character to exalt my Station." Although he went on to note that "my Youth excludes me from any hopes of immediate Preferment nor do I desire it, but I mean to prepare the way for futurity."[5]

He wasted little time in his preparations for a life beyond the islands. When he was sixteen he managed to have the *Royal Danish American Gazette* print poems that showed his mastery of rhyme as well as his knowledge of French. Although his poetry revealed more ambition than talent, his business correspondence reflected a maturity that lacked the presumption he had admitted in submitting his verses to the editor of the journal. Writing in November of that year on behalf of his employer, he admonished a supplier for sending flour from Philadelphia that "is really very bad, being of a most swarthy complexion & withal very untractable; the bakers complain they cannot by any means get it to rise." As a result of the inferior quality of the flour, "I conceive it highly necessary to lessen the price or probably I may be oblig'd in the end to sell it at a much greater disadvantage." With equal brashness he could instruct a ship's captain as to how he was to deliver a cargo and the schedule he was to follow. "Remember you are to make three trips this Season & unless you are very diligent, you will be too late as our Crops will be early in."[6] Such was the air of authority this youth conveyed. It was reasonable, then, for biographer Broadus Mitchell to conclude that "Cruger's countinghouse must have been his real school."[7]

It is tempting to find in Hamilton's youthful experiences the sources of his success in finance and of confidence in his managerial abilities. Given Cruger's illness, it was the sixteen-year-old Hamilton who oversaw the firm's accounts. He could give orders to a ship captain as if he were the proprietor, as he did in November 1771 when he told the captain of a ship owned by Cruger's firm to "proceed immediately to Curracoa [*sic*]. You are to deliver your Cargo there to Teleman Cruger Esqr. agreeable to your Bill of Lading, whose directions you must followe in every respect concerning the disposal of your Vessel after your arrival." He was equally comfortable in judging the differences between New York and Copenhagen flour. "There has been large quantitys of Rye Meal brought here lately from Copenhagen. . . . Tis true the quality is somewhat inferior to that of New York," but weighing the price differential, he was prepared to recommend the Danish imports.[8] It was reasonable for his absent employer to place his trust in his youthful assistant.

Most historians have accepted the foregoing versions of Hamilton's activities in the merchant house of Nicholas Cruger. The youth's correspondence is carefully recorded in the first volume of the authoritative collection, *The Papers of Alexander Hamilton*, edited by Harold C. Syrett and Jacob E. Cooke, but his signature is not appended to any of the business letters cited above. As Harold Larson has pointed out, the letters in the Hamilton Papers at the Library of Congress are copies, and, given the varying script, some of them may not be in Hamilton's hand. Larson concluded that Hamilton never really ran the business during the months that Nicholas Cruger was away, and that David Beekman managed its affairs. Young Hamilton "at best was the trusted chief clerk."[9] This skeptical look at the Hamilton saga was also speculative, fueled in good measure by the unlikelihood of a teenager's performing such responsible tasks in such a capable fashion. But even if Hamilton's wife and children put a misleading gloss on the early career of the distinguished husband and father, there could be no doubt that the countinghouse was a formative part of his education.

If the countinghouse was a teacher, so was the world in which his business operated. Danish St. Croix may have been a small island—nineteen miles long east and west and up to five miles in breadth—but its residents, English and Scots as well as Danes, were part of a larger world. This world was the vast North Atlantic community, extending from England and Spain to New York and the West Indies, inclusive of Dutch, French, English, and Spanish as well as Danish territories and populations. The economy of the island of St. Croix was built around trading its staple crop, primarily sugarcane, for supplies that only the mainlands of Europe and America could provide—lumber, livestock, foodstuffs, and manufactured goods. The contrast between the tiny Danish island and the wider world with which Hamilton dealt bred a cosmopolitanism that became a hallmark of the future leader. His circumstances were such that attachment to his native region on the order of that of a Thomas Jefferson or a John Adams was inconceivable. According to Richard Brookhiser, Hamilton's "country" was not a colony or state, as Virginia was to Jefferson or Massachusetts to Adams.[10]

His experience was initially with an Atlantic world, not just the islands of his childhood and early youth. And if he made New York his home, it was not as a New Yorker but as an American immigrant with the new nation as the object of his fealty. In this respect he was as fortunate as Napoleon. Both moved from an offshore island to what was essentially a new land, whether it was revolutionary France or revolutionary America. Bonaparte and Hamilton were twenty years old in 1789 and 1775, respectively. And both found the fluid social and political bonds sufficiently loose for an ambitious and intelligent outsider to rise to power and influence at an early age. War was a vehicle for both men. Given the opportunity the Revolution presented to young Hamilton, there was some justification for the fourteen-year-old apprentice to "wish there was a War."[11]

Even the most self-made leaders need patrons to advance their fortunes, and Hamilton was rarely without such support. His abilities won admiration not only from his employer but also from an influential Presbyterian clergyman, the Reverend Hugh Knox, through whose agency he was dispatched to New York for a more formal education. Knox's intervention could not have come too soon. Hamilton's vision of his future did not include a permanent connection with the Cruger house, particularly since his position had been reduced to that of a bookkeeper when his employer returned to St. Croix after recovering his health.

Biographer John Miller found, "It was not a war but a hurricane that gave Hamilton his opportunity of severing his connections with St. Croix."[12] When the tempest struck the island on the last day of August 1771, it left a scene of "horror and destruction . . . as if a total dissolution of nature was taking place." Such were the more reflective parts of the young man's florid account of the disaster. In another section, he anguished over the "ear-piercing shrieks of the distressed," which "were sufficient to strike astonishment into Angels." He went on to castigate himself for his "arrogance and self sufficiency . . . Oh! impotent presumptuous fool! how durst thou offend that Omnipotence, whose nod alone were sufficient to quell the destruction that hovers over thee, or crush thee into atoms."[13] This effusive elaboration on the impact of the hurricane, including his pious afterthoughts, found its way into the hands of Knox, by accident or not, who in turn passed it on for publication in the *Royal Danish American Gazette*. The hurricane was an act of nature; Hamilton's use of it was an act of will, an ability to exploit the catastrophe to advance his own fortunes. It was no coincidence that his piety included respectful reference to the role that the Danish governor-general played in helping the island to recover from the disaster.

Like Cruger, Knox was deeply impressed by the intellectual maturity of young Hamilton and proceeded to advance the ambitions of the talented youth. Unlike Cruger, he had an appreciation for the literary abilities Hamilton displayed and was impressed by his familiarity with the classics of Britain and the ancient world. It was Knox who took the initiative in dispatching him to America for the furthering of his education. Other patrons, including the Cruger family, joined in supporting Hamilton's budding career. His own family had nothing to offer. His mother's relatives had lost whatever fortune they once had, and his father continued to absent himself from Alexander's life. In place of a distant parent, poverty-stricken relatives, and a benevolent but intellectually

limited employer, Hamilton found in Knox the inspiration for scholarly achievement, moral improvement (including abhorrence of
slavery), and formal education in colonial America.

Knox's objective as a Presbyterian minister was to ready the
youth for entry into the College of New Jersey at Princeton, and so
he had him placed in a preparatory academy at Elizabethtown, New
Jersey, on the advice of the minister's influential friends, Elias
Boudinot and William Livingston. Boudinot was a trustee of the
College of New Jersey and Livingston was governor of the state. It
was through the Livingstons that Hamilton first made the acquaintance of the future Revolutionary leader, John Jay, who was married to William Livingston's daughter. Such were the valuable
political connections that the young immigrant made as he entered
the American colonies.

Hamilton's progress was rapid, although the end results were
not quite what Knox had anticipated. Given his lack of formal education, the challenge of mastering mathematics, Latin, and Greek
should have been formidable, requiring at least two to three years
for him to complete the curriculum. In fact, Hamilton, who arrived
in America in November 1772, was ready for college in less than a
year's time. But it was King's College in New York, an Anglican
school, not Presbyterian Princeton that accepted the young immigrant. Princeton rejected the terms Hamilton had proposed to that
institution, namely, to be admitted in whatever "of the classes to
which his attainments would entitle him but with the understanding that he should be permitted to advance from Class to Class
with as much rapidity as his exertions would enable him to do."[14]
This bold proposal, however, was acceptable to President Myles
Cooper of King's College.

The move from New Jersey to New York was also a move from
the Presbyterian piety that impressed Knox to King's Anglican milieu. Hamilton's piety did not change; it just seemed no longer
bound by theological divisions. A poem in the spirit of Alexander
Pope in 1772 displayed a religiosity that was ecumenical in spirit.
Robert Troup, his college roommate and lifelong friend, observed
his "habit of praying upon his knees both night and morning."[15]
This behavior may have reflected Knox's influence, and if so it
metamorphosed into an Anglican conformity in later years.
Princeton held republican sentiments fueled by the dissenting tradition, while King's College was attached to the Crown. Yet these
differences seemingly meant little at the time—or, perhaps, at any
time. Hamilton's religious sentiments were influenced by the con-

temporary deism that characterized the rationalist beliefs of most of the Founding Fathers. Hamilton's personality won him the respect and admiration of Presbyterian John Witherspoon of Princeton as well as the friendship and patronage of President Cooper of King's just as it had attracted Knox and so many other patrons and friends in his odyssey to America.

Formally, Hamilton was a student of medicine at King's, perhaps because Knox was a physician as well as a cleric, and his close friend from his St. Croix years, Edward Stevens, had also embarked on a medical career. Hamilton studied at King's just as he did at the Elizabethtown academy, quickly assimilating as much knowledge as he could as rapidly as possible in all the areas of learning. But it was his literary skills already displayed in St. Croix that claimed most of his time and attention, particularly as they could be applied to the political turmoil embroiling the colonies in 1774. They drew him away from his studies and into the political fray. In his plunge into pamphleteering and then into the Continental Army, he never bothered to take his degree, which was hardly necessary for talents that were in full flower by the time he reached his majority.

The Apprentice Years, 1773–1775

Hamilton's political career may be said to have begun with his leadership in a debating club at King's College. As Robert Troup put it, he "made extraordinary displays of richness of genius, and energy of mind."[16] The genius and energy were displayed in his writings as well. New to New York and the American scene though he was, he quickly grasped the meaning of the events of the day. Although his bias as an overseas islander initially inclined him toward monarchy, this sentiment dissolved, presumably upon hearing the news of the Boston Tea Party. New York was in many ways the right place for an ambitious patriot to make his mark. Unlike Boston or Philadelphia, the city was relatively sluggish in adopting an adversarial stand toward the mother country. The city's close commercial ties to Britain, its diverse population, and its conservative oligarchy all militated against the kind of radical sentiments that burst out of Massachusetts and Virginia. The situation in the colony was made to order for new blood to spark revolutionary fervor.

Hamilton arrived on the scene in the fall of 1773 just in time to be swept away by the emotions of the New York Sons of Liberty, who forced the ship carrying East India Company tea to leave the harbor without unloading its cargo. Biographer Nathan Schachner was skeptical of Troup's claim that a visit to Boston, the epicenter of the crisis, converted the young monarchist to the radical cause.[17] There was no need for such a journey, if it did actually occur. It is more likely that Hamilton led his debating club in denouncing British tyranny on this issue just as he took the initiative on other matters. Moreover, the Tea Party may have awakened memories of the resentment of British mercantilism in the West Indies, which had manifested itself in 1766 by the destruction of stamps in St. Kitts and Nevis at the hands of the Sons of Freedom. The presence of his mentor Hugh Knox and his friend Ned Stevens on the patriot side provided an added incentive.

While still an undergraduate, Hamilton has been credited with writing an essay on the "Defence of the Destruction of the Tea," in *Holt's Journal*, followed by a series of articles in the same journal. The articles won the attention of leaders of the colony, notably John Jay, although they were initially anonymous contributions. What catapulted him onto the public stage was a speech in the "Fields," where the Sons of Liberty had set up a liberty pole on July 4, 1774, and called upon New Yorkers to support Boston. Although the more radical candidates failed to win nomination as New York's delegates to the Continental Congress, young Hamilton, according to the account of his son, mounted the platform with the support of Captain Alexander McDougall, leader of the radicals, and stirred the audience with his denunciation of the Intolerable Acts against Boston.[18] Most notably, this new American urged national unity in resisting unconstitutional taxes imposed by the British Parliament. This was not a New Yorker speaking; it was a nationalist urging common action on the part of a nation.

It was Hamilton's good fortune that the social fabric of New York presented the opponents of Britain with more obstacles than in the other colonies. McDougall's failure to win nomination as a delegate to the Congress created an opportunity for new voices to be heard. His replacement by the moderate Jay was not substantively different from selections in Massachusetts and Virginia, where John Adams and Thomas Jefferson took control of the Continental Congress in September 1774. What was different was the Tory power in New York, which was increasingly upset by the behavior of the opponents of Britain's Coercive Acts. The Tories enjoyed more influence in New York than conservatives did in other colonies. But the King's College circle, which included President Cooper and the Reverend Samuel Seabury, provided just the kind of spur that

Hamilton needed to continue his upward march toward leadership of the colonial cause.

That the Tories were alarmed by the actions of the Continental Congress was hardly surprising. The protest against British actions in Massachusetts escalated in the course of its sessions. While independence was not on anyone's lips, the radicals managed to co-opt Jefferson and John Adams when these moderate leaders endorsed the enforcement of an embargo on British goods until colonial grievances had been remedied. More important, the Congress rejected a proposal by the Pennsylvania Loyalist Joseph Galloway to establish an American Grand Council chosen from colonial assemblies. Headed by a president-general appointed by the king, this body would have to approve acts of Parliament before they became valid. Galloway's plan admitted that the American parliament would be an "inferior" branch of the British Parliament, while Jefferson's and Adams's conception of the British Empire would have pledged colonial allegiance only to the Crown. It is worth noting that Adams's "Novanglus Letters" and Jefferson's "Summary View of the Rights of British America" centered American rights on each colony's parliament enjoying equality with Britain's. Hamilton's vision went beyond those of Jefferson and Adams and was more coherent than the ideas of the radicals. He was not thinking about a New York parliament but an American institution that would be on a par with Britain's.

Hamilton's support for a national rather than a colonial response to British authority was implicit in his reaction to the sentiments of "A. W. Farmer" (Samuel Seabury), who professed to offer "Free Thoughts on the Proceedings of the Continental Congress." Seabury appealed to the common sense of the essentially conservative farming community, urging it to consider the benefits gained by membership in the empire and to take into account what might be lost by riotous rebellion. The author condemned the Continental Congress for betraying the interests of the colonies by denying them British manufactures for the sake of an "abominable scheme" of independence from the mother country.[19] Moreover, "Farmer" asserted that commercial blackmail would not work; the produce that the Congress denied the West Indies could be replaced by sources in Canada or Georgia. City merchants, not the farmers, were the only potential winners. The author of this broadside intended to expose a plot of New York businessmen to bleed farmers by selling their stocks at high prices at the same time that the countryman was prevented from selling his goods by the Continental

Congress's nonexportation arrangements. "Will you submit to them? . . . by Him that made me, I will not.—If I must be enslaved, let it be by a King at least, and not by a parcel of upstart lawless Committee-men. If I must be devoured, let me be devoured by the jaws of a lion, and not *gnawed* to death by rats and vermin."[20]

Deepening the division between merchants and farmers, between conservative New York countrymen and the radicals of Virginia and Massachusetts was the major aim of Seabury's attack on the Continental Congress and the policies advocated by its members. Admitting that there were legitimate grievances on the part of townspeople as well as farmers, he urged his readers to listen to their representatives in the more moderate New York Assembly who would resolve their problems through petition, rather than to the fire-eaters who would tar and feather any dissenter.

Given his connections at King's College it did not take Hamilton long to identify "Farmer" as Seabury, an intimate of President Cooper and a leading figure among New York Loyalists. There was nothing to connect him with the plain yeoman of his pamphlet, and young Hamilton took full advantage of this ruse. Once again the new American, little more than a year after his migration to New York, saw an opportunity to advance his name as well as the cause of his new country, and he took it. He was ready to move from orator to pamphleteer, and Seabury provided a ready vehicle for his ambitions. His response to Seabury in "A Full Vindication of the Measures of the Congress, from the Calumnies of Their Enemies" was filled with examples of his erudition, his passion, and his immaturity. It was also as effective as any propaganda that the apologists for the Continental Congress could want. The zeal with which he assailed the establishment that had nourished him on his arrival in New York suggests a traditional youthful rebellion against authority figures, but one accomplished with far more sophistication than an ordinary undergraduate would display. Hamilton was reaching for an appreciative audience of colonial leaders, and he found it.

The language and images he employed were those of the dissenters, and he shared with friends and opponents a delight in hyperbole. The spirit of the Enlightenment was also evident in his asking "these restless spirits, whence arises that violent antipathy they seem to entertain, not only to the natural rights of mankind, but to common sense and common modesty." He wanted the reader to accept without question the assumption that Seabury and his like-minded friends were "enemies to the natural right of mankind" because they proposed that the colonies be enslaved to the mother country. As for common sense, he argued that it was ridiculous to think that the "contest with Britain is founded entirely upon the petty duty of 3 pence per pound on East India tea." The world knew that the real issue with the mother country was whether "the inhabitants of Great-Britain have a right to dispose of the lives and properties of the inhabitants of America, or not."[21] The Continental Congress so maligned by Seabury spoke for the freedom and future prosperity of America.

The arguments Hamilton presented in favor of economic pressure on Britain were similar to those articulated by leaders of Congress: "that Americans are intitled to freedom, is incontestible upon every rational principle. . . . No reason can be assigned why one man should exercise any power, or pre-eminence over his fellow creatures more than another; unless they have voluntarily vested him with it. Since then, Americans have not by any act of their's [*sic*] impowered the British Parliament to make laws for them, it follows they can have no just authority to do it."[22] Shrewdly he linked the "fundamental principles of the English constitution" and the charters of the colonies to observe that they "preclude every claim of ruling and taxing us without our consent. . . . What then is the subject of our controversy with the mother country? It is this, whether we shall preserve that security to our lives and properties, which the law of nature, the genius of the British constitution, and our charters afford us; or whether we shall resign them into the hands of the British House of Commons, which is no more privileged to dispose of them than the Grand Mogul?"[23] The sarcasm aside, this expression of a federal conception of the British Empire was essentially that of the writings of Jefferson and John Adams in 1774. Loyalty to Great Britain did not mean loyalty to Parliament, but to a king who was ruler of America by a compact between the Crown and the colonies.

Hamilton also addressed Seabury's specific issues. Answering the assertion that the patriots' association enforcing nonimportation and nonexportation would ruin farmers, he claimed that, on the contrary, submission to Parliament would be the source of their suffering. If Americans accepted the tax on tea, "perhaps before long, your tables, and chairs, and platters, and dishes, and knives, and forks, and every thing else, would be taxed. Nay, I don't know but they would find means to tax you for every child you got, and for every kiss your daughters received from their sweet-hearts; and, God knows, that would soon ruin you."[24] The college humor notwithstanding, he made the point that if New Yorkers sacrificed the interests of Massachusetts, they in turn would be the next victims. It was the obvious hope of "Farmer" that the natural divisions in America—between merchants and farmers, between one colony and another—would fracture the unity fashioned by the Continental Congress. Hamilton disagreed with this dichotomy on the grounds that a flourishing commerce and industry would embrace farmers within a self-sufficient economy.

As for the colonies suffering from the self-imposed embargo, he contended that Britain would suffer more. The mother country might appear to be immune to colonial action, but "in the calm unprejudiced eye of reason . . . she is oppressed with a heavy national debt, which it requires the utmost policy and oeconomy ever to discharge . . . and the continual emigrations, from Great-Britain and Ireland, to the continent, are a glaring symptom, that those kingdoms are a good deal impoverished."[25] While his estimates of the damage to Britain's prosperity were for the most part speculative, he was on safer ground when he spoke of the economy of the West Indies. Those islands were dependent on the American trade. Hamilton wrote knowledgeably about the side effects of the islands' concentration on the cultivation of sugarcane; the consequence was that the proprietors were neglecting to raise sufficient food to sustain the inhabitants. He claimed that Seabury's suggestion that Canada or the Floridas could replace the Thirteen Colonies as suppliers of food was illusory. In sum, America possessed the power to force Britain to change its ways, not through petitions but through the economic action of denying the mother country the West Indies' agricultural exports.

With more than a touch of condescension he hailed the farmers of New York as "MY GOOD COUNTRYMEN" and professed the reason for addressing them was simply out of concern for truth and not because he was "one of your number." By contrast he pointed out that "the true writer of the piece signed A. W. FARMER, is not in reality a Farmer. He is some ministerial emissary, that has assumed the name to deceive you."[26] Having assured his readers of his objectivity as well as his honesty, he asked, "Will you, then, my friends, allow yourselves to be duped by this artful enemy? . . . I am sure you will not. I should be very sorry to think any of my countrymen would be so mean, so blind to their own interest, so lost to every generous and manly feeling."[27]

Reading these bold words, there is some pathos as well as arrogance in the lengthy peroration, often repetitious, occasionally cal-low, and replete with unproven allegations. It is tempting to read into his defense of the Continental Congress portents of Hamilton's future. There certainly was not much of his past, beyond his first-hand knowledge of the economy of the West Indies. The young immigrant took on a new American persona to replace his personal history, as if the farmers had always been his "countrymen." But the hints of his future policies may be conjured up from the positions he seemed to advocate in the text. His defense of business-men against the charges of exploiting the farmer was based on the mutuality of interests linking the farmer to the tradesman and merchant. He was convinced that patriots would not suffer from the loss of British goods because America had the raw materials to become a manufacturing equal of the mother country: "Those hands, which may be deprived of business by the cessation of commerce, may be occupied in various kinds of manufactures and other internal improvements. If . . . manufactures should . . . take root among us, they will pave the way, still more, to the future grandeur and glory of America."[28] Was this the beginning of the national economy that his reports of 1791 recommended? Such speculation may be wide of the mark. Young Hamilton was assimilating the ideas of his environment in pre-Revolutionary New York, which his talents permitted him to rephrase and even to extend. They covered the whole spectrum of eighteenth-century polity; his choice of specific directions had not yet been made in 1774.

Did he go too far in absorbing the language as well as the views of the leaders around him, Tory as well as Whig? His closing note—"May God give you wisdom to see what is your true interest, and inspire you with becoming zeal for the cause of virtue and mankind"—may have been a benediction he heard in daily services at King's College, perhaps even from the Reverend Samuel Seabury himself.[29] Whether or not Seabury was the inspiration for his final lines as well as the object of the address itself, there is no doubt that the College establishment heard and paid attention to Hamilton's broadside. The student's pamphlet had attracted so wide an audience that Seabury treated the author as a peer, complimenting him with a response, even though, like Seabury's first effort, it was published anonymously. Like others of his generation, the minister had difficulty in accepting the fact that his antagonist was a teenager and a King's College student. Seabury thought it was written by "an old experienced practitioner" such as John Jay. President Cooper could not believe that his student was the author. He expressed his doubts to Troup, who replied that "all the political tracts were written when the General and I were in college together & I saw them in manuscript before they were sent to press."[30]

Seabury's rejoinder took to task the young pamphleteer for misleading generalizations, such as his interpretation of natural rights. There was no inherent natural right for a colony to legislate for itself. Such rights as the colonies enjoyed came from their charters, and New York lacked even a charter to justify the assertions of "A Friend to America." To make a distinction between Crown and Parliament was to break the bonds of empire; the two were indivisible in protecting all parts of the realm.[31]

Although Hamilton was not cowed by these criticisms, he was aware of some errors in his "full" vindication of the colonial cause and had his publisher, James Rivington, print corrections. He prepared a counterblast to Seabury's refutations, one with much more documentation than his first broadside contained. In February 1775, a little more than two months after his first response to Seabury, he published "The Farmer Refuted: or A more Impartial and Comprehensive View of the Dispute Between Great-Britain and the Colonies," in which he provided exhaustive details to prove his points, delving into the histories of the colonies and citing with considerable flourish a list of philosophers to support his counterattack. But this serious rebuttal was preceded by an intemperate indictment of Seabury's response that claimed that "the spirit that breathes throughout is so rancorous, illiberal and imperious: The argumentative part of it so puerile and fallacious: The misrepresentations of facts so palpable and flagrant: The conceits so low, sterile and splenetic, that I venture to pronounce it one of the most ludicrous performances which has been exhibited to public view, during all the present controversy."[32]

After delivering these barbed words, Hamilton challenged Seabury's implication that he did not understand such terms as "natural rights of mankind" or realize that New York had no charter. On the matter of natural rights, the student displayed the breadth of his scholarship by throwing at the "Farmer" the authority of most of the great philosophers of the past two centuries —from Grotius and Locke in the seventeenth century to the contemporary Montesquieu and Blackstone. Whether he had studied their writings in his college courses or prepared himself specifically for this pamphlet, he marshaled citations in support of almost all the claims he had made in his first essay, with the notable exception of the statement that anyone "governed by a will of another" was enslaved.[33]

Hamilton's rejoinders in this broadside were filled with examples of his familiarity with the ideas of the Enlightenment. He took Blackstone's works for his guide in showing that the law of nature was divinely given and binding in all countries at all times. He vilified Seabury by associating his views with those of Hobbes, who "held, as you do, that he was, then, perfectly free from all restraint of *law* and *government*" without a deity to mitigate the relations between man and society.[34] But Hamilton overdid his show of erudition in lecturing Seabury: "If you will follow my advice, there still may be hopes for your reformation. Apply yourself, without delay, to the study of the law of nature," from a reading list he provided.[35] Even if he did not know the identity of "Farmer," the so-called advice was intentionally and needlessly insulting. In fact, Hamilton revealed his own confusion over distinctions between Hobbes and Blackstone, and between Blackstone and Seabury. They were not quite so far apart as he asserted—nor was Hamilton himself. They all could agree that "there must be a supreme power, to which all members of that society are subject, for, otherwise, there could be no supremacy, or subordination, that is, no government at all."[36] The importance attributed to law and order is a factor in Hamilton's polity that would surface repeatedly in the future—indeed, within the year.

Hamilton was not fazed by the issue of charters. After demonstrating that the colonial charters were outside the jurisdiction of Parliament, he turned to the case of New York. "It is true, that New-York has no Charter. But if it could support it's [*sic*] claim to liberty in no other way, it might, with justice, plead the common principles of colonization, for it would be unreasonable, to seclude one colony, from the enjoyment of the most important privileges of the rest." He then swept away legal arguments with colorful language: "There is no need, however, of this plea: The sacred rights of mankind are not to be rummaged for, among old parchments, or musty records. They are written, as with a sun beam, in the whole *volume* of human nature, by the hand of divinity itself, and can never be erased or obscured by mortal power."[37] There is a seeming paradox in Hamilton's asserting the power of natural rights more strongly than did Jefferson and Adams in their writings in 1774. The paradox may be more apparent than real. Given the absence of a royal charter that buttressed the case for Massachusetts or Virginia, Hamilton

had to compensate for this lack, as political scientist Gerald Stourzh
suggests, by a special emphasis on natural rights.[38]

The main thrust of his second pamphlet was not essentially
different from the first. He sought to demonstrate that the supreme
authority over the American colonies was the king, not Parliament.
The differences were largely in the documentation, he added. He
invoked the Scottish philosopher David Hume in "asserting that
the authority of the British Parliament over America, would, in all
probability, be a more intolerable and excessive species of despo-
tism than an absolute monarchy."[39] And he mocked Seabury's pro-
nouncement that there were no differences between Americans and
Britons in their allegiance to authority. Playing with a syllogism
equating man with a horse, he flaunted his knowledge of both Latin
and logic in reciting "*Homo est* animal": *equus est* animal, *Ergo, homo
est equus,* which he translated into "Britons are men; Americans are
the *same*: Therefore Britains [*sic*] and Americans are the *same.*"[40]

There is little to distinguish Hamilton's arguments from those
of the Jeffersonian positions in 1775. His pamphlet revealed a remarkable sophistication in the presentation of these views and in
an innovative eclecticism mature beyond his years, even as they
were occasionally expressed in sophomoric language. But those
outbursts were not beyond the bounds of the invectives of his el-
ders. Even his conclusions echoed Jefferson's, in his appreciation
of the British tradition of liberty, in his pious if not fully sincere
laments over "the unnatural quarrel, between the parent state and
the colonies," and in his professed "wish for a speedy reconciliation, a perpetual and *mutually* beneficial union." He assured his
readers that he was "a warm advocate of a limited monarchy, and
an unfeigned well-wisher to the present Royal Family."[41]

The young Hamilton did more than parade his familiarity with
the philosophers of the Enlightenment or replicate the political ideas
of the older Founding Fathers. Running through the two pamphlets
was the assumption that the colonies had the power to shape their
own destiny if the mother country did not respond to their grievances. He projected a vision of an America whose separate parts
would complement each other to create ultimately a powerful en-
tity on the American continent. Whatever role he would assign to
Britain in the establishment of an American foreign policy, the fun-
dament would not be Anglophilic. The basis for his confidence in
the future of America lay in the economic weight it could wield.

Within three months of the exchange between Hamilton and
Seabury, the political scene in America had changed radically. The

Battle of Lexington and Concord had escalated the controversy between the mother country and the colonies. Britain seemingly had done what the youthful polemicist had considered "the grossest infatuation of madness itself" in employing military means to subdue the colonies.[42] Hamilton's reactions reflected the changed relationship. Using as his vehicle for protest the Quebec Act of 1774, whereby Britain granted French Canadians protection of their religious and judicial systems, he claimed to have seen what otherwise might be considered an enlightened act on the part of Britain as a conspiracy to force an alien religion on Anglo-America. Hamilton exploited anti-Catholic prejudice to assert that freedom of religion in a Quebec that extended to the Ohio River would result in the subjugation of Protestants.

For the first time he blurred the distinction between Crown and Parliament; the thrust of his two pamphlets on the Quebec Act was to transfer the odium hitherto attached to acts of Parliament to the king himself. "What can speak in plainer language," he asked, "the corruption of the British Parliament, than its act; which invests the King with absolute power over a little world."[43] As a subtext to his broadside, he asked rhetorically why Britain "has also added the immense tract of country that surrounds all these colonies to that province." He hinted of a plot not only to "establish" rather than "tolerate" the Roman Catholic religion in Quebec, "as stipulated by the treaty of peace" (which had terminated the Seven Years War in 1763), but also to deny Americans access to the West by extending the boundaries of Catholic Quebec.[44] Two issues were thereby exposed as the gaps within the empire grew wider. One was the action to prevent the colonies from taking their share of the West that had been wrested from France; the other was the less than subtle shift of responsibility from Parliament to the king, in apparent preparation for a more serious break with the mother country.

Whether or not he specifically anticipated war, Hamilton was quick to join with his friend Troup in a company of fellow students to drill with their muskets at the churchyard of St. George's Chapel before going to class. But an incident in May 1775 checked to some degree the ardor that had appeared in his writings. Inflamed by the reactions to the Massachusetts farmers' confrontation with British troops at Concord and Lexington in April and by rumors that President Cooper of King's College was the leader of a Tory ring, a New York mob marched on the president's house on May 10 with the intention of tarring and feathering him—or worse. Young Hamilton, according to the account of Robert Troup, addressed the mob and held them off long enough for Cooper to slip away to the safety of a British warship.[45] The accuracy of this account hangs on the memory of a devoted friend who recorded the incident many years later. However much the story may have been embellished, it is clear that the King's College student's defense of his old teacher and current adversary was a testament to his elevation of law and order to the same plane as liberty and freedom. Hamilton's dislike of mob action was displayed again in November 1775 when he confronted Connecticut militiamen who had ransacked James Rivington's printshop because of his Tory sentiments. Rivington had printed Seabury's pamphlets, but he had also published Hamilton's responses.

It was his sense of order rather than gratitude for Rivington's past services as his printer that animated the young patriot. He made his position clear in a letter the same month to John Jay: "Though I am fully sensible how dangerous and pernicious Rivington's press has been, and how detestable the character of the man is in every respect, yet I cannot help disapproving and condemning this step." He was worried about "the great danger of fatal extremes" when "the passions of men are worked up to an uncommon pitch." Despite all his youthful revolutionary fervor, he feared that opposition to tyranny and oppression on the part of the "unthinking populace" could lead to "a contempt and disregard of all authority."[46] It is worth noting that the collegian was presenting himself as an equal to John Jay, a leader of the New York delegation to the Continental Congress with whom he had had only a slight connection during his brief stay in Elizabethtown.

Neither his vigorous denunciation of mob violence nor his actions in defense of potential victims indicated any intention of joining the Tory cause. He blamed New Englanders for imprudent if not dangerous acts of repression as they moved into New York. But, as he recommended in his letter to Jay, "a few regiments of troops, raised in Philadelphia, the Jerseys or any other province except New England . . . will suffice to strengthen and support the Whigs who are still I flatter myself a large majority and to suppress the efforts of the tories."[47] Hamilton feared that the royal governor, who had withdrawn to a British warship in New York harbor in October 1775, might try to mobilize Loyalist supporters of the old Assembly to overthrow the Provincial Congress elected in November.

As for the ardent young patriot, he was no longer on the sidelines as a pamphleteer or even as a student volunteer member of the "Corsicans" who braved British fire in August 1775, according to the memories of his friends, when he went to the Battery in lower Manhattan to remove its cannons. By January 1776, he was ready and anxious to abandon his studies and join the war. On the recommendation of the former leader of the Sons of Liberty, Alexander McDougall, Hamilton was commissioned a captain of the Provincial Company of Artillery.

Notes

1. Adams to Jefferson, July 12, 1813, in Lester J. Cappon, ed., *The Adams–Jefferson Letters*, 2 vols. (Chapel Hill: University of North Carolina Press, 1959), 2:354.
2. Broadus Mitchell, *Alexander Hamilton: Youth to Maturity, 1755–1788* (New York: Macmillan Co., 1957), 6; Forrest McDonald, *Alexander Hamilton* (New York: W. W. Norton & Co., 1979), 8.
3. Quoted in John C. Miller, *Alexander Hamilton: Portrait in Paradox* (New York: Harper & Brothers, 1959), 3.
4. See, in particular, McDonald, *Alexander Hamilton*, 7 and 366–67; Robert A. Hendrickson, *The Rise and Fall of Alexander Hamilton* (New York: Van Nostrand Reinhold Co., 1981), 6–7; Mitchell, *Alexander Hamilton*, 1.
5. AH to Edward Stevens, November 11, 1769, in Harold C. Syrett and Jacob E. Cooke, eds., *The Papers of Alexander Hamilton*, 27 vols. (New York: Columbia University Press, 1961) 1:4. Hereafter cited as Syrett and Cooke.
6. AH to Nicholas Cruger, November 12, 1771, in ibid., 11; AH to Captain William Newton, November 16, 1771, in ibid., 14.
7. Mitchell, *Alexander Hamilton*, 19.
8. AH to Newton, November 16, 1771, in Syrett and Cooke, I: 14; AH to Walton and Cruger, November 27, 1771, ibid., 17.
9. Harold Larson, "Alexander Hamilton: Fact and Fiction," 3rd ser., *William and Mary Quarterly* 9 (January 1952): 148.
10. Richard Brookhiser, *Alexander Hamilton: American* (New York: The Free Press, 1999), 8.
11. AH to Edward Stevens, November 11, 1769, Syrett and Cooke, 1:4.
12. Miller, *Alexander Hamilton*, 5.
13. AH to *Royal Danish American Gazette*, September 6, 1772, Syrett and Cooke, 1:35–36.
14. Quoted from the biographical sketch of Hamilton's friend, Hercules Mulligan, in Nathan Schachner, ed., "Alexander Hamilton Viewed by His Friends: The Narratives of Robert Troup and Hercules Mulligan," 3d ser., *William and Mary Quarterly* 4 (April 1947): 209.
15. "Narrative of Colonel Robert Troup," March 22, 1810, in Schachner, "Narratives," 213.
16. Ibid.
17. Nathan Schachner, *Alexander Hamilton* (New York: A. S. Barnes & Co., 1946), 30–31.
18. John Church Hamilton, *Life of Alexander Hamilton*, 2 vols. (New York: D. Appleton & Co., 1840), 1:22–23.
19. Quoted in Mitchell, *Alexander Hamilton*, 67.
20. Ibid.

21. "A Full Vindication of the Measures of the Congress," December 15, 1774, Syrett and Cooke, 1:46.

22. Ibid., 47.

23. Ibid., 47–48.

24. Ibid., 67.

25. Ibid., 57–58.

26. Ibid., 65.

27. Ibid., 77.

28. Ibid., 56.

29. Ibid., 78; Hendrickson, *Rise and Fall*, 45.

30. "Narrative of Robert Troup," 214.

31. Cited in James Thomas Flexner, *The Young Hamilton: A Biography* (Boston: Little, Brown & Co., 1978), 70–71.

32. "The Farmer Refuted, etc.," February 23, 1775, Syrett and Cooke, 1:81–82.

33. Ibid., 47.

34. Ibid., 87.

35. Ibid., 86.

36. Ibid., 98.

37. Ibid., 121–22.

38. Gerald Stourzh, *Alexander Hamilton and the Idea of Republican Government* (Stanford: Stanford University Press, 1970), 14.

39. "The Farmer Refuted," February 23, 1775, Syrett and Cooke, 1:100.

40. Ibid., 101–2.

41. Ibid., 164.

42. Ibid., 54.

43. "Remarks on the Quebec Bill: Part Two," June 22, 1775, ibid., 175.

44. Ibid., 174.

45. "Narrative of Robert Troup," 219.

46. AH to John Jay, November 26, 1775, Syrett and Cooke, 1:176.

47. Ibid., 178.

2

The War as Opportunity

1775–1782

A comparison with the meteoric career of Napoleon Bonaparte was suggested briefly in Chapter 1 and will appear again in subsequent chapters. It is not that their trajectories were identical, or even that their circumstances were similar; they were not. Bonaparte may have come from an offshore island but, unlike Hamilton, he grew up in a close-knit and devoted family who sponsored his education in France and whom he carried up the ladder of success with him over the next generation.

Such was not the experience of the young West Indian. Hamilton was the product of a dysfunctional family and never achieved the power that the Corsican enjoyed. Bonaparte was a general in the French Revolution, and Hamilton a lieutenant colonel in the American Revolution, but both men quickly recognized the opportunities that a revolutionary society opened to them. Both immersed themselves in a wide variety of studies to exploit their knowledge of the arts of war and of government. Toward this end, they published pamphlets early in their careers that drew the attention of influential friends who were impressed by their charm, intelligence, and qualities of leadership.

The Militia Captain

It was revolution and war that permitted their ambitions to be realized. Hamilton, like Bonaparte, knew what would serve his interests from the outset of his career. Given the connections he had made at Elizabethtown and New York, he could have had a prestigious post as an aide-de-camp to General William Alexander, also known as Lord Stirling, who was in charge of the defense of New York City in George Washington's Continental Army. Indeed, Elias Boudinot, a patron from Hamilton's school days, went out of his way to win Alexander's support. But the twenty-one-year-old youth turned down this opportunity; he wanted an active command, not a staff position. Hamilton preferred to accept a commission as captain in an artillery company that the New York Provincial Assembly raised for the defense of the city simply because this assignment promised action.

The intervention of (now) Colonel Alexander McDougall, seconded by John Jay, another early patron, overcame the Assembly's doubts about the young man's qualifications, even though there were reasons enough to question his credentials as a line officer. Such experience as he had was the equivalent of that of reserve officers training in twentieth-century universities. His one encounter with artillery had been as a volunteer militiaman in August 1775, dragging cannons away from the Battery in the face of gunfire from a British sloop. His appearance was not in his favor. Slight and short, he looked younger than his years. Some months later, during the American retreat across New Jersey, an officer described him as "a youth, a mere stripling, small, slender, almost delicate in frame, marching beside a piece of artillery, with a cocked hat pulled down over his eyes, apparently lost in thought, with his hand resting on the cannon and every now and then patting it as he mused, as if it were a favorite horse or pet plaything."[1]

Yet it was more than his connections that determined his fitness for the post. He had studied for the examination that the Assembly required and probably knew as much about the subject of artillery as his examiner. It was his intelligence and drive as well as his air of authority that won him advancement then and later. On March 14, 1776, Hamilton was appointed "Captain of the Provincial Company of the Artillery of this Colony."[2]

The captaincy was a position of considerable importance. He was in command of the sole artillery company of the colony of New York, with unusual access to the legislature that had appointed him. Captain Hamilton made the most of his special status. He impressed his sponsors by a display of zeal in raising, supplying, and drilling his company. He was effective, even if his success in equipping his men absorbed, according to his friend Hercules Mulligan, "the remnant of the second and last remittance from St. Croix."[3] He also made sure that the Assembly appropriated suitable pay for his men.

And for an officer ambitious to be admitted to the ruling class, he made an unusual effort to promote a sergeant to the rank of "officer and gentleman." As he informed the Convention of the Representatives of the State of New York (successor to the Provincial Congress) on July 12, 1776, "I verily believe he will make an excellent lieutenant, and his advancement will be a great encouragement and benefit to my company particularly, and will be an animating example to all men of merit, to whose knowledge it comes."[4] Whatever insecurity the young officer may have felt about his own status in society was not transformed into a temptation to deny others what had been given to him.

What is unusual about the foregoing correspondence was the ease and confidence Hamilton displayed in writing to the legislators. Just as in his business correspondence from St. Croix, his language was not that of a low-level functionary; he wrote as an equal to his civilian superiors. On the matter of rations for his men, he had no compunction about complaining that they fell below the standard of the Continental Army: "My men, you are sensible, are by their articles, entitled to the same subsistence with the Continental troops, and it would be to them an insupportable discrimination as well as a breach of the terms of enlistment to give them a third less provisions. . . . I doubt not you will readily put this matter upon a proper footing."[5] Notwithstanding the imperious tone, he won his case; even more provisions were allotted than he had anticipated. Such was the advantage he enjoyed through the friendships of leading figures in the new legislature.

Hamilton's role as drillmaster and provisioner was only part of his record in 1776. The latter half of the year afforded him a taste of combat and a glimpse of the glory that active participation in war might bring. After the siege of Boston had been lifted in March, the battle scene moved to the middle states, especially New York. It was not a happy time for the new nation. A more powerful British force than had been present in New England confronted Washington's 10,000 Continental troops and the 12,000 militiamen that included Hamilton's Provincial Artillery Company. Its captain was with Washington's army as it retreated from Long Island to New York City and then to New Jersey.

It was in these circumstances that Hamilton may have attracted the attention of General Washington. Whether the captain was with the general in the Battle of Long Island, as his son later claimed, is moot.[6] What is more verifiable was the failure of most militiamen to hold the line in Manhattan. The commander in chief may have

witnessed the contrast between their panicked flight and the behavior of Hamilton's disciplined artillery company. Hamilton family lore notwithstanding, it was in New Jersey, particularly in the
crossing of the Delaware and the surprise attack against the Hes-
sian garrison in Trenton on December 26, culminating in the recapture of Princeton on January 2, 1777, that the artillery captain caught
the eye of the general.

Washington's Aide-de-Camp

Three weeks after his victory at Princeton, Washington asked about
the suitability of Hamilton as an aide-de-camp; on March 1, 1777,
he appointed him to that post. Although it is likely that Hamilton's
exploits in battle, embellished as they were in the retelling, played
a role in the appointment, Generals Henry Knox and Nathanael
Greene also gave their support to Washington's decision. Knox was
a trusted associate of the commander in chief and had observed
firsthand the service that the militia captain had rendered to his
Continental troops. Greene reputedly had been favorably impressed
with Hamilton's drilling of his company in the course of a visit to
Washington's headquarters in the summer of 1776.

In light of Hamilton's reputation, it was not surprising that
Washington chose him for his staff. What is superficially surprising was Hamilton's acceptance of the appointment. The idea of serving as a glorified clerk, which was how he occasionally described
the position, had been his reason for rejecting General Alexander's
offer. Why the change of mind less than a year later? One reason
certainly was the dissolution of his militia company. Most of its
members had drifted away when their contracts expired. Five days
after his acceptance of Washington's offer, he wrote to the New York
State Convention that with death, desertions, and expiration of enlistments, the company was reduced to twenty-five men: "As the
rest [of] the Company can hardly answer any good purpose to the
s[tate, I] imagine you will resolve to resign it. There will be no (difficulty) in having it transferred to the Continental establishment."[7]

More than the coincidental collapse of his militia company ac-
counted for Hamilton's decision. Although an aide-de-camp was a
staff officer, joining Washington's circle catapulted him to the center of action. He felt that it was worth exchanging a line officer's
post for the honor that proximity to the commander in chief would
bring, especially since prospects for military glory were dim in 1777.

Nor did it escape his attention that admission to the elite group surrounding the general was also confirmation of his status as a gentleman. The "family" he joined was composed mostly of young men of considerable talents. Many of the aides, such as James McHenry and Timothy Pickering, would become important figures in the new Republic and remain loyal friends of Hamilton the statesman. Membership in this circle would provide him with a family he never had—and a family at the top of the social ladder.

The new lieutenant colonel recognized potential drawbacks as an aide. His rank carried no congressional commission; it was valid only so long as he was an aide. It must also have been dispiriting for a man of Hamilton's temperament to know that an aide was not allowed to bear arms. But considering his ambitions for distinction, the appointment was an opportunity he could not afford to dismiss. One biographer emphasized his propensity to look at the world from a panoramic perspective, to see America in the broadest terms. As James Thomas Flexner observed, "For a man so disposed, the outlook of an artillery captain seemed almost blindness. But a member of the Commander-in-Chief's staff would stand on the highest lookout tower."[8]

An opportunity came quickly. The general found in Hamilton just the kind of amanuensis he required. A quick mind, a fluent pen, a command of French, and an ability to read the chief's thoughts made the new aide indispensable. Both men shared a love of order and a continental perspective on the problems of the new nation. In this respect, Washington was no more a Virginian than Hamilton was a New Yorker. They were both nationalists. For the general, the diminutive aide was his "boy." For Hamilton, the relationship was more complex.

In some ways the general served as a surrogate father, possessing qualities that Hamilton's own father totally lacked. It was inevitably a close and trusting relationship, since Hamilton's skill in putting Washington's ideas on paper made him the principal aide. Yet it was in most ways formal, far removed from the intimacy displayed in the correspondence between Washington and Lafayette, or between Hamilton and fellow aide-de-camp John Laurens. To Hamilton, the general was always "His Excellency," and while the respect, even awe, of the younger man was genuine, there was always a certain reserve on Hamilton's part, the product of impatience with his station as a subordinate as well as of some doubts about his leader's intellectual capacities.

An Advantageous Marriage

The advantages of Hamilton's situation far outweighed the disadvantages. Not least among the former was the chance to shine in the social milieu of Washington's winter headquarters. The young officer's charm and wit sparkled as he played the gallant with the ladies of Martha Washington's circle. Enjoying as he did the company of impressionable young women, he was aware of the importance of a well-placed marriage to his standing in society and to his future career. From John Laurens, Hamilton demanded, tongue in cheek, that he find a wife for him in Carolina and then proceeded to state his requirements: "She must be young, handsome (I lay most stress upon a good shape) sensible (a little learning will do) well-bred . . . of some good nature, a great deal of generosity (she must neither love money or scolding). I dislike equally a termagant and an oeconimist [*sic*]." Embodied in this lighthearted list was a serious note, though frivolously expressed: "as to fortune the larger stock of that the better. . . . You know my temper and circumstances and will therefore pay special attention to this article in the treaty."[9]

This letter was written in April 1779, and by fall of that year he had found his wife, not in Carolina but in Morristown, New Jersey. His choice was Elizabeth Schuyler, a daughter of the powerful New York patroon, General Philip Schuyler. The impecunious lieutenant colonel could not have found a more suitable bride. Apparently, it was love at first sight, or almost at first sight, on both their parts. They became engaged in March 1780 after a brief but characteristically ardent courtship. She was as captivated by the dashing young officer as he was by her.

Writing to Laurens about his fiancée in June 1780, he called himself a "lover in earnest,"[10] although he was well aware of the impact of his impending marriage upon his career. The one potential obstacle was the Schuyler family, particularly its aristocratic head. Under ordinary circumstances, the admission of a West Indian bastard to one of the first families of New York was unlikely, if not impossible. But the circumstances of 1779 were such that General Schuyler had known and admired Hamilton before the young aide met his daughter. The suitor's manners were those of a gentleman, and his connections to the Hamiltons of Scotland gave a reality to that impression. Schuyler gathered this information from his future son-in-law, but he did not elicit much information about his West Indian parents. Conceivably, the general did not wish to know more. Hamilton did allude elliptically to his shadowy background, but it requires a leap of imagination to conclude that "the instance of delicacy"[11] found in the general's correspondence was a confession of his illegitimacy.

General Gates and the Conway Cabal

Hamilton's courtship of Betsy Schuyler was an interlude, though an important one, in the aide's busy life on Washington's staff. Acting on behalf of the commander in chief, he usually saw the war through the general's eyes and was privy to events and actions incidental to his privileged position. As a member of the inner circle, he followed the conduct of the war from the inside. Not that he was the only confidant; Washington needed and valued the services of every one of his thirty-two aides. They, in turn, were fiercely loyal to their leader, especially in the middle years of the war when Washington was challenged by the machinations of General Horatio Gates and denigrated by an unsympathetic Continental Congress. In this context, Hamilton was Washington's chief agent as letter writer, intelligence informant, diplomatic correspondent, and special agent to field commanders.

In these capacities he was present at some of the most critical moments of the war. And it was in these moments of crisis that he displayed his appreciation of his commander's virtues even when he occasionally questioned his judgments. Hamilton shared Washington's frustrations with generals nominally under his command. The most notable conflict was with General Gates, a veteran British officer who had won unearned glory in New York State at the crucial battle of Saratoga in October 1777, at a time when Washington was losing ground in Pennsylvania. Gates was an ungracious victor, denying credit to the vital role of General Benedict Arnold in the defeat of British General John Burgoyne. He was also a personal enemy of Philip Schuyler. Small wonder, then, that Hamilton fully empathized with his general's conviction that Gates was conspiring with members of Congress to replace Washington as commander in chief.

Hamilton's dislike was exacerbated by a personal encounter. While Gates was triumphant in New York, Washington barely managed to keep his forces intact in Pennsylvania. He badly needed reinforcements from Gates and dispatched Hamilton to Albany. Instead, the young aide encountered a host of excuses for Gates's not following Washington's order. Although embarrassed and annoyed at Gates's behavior, the young officer took it upon himself to refrain from insisting on the dispatch of more troops than Gates was willing to send and gave his reasons: "Should any accident or inconvenience happen in consequence of [Washington's order], there would be too fair a pretext for censure."[12] He worried that Gates would use his influence in the Continental Congress to put the order in the worst possible light.

Here was a clear case of an aide-de-camp, only six months in Washington's service, presuming, despite some uneasiness, to "have done, what considering all circumstances, appeared eligible and prudent."[13] Even though he recognized that Gates was shortchanging Washington by sending the weakest of his brigades, he also recognized the dangers that Gates's proclivity for intrigue posed to the commander in chief. In fact, Hamilton was able to pry loose from Gates more troops than the victor of Saratoga intended to give. The offended general then complained to Washington about the young officer's unseemly pressure: "Although it is customary & even Absolutely necessary to direct Implicit Obedience to be paid to the Verbal Orders of Aids [*sic*] de Camp in Action . . . yet I believe it is never practiced to Delegate that Dictatorial power to one Aid de Camp sent to an Army 300 miles away."[14]

Instead of upbraiding Hamilton for exceeding his instructions or for insulting a senior officer, Washington was grateful for his aide's perceptive appraisal of Gates's attempts to undermine the commander in chief and for his efforts to counter them. That Gates sought to curry favor with the Board of War by denigrating Washington's abilities seemed to have been confirmed by what has been called with some exaggeration the "Conway cabal." General Thomas Conway, a Frenchman of Irish extraction on leave from the French Army, pressed Gates's candidacy with the Board of War to succeed the failing Washington. The Continental Congress might have elevated Gates had Major James Wilkinson, one of Gates' aides, not inadvertently allowed a letter from Conway to Gates to fall into Washington's hands. The letter insinuated that only Gates could save the country from the failures of a "weak general."[15]

Once again, Hamilton played a part, though unintentionally, in the contest between the two generals. Gates accused him of stealing the letter during his mission to Albany and then showing it to Washington, perhaps with the connivance of Robert Troup, another of Gates's aides and Hamilton's college classmate. When Gates publicly charged Washington with conspiring with Hamilton to discredit him, the commander in chief revealed that his source was an inebriated Wilkinson who blurted out its contents, which were subsequently reported to Washington. Hamilton bitterly condemned both Gates and Conway, with special attention to the latter as "one of the vermin bred in the entrails of this chimera dire, and there does not exist a more villainous calumniator and incendiary."[16]

The Conway "cabal" collapsed in the spring of 1778, with Conway disgraced and Gates embarrassed, although the latter's influence in Congress was strong enough to secure an appointment as commander in the south. Although Washington and Hamilton may have exaggerated the nature of the cabal, their contempt for Gates's leadership seemed confirmed in 1780 by his behavior in the Battle of Camden in South Carolina. He fled, leaving his army to fend for itself, thereby prompting Hamilton to mock him as a man who ran away from combat. As he informed Betsy, it was obvious that "age and the long labors of military life had not in the least impaired his activity; for in three days and a half, he reached Hills borough, one hundred and eighty miles from the scene of action. . . . He has confirmed in this instance the opinion I always had of him."[17] General Greene, a more reliable leader, replaced Gates.

The Gates episode was just one of a number of occasions for Hamilton to display his loyalty to Washington and to appreciate the burdens his commander in chief had to endure in the course of the war. Another one of his senior generals, Major General Charles Lee, like Gates a former British officer, replicated Gates's behavior by taking improper credit for the defense of Charleston in 1776 and then failing to support Washington after the defeat at White Plains later that year. Lee was to demonstrate his incompetence again at the Battle of Monmouth in June 1778 in New Jersey. By disobeying Washington's orders to hold the line until the commander in chief could bring his troops from Valley Forge, Lee sabotaged a potential victory.

Hamilton observed from the sidelines as Lee frittered away an opportunity to destroy Sir Henry Clinton's forces. The new French ally had sent a fleet to close the Delaware in June 1778, forcing the British to evacuate Philadelphia. New York might have been taken as well if Admiral Comte d'Estaing had moved more quickly. In any event, Washington hoped to exploit the British retreat through New Jersey and sent Hamilton and other aides-de-camp to survey possibilities for attack. When the encounter at Monmouth Courthouse failed to cut off Clinton's troops, the impatient colonel placed some of the blame on the excessively cautious advice of

Washington's generals, but primarily on the dithering of General Lee. With his customary self-confidence, Hamilton assailed Lee as a "driveler in the business of soldiership or something much worse."[18]

His commander in chief shared his aide's condemnation of Lee's conduct on the battlefield and saw to it that Lee was brought to a court-martial. There was probably some hyperbole in the charges that Laurens and Hamilton had made over the general's panicking in the crisis, and Washington's instructions left some leeway in interpretation. Still, Lee lost his command and was humiliated in a duel with Laurens over insulting remarks about the commander in chief. That Gates and Conway wanted to remove Washington from his command was obvious; that there was a coherent plot to do so is less certain. Similarly, that Gates was an erratic, self-promoting adventurer was equally obvious; that he was quite the bumbler that Hamilton made him out to be was less so.

Despite Lee's disgraceful behavior, the battle at Monmouth Courthouse could still be claimed as a victory of sorts, and, if so, Hamilton was convinced that "America owes a great deal to General Washington for this days work. . . . A general route [sic] dismay and disgrace would have attended the whole army in any other hands but his. By his own good sense and fortitude he turned the fate of the day."[19] In these conflicts with Washington's rivals, his aide invariably took a strong stand by the general's side. But it should also be noted that Hamilton frequently made observations to his wife and friends that projected a stream of mature comments on just how the war should be fought, even as he displayed at the same time the romantic and impulsive side of his temperament. He would have exhorted the commander in chief to ignore the counsel of his advisers and behave as boldly as he himself would. Hamilton identified himself with Washington, supported him passionately, and yet had doubts about the quality of his mind.

Benedict Arnold and Major André

Hamilton's ambivalence toward the head of his official family grew in the next crisis that he shared with his commander in chief. The treason of General Benedict Arnold and the hanging of the British spy, Major John André, was an emotional issue that separated Washington from Hamilton even as the younger man understood the reasons for his commander's decision. As in so many instances during the war, Hamilton was at the scene of a dramatic situation, this time when Arnold, then American commander at West Point, was preparing to turn over plans of its fortifications to the British. Arnold, the true hero of Saratoga and arguably the most gifted general in the Continental Army, had been progressively frustrated by Congress's refusal to give appropriate recognition to his contribution. Encouraged by his wife's connections with Tory Philadelphia, this Connecticut Yankee betrayed his country.

Washington and his staff were en route to West Point in September 1780 when they learned of both the capture of Major André, the British middleman, and Arnold's escape to British protection in New York. Hamilton was shocked by Arnold's "treason of the deepest dye" and angry over his failure to catch the traitor as he made his way to New York.[20] Even more noteworthy was the display of his romantic spirit. When he met Arnold's wife, he "saw such an amiable woman frantic with distress for the loss of a husband she tenderly loved—a traitor to his country and to his fame, a disgrace to his connections. It was the most affecting scene I ever was witness to." Hamilton clearly was deceived by the clever woman who played on his empathy for "all the sweetness of beauty, all the loveliness of innocence, all the tenderness of a wife and all the fondness of a mother." The susceptible recent bridegroom went on: "Could I forgive Arnold for sacrificing his honor, reputation, and duty, I could not forgive him for acting a part that must have forfeited the esteem of so fine a woman."[21] He failed to recognize that Arnold's wife too was acting a part; she was deeply involved in the plot.

The romantic strain in Hamilton's character was equally apparent in his sentimental admiration for the British spy, Major André, who was executed for his role in Arnold's treason. André, adjutant-general of Sir Henry Clinton, was captured in civilian clothes, and so he was hanged rather than shot as an officer and gentleman. Hamilton was deeply affected by André's possession of "a peculiar elegance of mind and manners, and the advantages of a pleasing person. His sentiments were elevated and inspired esteem."[22] His admiration may have been prompted by his conception of the doomed major as his doppelgänger, or at least as a model of courage under the most trying circumstances. Hamilton's concern for André's fate was deep enough to elicit a proposal that he suggest an exchange of André for the traitor Arnold. Such an idea offended Hamilton's sensibilities. As he told Betsy, "I knew I should have forfeited his esteem by doing it, and therefore declined it. As a man of honor he could not but reject it and I would not for the world have proposed such a thing."[23] The same sense of noblesse oblige that precluded any effort to free André led to Hamilton's urging Washington to allow death by a firing squad rather than by hanging, as befit a man of character. Although the general himself was favorably impressed by André's conduct, he rejected his aide's recommendation.

The Breach with Washington

Hamilton's resentment of Washington's decision was hardly reason enough to cause a break between the two men. It was the culmination, however, of almost four years of perceived slights and, more important, continued refusal on the part of Washington to give his aide an opportunity to take up the sword once again. Much of the trouble lay with Hamilton's immaturity. Although he was respectful of Washington's leadership, his appreciation was always qualified. And while he was loyal in a crisis, he was increasingly impatient with his role as aide and could not appreciate the many advantages that his position in Washington's family had given him. After the Arnold affair, he had time to reflect on his situation. Not only was he ready for action, but he also felt he deserved promotion. He complained that officers with field commands moved ahead while he languished.

His patron disappointed him at every turn. When General Lafayette, three years his junior, proposed, with Hamilton's advice, an attack against New York, Washington demurred. When the commander in chief did allow further planning, the lieutenant colonel envisioned himself leading two hundred men in this campaign. For this prospect to materialize, he needed Washington's approval. Although the general had said in the past that he would grant him a chance "to act a conspicuous part in some enterprise that might perhaps raise my character as a soldier above mediocrity," Washington rejected the application, partly because Hamilton's service as an aide was so important to him, and partly because of the jealousy that his promotion would provoke among his peers.[24] None of Hamilton's justifications swayed the general. Nor did the intervention of his friend Lafayette move the general, despite the paternal attention Washington usually gave to Lafayette's judgments. The young Frenchman was convinced that "the general's friendship and gratitude for you, My Dear Hamilton, both are greater than you perhaps imagine. I am sure he needs only to be told that something will suit you and when he thinks he can he certainly will."[25]

Hamilton was not convinced. Newly married in December 1780, he was all the more frustrated when he saw no early outlet for his ambitions. In retrospect, his break with Washington in February 1781 should not have come as so great a surprise as it apparently did to his father-in-law, Philip Schuyler. Hamilton's confidence in his own military talents, combined with an elliptical denigration of Washington's abilities, served as a trigger to his impulsive tendencies when a suitable moment arrived. It was not that he consciously set out to undermine his leader; he shared most of Washington's biases with respect to the conduct of the Continental Army and the Continental Congress. But, as noted earlier, the ties lacked the intimacy that bound Washington to Lafayette. The breach erupted suddenly and seemingly unpremeditatedly. As he told his father-in-law, the general asked to speak with him as they passed each other on the stairs, and he, of course, agreed. But on the way up to Washington's room, Lafayette stopped him on the staircase "about a minute on a matter of business." When Hamilton broke away to rejoin Washington, the general was waiting for him at the head of the steps and "in a very angry tone" accused him of keeping him waiting ten minutes, adding: "I must tell you Sir you treat me with disrespect." His aide responded "without petulancy," he claimed: "I am not conscious of it Sir, but since you thought it necessary to tell me so we part."[26] Such was the apparent cause of the break between them.

Schuyler was confused by Hamilton's account and asked him to consider the consequences. Although abstaining from judging the propriety of Hamilton's behavior, he felt that "quitting your station must therefore be productive of very material injuries to the public, and this consideration, exclusive of others impels me to wish that the unhappy breach should be closed, and a mutual Confidence restored." Washington, he noted, admitted that he was "the Agressor [sic], and that he quickly repented of the Insult."[27] Schuyler was correct in concluding that Washington regretted the harsh words and was prepared to resume the old relationship. Hamilton, however, had no wish for reconciliation unless a command was in the offing. It is a tribute to Washington's patience and magnanimity that he was not offended by the rude rejection of his efforts to put the incident behind them. In contrast, the younger man boasted to fellow aide James McHenry that "the Great Man and I have come to an open rupture" and seemed to revel in his own inflexibility.[28]

Despite the bravado of the foregoing letter to McHenry, Washington's ambitious and impulsive aide did not cut all his ties.

He admitted that the "Great Man" was also a man of integrity, unlike most of his detractors. And, more important, the general was essential to the American cause: "these considerations have influence[d] my past conduct respecting him, and will influence my future. I think it necessary he should be supported."[29]

How much of this grudging respect was granted to appease his father-in-law's sensibilities, how much to keep alive his hopes for a field command, and how much really reflected his awareness of Washington's distinction as a leader despite his disaffection for him as a person, has to be speculative. What is verifiable was Hamilton's continuing presence on the general's staff in the winter and spring of 1781, and Washington's continuing willingness to condone the reason for his former protégé's behavior. Although the general still would not grant Hamilton a regimental command for fear of offending other officers equally worthy, he did give him a line commission as a lieutenant colonel. This was not sufficient compensation for the impatient Hamilton, who was prepared to surrender his newly gained commission and return to civilian life.

Toward Yorktown

Writing to his wife in July 1781, Hamilton exulted in achieving his goal at last. Washington yielded, and "though I know my Betsy would be happy to hear that I rejected his proposal, it is a pleasure my reputation would not permit me to afford her. I consented to retain my commission and accept my command."[30] Hamilton was not aware, however, that if Washington gave in to his former aide's importunities, it was because of the pressure exerted by Generals Greene and Lafayette. In his eagerness for combat the potential battalion commander would have accepted a post in either the north or south. Washington's preference was to mount an assault against Clinton in New York, but the French ally, finally mobilizing its resources, preferred to take on Lord Cornwallis in Virginia. Despite a pregnant wife in uncertain health, the new commander of a light infantry unit marched happily with his French friends south to Virginia.

This mission might be his last chance for glory on the battlefield, as the war seemed to be coming to an end. He recognized that news of Admiral Comte de Grasse's ships being sighted off the Virginia capes meant that "our operations will be expeditious, as well as our success certain."[31] In this context his overblown sentiments of despair over being parted from his wife sounded hollow. Was he deceiving Betsy and himself when he claimed the "intention of renouncing public life and devoting myself wholly to you"? "Let others waste their time and their tranquillity in a vain pursuit of power and glory; be it my object to be happy in a quiet retreat with my better angel."[32] Such was the rhetoric that marked Hamilton's correspondence with his wife, even as he pursued the "power and glory" that he professed to renounce.

After years of service as an aide-de-camp, Hamilton found at Yorktown the joy of combat he had been seeking since drilling with his college classmates in the churchyard of St. George's Chapel in 1775, and even earlier as a clerk in St. Croix envisioning war as a path to a better future. Side by side with his friend Lafayette, he attacked a well-fortified British bunker. Leaping over a moat in advance of his men, he emerged from the fracas without a scratch. In his report to Lafayette, he praised the performance of his fellow officers, particularly that of John Laurens, but he modestly omitted his own role. Calling attention to his own gallantry was unnecessary; there were others to do it for him. In his portrait of the surrender scene, artist John Trumbull placed Battalion Commander Hamilton in a position of honor among Washington's officers. And the Confederation Congress, in January 1782, cited his contributions to the victory at Yorktown in October 1781.

The French Connection

In retrospect, the war had given the young immigrant all that he could have hoped for when he rallied patriotic sentiment as a college student in New York. His experiences included access to the highest social circles in America, including an upwardly mobile marriage; familiarity with most of the military leaders of the Revolution through his appointment to Washington's staff; a deepening relationship with the new political elite, which had begun with McDougall and Jay in 1775; and, not least, exploiting an advantage that his knowledge of French conferred at a time when France played an important part in the war. Even after his break with Washington, his command of the language made him a valuable connection with General Comte Rochambeau as the allies planned what would be the final chapter of the war on American soil.

Hamilton was able to take advantage of his mother's Huguenot background (at least as far as language was concerned) from the beginning of his service as aide. His acquaintance, even intimacy, with prominent French officers opened another window of opportunity for advancing his political education, and particularly for developing insights into the imperatives of American foreign policy. He quickly recognized the importance of bringing France into the war, but he also saw obstacles in winning over this potential ally. As he informed his old mentor, the Reverend Hugh Knox, France's self-interest would be served by reducing British power, which explained French surreptitious support early in the war "both by their intrigues in foreign courts and by supplies of every kind." He also understood that country's understandable reluctance to be drawn into the conflict "unless she finds our affairs to require it absolutely."[33]

Once France made an alliance with the new nation after Saratoga, Hamilton was embarrassed by the apparent willingness of too many Americans to relax their efforts and turn the war over to their new ally. With the customary hyperbole that he exhibited in private correspondence, he complained to Laurens that "our countrymen have all the folly of the ass and all the passiveness of the sheep in their composition. They are determined not to be free and they can neither be frightened, discouraged nor persuaded to change their resolution. If we are saved, France and Spain must save us."[34] At the same time, he felt that it was not in France's interest to abandon the United States because of its failures. In fact, he urged James Duane, a prominent New York member of the Continental Congress, to make use of this knowledge to extract more funds from the ally: "The most effectual way will be to tell France that without it, we must make terms with Great Britain. This must be done with plainness and firmness, but with respect and without petulance, not as a menace, but as a candid declaration of our circumstances."[35]

The young officer's sangfroid in observing the French factor in American policy and in advising policymakers of the course that should be taken would have done credit to the wiliness of Benjamin Franklin. Like Franklin, he knew when to yield to France's prejudices. In the notorious feud between Silas Deane and Arthur Lee as they worked uneasily together in Paris to bring France into the war, Hamilton sided with Foreign Minister Comte de Vergennes against Lee, even though he was no admirer of the speculator Deane. If both Versailles and Madrid distrusted Lee, "This disqualifies him absolutely for representing our interests in either of those Courts—at least at the present juncture. . . . At another period, I should not be fond of removing a Minister from a Court. . . . But we ought to accommodate our conduct to circumstances. This is a time to yield. I repeat it; the friendship of France is our *unum necessarium.*"[36]

Hamilton's tolerance for the many French volunteers seeking service in Washington's army extended only up to the point where they would be useful to the United States, or where their unhappiness with conditions in the army might damage American relations with France. Writing to John Jay in 1779, he noted that the Marquis de Fleury, who was en route home, might return as secretary to the next embassy to the United States. If so, he is "such a person as we ought to wish to possess influence in the affairs of France and in the councils of the man entrusted with the management of her concerns in America."[37] Three months later, Hamilton was less optimistic about the uses to which Fleury might be put: "Indeed, I should be loth to trust him with any of our present ministers. He is a fellow of too much intrigue and penetration, to be placed near any but a man who would know how to make use of these talents."[38]

Given his sophistication in the ways of statecraft, Hamilton would have been a fitting candidate for the post of secretary to the American minister to Paris or as special envoy to secure new loans in 1781. The missions never materialized. In winter and spring 1781, Hamilton would have seized any chance to escape Washington's camp, and he would have made the most of this particular opening. He understood both the importance of a strong financial base for America and the service France might provide in achieving this objective. Moreover, he might have smoothed Franklin's path in exploiting both France and Britain as the new nation moved toward full freedom from European control. Not incidentally, his friendship with Jay might have mitigated that Francophobe's hostility to Franklin's devious negotiations. It was unlikely that his uncharacteristic outburst of self-pity earlier in 1780 when he was denied the secretaryship was the reason for his failure to win the approval of the Continental Congress in December of that year. His lament lacked credibility. In fact, it may have been the very depth of his "connexions" that spoiled his application for a post abroad. Washington continued to be dependent on his aide, and his future father-in-law did not want to postpone his daughter's wedding for the sake of Hamilton's career.

Junior Statesman in Wartime

The streak of immaturity that may be attributed in part to his impatient ambition was usually exhibited when he found his hopes thwarted. They devolved for the most part on personal relations. When it came to matters of state, Hamilton was a font of good sense, and his advice was appreciated by the nation's leaders even when it could not always be followed. Even before he joined Washington's staff, his correspondence was filled with commentary not only on how the war should be managed but also on the directions the new nation should take.

In a sense, Hamilton's involvement in affairs of state in the course of his military duties represented a natural progression from his activities as a college student. In that period he had become acquainted with such leaders as Alexander McDougall and John Jay and made contributions to the polemics of the Revolutionary movement. Hence, it was not surprising that, in March 1777, a three-man standing committee of the New York legislature, which included Jay, invited him to offer his observations about the state of the army and of the nation itself as he saw them from his perch on General Washington's staff. The newly appointed aide-de-camp did not hesitate to make his views known—and make them known frequently and confidently. Inevitably, many of his communications centered on the progress of the war on the battlefields. He was occasionally mistaken in his predictions, but even when he admitted, in April, that "the opinion I advanced respecting the Enemy's not moving before the beginning of May seems to be Shaken," he still thought it might not be "entirely overthrown by some present appearances."[39] The enemy, he judged, was running a great risk in moving from New York to the Delaware.

While he may have misjudged British abilities in the foregoing instance, he was more perceptive in his judgment that General Burgoyne could not successfully invade New York from Canada. When the British general captured Fort Ticonderoga en route south, the stroke was "heavy, unexpected and unaccountable." Actually, Hamilton did account for the loss in suspecting cowardice or treachery on the part of the American commander but then went on to predict that Burgoyne's "success will precipitate him into measures that will prove his ruin."[40] Burgoyne's disaster at Saratoga two months later proved Hamilton's point.

The conduct of the war was not the young officer's primary interest in communications with the New York legislature, the Continental Congress, and later the Confederation Congress. Running throughout his commentaries was a concern first for making laws that would apply to all the states, whether it be, as he instructed the legislature, about the virtues of a uniform standard for courts-martial or about the importance of including a strong chief executive in the state constitution that New York was creating in 1777. In an exchange of correspondence with Gouverneur Morris, a member of the New York Committee of Correspondence, Hamilton generally approved of the new state constitution but was quick to point out its defects. Morris admitted that there were faults; specifically, it was "deficient for the Want of Vigor in the executive, unstable from the very Nature of popular elective Governments and dilatory from the complexity of the Legislature."[41] Hamilton agreed with Morris's judgment of the executive but disagreed with him about the instability of popular governments. From his examination of historical records, "A representative government, where the right of election is well regulated & the exercise of the legislative, executive, and judiciary authorities, is vested in select persons, chosen *really* and not *nominally* by the people, will in my opinion be most likely to be happy, regular and durable."[42] Here is the young soldier functioning as a statesman and projecting ideas that would become an integral part of his political philosophy. Implicitly he accepted democracy, the judgment of the people, provided it was interpreted by "select persons."

His philosophical reflections on the nature of government were less in evidence during the war than his impatience with the inability of the Continental Congress to manage the war properly. As he informed Isaac Sears in 1780, "It is impossible the Contest can be much longer Supported on the present footing. We must have a Tax in kind. We must have a Foreign Loan. We must have a Bank on the true principles of a Bank. We must have an Administration distinct from Congress and in the hands of Single Men under their orders. We must above all things have an army for War, and an Establishment that will Interest the Officers in the Service."[43] To James Duane, he went into greater detail about the defects of the Congress, notably its lack of power. Granting its successes in declaring independence, levying an army, and making alliances, the new Confederation "is defective and requires to be altered; it is neither fit for war, nor peace. The idea of an uncontrolable [sic] sovereignty in each state, over its internal police, will defeat the other powers given to Congress, and make our union feeble and precarious."[44]

Three serious defects needed to be addressed, he advised Duane. First, he deplored the Confederation's giving the power of the purse to state legislatures. Second, there was no effective executive. Single individuals must be given the responsibility of managing executive departments, and "as these men will be of course at all times under the direction of Congress, we shall blend the advantages of a monarchy and republic in our constitution."[45] A third defect—obviously his most immediate concern—was the absence of appropriate controls to provision the army. He criticized the dependence on state purchases for supplying its needs. Corruption and inefficiency were rife. "Without a speedy change, the army," he feared," must dissolve; it is now a mob, rather than an army, without cloathing, without pay, without provision, without morals, without discipline."[46]

His solution was to grant Congress powers to use the sale of unoccupied lands to raise revenue. The agency for this change would be "a convention of all the states with full authority to conclude finally upon a general confederation," although his preference was that Congress resume exercising "the discretionary powers I suppose to have been vested in them for the safety of the states."[47] Admitting that this recommendation was too radical to be accepted, he still hoped that the new confederation would "give Congress complete sovereignty, except as to that part of internal police, which relates to the rights of property and life among individuals and to raising money by internal taxes." These are the appropriate functions of state legislatures, but "Congress should have complete sovereignty in all that relates to war, peace, trade, finance, and to the management of foreign affairs, the right of declaring war."[48]

Of all the problems confronting the new nation, Hamilton believed that the financial bind was the most important for the immediate future. It affected every aspect of governance. The plain fact was the insufficiency of financial resources to fight a prolonged war. To raise supplies, Congress was obliged to "go on creating artificial revenues by new emissions, and as these multiplied their value declined. . . . It was in a great degree necessary."[49] The only way to stem the rise of inflation was to secure foreign loans. And to win over foreign lenders he proposed an American bank under the name of the Bank of the United States subscribed to by the monied class. Men of wealth and standing would be further attached to the government through a partnership with a trading company that would furnish capital to the bank and draw commensurate profits. Such were the mature reflections of Washington's aide, who in the midst of war composed a plan of government that would be the bedrock of his political future.

Hamilton had a candidate for the head of a financial department in Robert Morris, whom he named directly in his long letter to Duane and whom he addressed both before and after Morris was appointed superintendent of finance by the Confederation Congress. Given the detailed advice drawn from the young man's remarkable knowledge of the financial history not only of the British colonies but also of Britain, France, Sweden, and the Netherlands, it was Hamilton himself who could have filled the position. He was offering his informed advice in the midst of war and in the midst of his own quarrel with Washington. The contrast between his petulant behavior toward the general in February and the worldly-wise advice to Morris in April 1781 is striking. It was all the more so when one considers that he seemed absorbed in plans to reconstruct the nation on the eve of the Battle of Yorktown. Indeed, he published the third of his six pamphlets, "The Continentalist," a learned discourse on the necessity for increasing congressional powers, on August 9, 1781, at a time when he was eagerly looking forward to a combat command.

There was nothing of the dashing soldier yearning for glory in his correspondence with the leaders of the nation. He communicated as an equal and, indeed, was regarded as such. When General John Sullivan asked Washington his opinion of Hamilton as a financier, he answered that, although he had never talked about the subject with him, "I can venture to advance from a thorough knowledge of him, that there are few men to be found, of his age, who has a more general knowledge than he possesses."[50] His age notwithstanding, Sullivan would have nominated Hamilton as the nation's financier if Congress had not preferred Morris.

It was not just age that persuaded Congress to bypass Hamilton. Rather, it was his perpetual willingness to go public with his condemnations as well as his plaudits. Outraged at the maneuvers of Samuel Chase, a Maryland delegate to Congress, to profit illegally from supplying flour to the French fleet, Hamilton published a jeremiad against profiteers who used inside information to enrich themselves by betraying the public trust. It was published in the *New York Journal* in its October–November 1778 issue under the name of "Publius." His attack was intemperate but anonymous. More open was his feud with historian Dr. William Gordon, who reported that Hamilton was overheard in a coffeehouse to declare that the people should rise up and help Washington overthrow Congress. Hamilton was as passionate in his attacks against enemies as he was in support of his friends. It was not surprising that as the war was coming to a close, one of the heroes of Yorktown failed to receive a call to civilian service—at least in 1781.

Washington's caution suggested reasons why Hamilton's cause in Congress, whether it was as an envoy to France or as an official in the executive department, was turned aside. It was his youthful impulsiveness and propensity for making as many enemies as friends that postponed his entry into public life, if only briefly. His professed purpose in the winter of 1782 was to return to the bosom of his family, a prospect made all the more desirable by the birth of the first of his eight children.

He left the army in March 1782, frustrated over the lack of any prospects for advancement, with a characteristically extravagant gesture of renouncing "from this time all claim to the compensations attached to my military station during the war or after it." But even as he turned his talents toward the law, he made a point of noting that he took "this opportunity to declare, that I shall be at all times ready to obey the call of the public, in any capacity civil, or military . . . in which there may be a prospect of my contributing to the final attainment of the object for which I embarked in the service."[51] His new career would be as a lawyer, studying in the office of his old friend, Robert Troup. Hamilton certainly needed the money that a career in law would bring. He may have convinced himself for the moment that he had lost "all taste for the pursuits of ambition. The ties of duty alone or imagined duty keep me from renouncing public life altogether. It is however probable I may not be any longer actively engaged in it."[52] He did become a lawyer, but his absence from public life did not survive the year.

Notes

1. Quoted in Brookhiser, *Alexander Hamilton*, 28.

2. Quoted in Schachner, *Alexander Hamilton*, 45.

3. Schnackner, ed., "Narrative of Hercules Mulligan of the City of New York," *William and Mary Quarterly* 4 (April 1947): 210.

4. To the Convention of the Representatives of the State of New York, August 12, 1776, in Syrett and Cooke, 1:187.

5. To the Convention of the Representatives of the State of New York, July 26, 1775, ibid, 1:186.

6. Hamilton, *Life of Alexander Hamilton*, 1:54–56.

7. To the Convention of the Representatives of the State of New York, March 6, 1777, Syrett and Cooke, 1:200.

8. Quoted in Flexner, *Young Hamilton*, 137.

9. AH to Lieutenant Colonel John Laurens, April 1779, Syrett and Cooke, 2:37.

10. AH to Laurens, June 30, 1780, ibid., 348.

11. Cited in Broadus Mitchell, *Alexander Hamilton*, 1:200.

12. AH to George Washington, November 6, 1777, Syrett and Cooke, 1:354.

13. Ibid.

14. Quoted in Hendrickson, *Rise and Fall*, 79.

15. Washington to Brigadier General Thomas Conway, November 9, 1777, in John C. Fitzpatrick, ed., *The Writings of George Washington*, 39 vols. (Washington, DC: Government Printing Office,, 1931–1944), 10:29.

16. AH to George Clinton, February 13, 1778, Syrett and Cooke, 1:428.

17. AH to Elizabeth Schuyler, 1780, ibid., 2:422.

18. AH to Elias Boudinot, June 5, 1778, ibid., 1:510.

19. Ibid., 512.

20. AH to Elizabeth Schuyler, September 15, 1780, ibid., 2:441.

21. Ibid., 441–42.

22. AH to Laurens, October 11, 1780, ibid., 467.

23. AH to Elizabeth Schuyler, October 2, 1780, ibid., 449.

24. AH to George Washington, November 22, 1780, ibid., 509.

25. Lafayette to AH, November 28, 1780, ibid., 517.

26. AH to Philip Schuyler, February 18, 1781, ibid., 563–64.

27. Schuyler to AH, February 25, 1781, ibid., 576.

28. AH to Major James McHenry, February 18, 1781, ibid., 569.

29. AH to Philip Schuyler, February 18, 1781, ibid., 567.

30. AH to Elizabeth Schuyler, July 10, 1781, ibid., 647.

31. AH to Elizabeth Schuyler, September 6, 1781, ibid., 675.

32. Ibid.

33. AH to Hugh Knox, July 1777, ibid., 1:301.

34. AH to Laurens, June 30, 1780, ibid., 2:347.

35. AH to James Duane, September 3, 1780, ibid., 41.

36. AH to Laurens, May 22, 1779, ibid., 53.

37. AH to John Jay, July 25, 1779, ibid., 111.

38. AH to Jay, September 29, 1779, ibid., 191.

39. AH to the New York Committee of Correspondence, April 5, 1777, ibid., 1:219.

40. AH to Jay, July 13, 1777, ibid., 285–86.

41. Gouverneur Morris to AH, May 16, 1777, ibid., 253–54.

42. AH to Gouverneur Morris, May 19, 1777, ibid., 255.

43. AH to Isaac Sears, October 12, 1780, ibid., 2:472.

44. AH to James Duane, September 3, 1780, ibid., 402.

45. Ibid., 405.

46. Ibid., 406.

47. Ibid., 407.

48. Ibid., 407–8.

49. AH to ——[Schuyler?], December 1770–March 1780, ibid., 239.

50. Washington to John Sullivan, February 4, 1781, in Fitzpatrick, ed., *Writings of George Washington*, 21:181.

51. AH to Washington, March 6, 1782, Syrett and Cooke, 3:5.

52. AH to Richard Kidder Meade, March 1782, ibid., 69–70.

3

Toward the Constitution

1782–1789

When Hamilton ostentatiously laid down his arms after Yorktown to return to the bosom of his family, he had reason enough to remove himself from public life. The war continued, but opportunities for glory were unlikely in the future. Always short of funds, he needed to find employment that would provide an income for his growing family; his pride would hardly permit him to live very long as a ward of his father-in-law in Albany. Not that Philip Schuyler wished to remove the Hamiltons from his estate. Schuyler's admiration for his daughter's husband increased rather than diminished as the war drew to a close. If he was anxious to win Hamilton a place as a New York delegate to the Continental Congress in 1782, it was primarily in appreciation of his talents.

Hamilton stayed in Albany for a crash course in the law, a calling that would earn him a living. As always, he was a young man in a hurry. For a period of three months, from April through June 1782, he had the help of his former classmate, Robert Troup. His friend's tutorials were useful but not vital to the aspiring lawyer's success. Hamilton's writings since 1775 displayed a knowledge of such luminaries as Blackstone, Pufendorf, and Grotius that accelerated the progress of his studies. He quickly assimilated the discipline, and before he took the bar examination he had gathered his systematically compiled notes into a manual that became a model for future students of the law.

In July 1782 he was accepted as an attorney entitled to practice before the New York Supreme Court. And in

November the Supreme Court, finding him "of sufficient ability and Competent learning to practice as Counsel in this Court Ordered that he be admitted accordingly."[1] New York followed the British practice of separating the solicitor, who prepared cases, from the barrister, who argued them in court. In nine months, Hamilton qualified for both positions.

Hamilton was fortunate in having the ordinary three-year apprenticeship for the bar waived because of a loophole in the state law. In January 1782 special consideration was allowed to those students whose careers had been interrupted by wartime service. On the strength of his undergraduate studies at King's College, Hamilton claimed, with pardonable exaggeration, that he was a law student manqué as early as 1775. As he informed Lafayette in the fall, "I have been studying the art of fleecing my neighbors" over the past ten months.[2]

There is no doubt that Hamilton's skill as a lawyer could have fleeced more clients than just his neighbors. Almost immediately, he was recognized as a litigator of formidable talent. But his remark to Lafayette was more playful than serious. He undermined the sentiment by adding that he would "soon be a grand member of Congress. The Legislature at their last session took it into their heads to name me pretty unanimously one of their colleagues."[3] After some months he would return to the law—or so he said.

What his career reveals over the years is the continual temptation of public life that almost always superseded his desire for personal wealth, no matter how depleted his financial resources were. His law practice was intermittent, pursued by him whenever matters of state did not intrude—and those times were comparatively rare. Throughout the years of the Confederation, he was on the sidelines much of the time, at best a peripheral player—as tax collector in New York for the Confederation, as a New York delegate to the Confederation Congress, as New York Assemblyman, and as a member of the New York delegation to the Constitutional Convention of 1787. But no matter how minor his formal role was, his words were attended to closely. Polemical pamphlets followed a pattern that had its origins in the Revolution and would continue into the Federalist period. In or out of office, he spoke and wrote consistently of the need for a unified nation with a viable economic system under a strong central government. The reformed government's function was not only to achieve economic prosperity for the new nation but also to cope with the potentially malevolent power of the two European nations—Britain and France—that could challenge the future independence of the United States.

Tax Collector, 1782

His letter to Lafayette was written in November, but his civil service had begun while he was still studying law. At the urging of Robert Morris, superintendent of finance for the Confederation Congress, Hamilton accepted the position of receiver of continental taxes for the State of New York. His salary would be 4 percent on such monies as he collected. Tempted as he was by the call to service and by the importance of tax collection to the future of the Confederation, the law student demurred at first. He and his family could not live on the meager funds he figured to gather, and he consented only when Morris promised to pay the percentage on the state quota whether or not it was actually collected. Hamilton's was not the spirit of avarice but a realistic assessment of the deficiencies in the confederal system.

The cause itself fitted Hamilton's conception of the proper governance of the United States, and despite his skepticism he put his considerable energy and eloquence into seeing to it that New York paid its allotted contributions to the central government. Morris recognized the qualities his young friend could bring to the cause: useful army experience, connections with a powerful family, and "perfect knowledge of men and measures, and the abilities heaven has blessed you with."[4] Hamilton responded much as Morris had anticipated; he vigorously lobbied members of the legislature as well as the governor himself, and seemingly made progress. The legislature passed a resolution, ostensibly in favor of a Congress strong enough to raise funds more effectively, and it went on record as urging a convention of the states to revise the Articles of Confederation.

The New York legislature's actions were momentary. What was needed was a full examination and reformation of the requisition system. Asking states to fulfill quotas without the ability to enforce the requests was a prescription for failure. Dependence upon France during the war was the result of the Continental Congress's inability to collect taxes. Requisitions could not work for it, or for its successors in the Confederation. To effect change, Hamilton understood that "mountains of prejudice and particular interest are to be leveled."[5] The declining fortunes of France as the war was drawing to a close made change all the more pressing.

Hamilton used the sixth essay of his "Continentalist" series, written in July 1782, to expand his views not only on the collection of taxes but also on the need for the federal government to regulate trade among states. Much of his argument had been prefigured in his correspondence as a soldier. But it took on urgency as French support dwindled and as his experience in New York raised his fears about the very survival of the new Republic. There is a note almost of despair in his plaint: "It would seem as if no mode of taxation could be relished but that worst of all modes which now prevails, by assessment."[6] Although a land and poll tax would be the simplest to levy and the easiest to collect, he thought that this idea seemed doomed both from the avarice of landholders wishing to transfer the burden to others and from the ignorance of those who held that a fixed poll tax would be unfair to the poor.

This sixth "Continentalist" was his farewell address to the New York legislature and an unhappy termination of his position as receiver of taxes. He left with a sense of failure. New York's economy was in a precarious state. Five of its fourteen counties, including New York City, were still in British hands; foreign trade was for all practical purposes nonexistent, and there was little hard money anywhere in the state. Of the $365,000 Congress had assessed New York, Hamilton was able to collect less than 2 percent. It was small comfort that Virginia with a much larger quota had paid nothing, or that Georgia and South Carolina had equated their supplies to the army with their contributions to the nation's finances. One of the few consolations in this dismal situation was Hamilton's appointment as a delegate from New York to the Continental Congress where his voice might carry more weight.

Delegate to Congress, 1782–1783

Hamilton was elected in July, and he arrived in Philadelphia in November. It was unlikely that he anticipated greater success in his support for a stronger central government, but Philadelphia, as opposed to Albany, provided a national arena for his cause. Actually, there was little opportunity in the eight months he spent as a delegate to evangelize his colleagues with any prospect of success. For one thing, the chamber was frequently short of the delegates from the requisite nine states required to act on issues. Few of those who did attend were sufficiently interested to take on committee duties or even to engage in debate.

But there were kindred spirits in Philadelphia, such as James Madison of Virginia and Robert Morris, in what passed for a central government. With Hamilton's support, Morris sought to secure the adoption of Congress's impost resolution of 1781. Although customs duties would not solve the nation's debt in the long run, they could be, as historian E. James Ferguson has noted, "an entering wedge to establish the principle of federal taxation."[7] Once the impost was accepted, taxes on polls, property, and commodities might follow, and public credit would be established.

Hamilton's residual skepticism about New York's commitment to the nation appeared justified when Congress failed to adopt an impost or any other tax. Rhode Island, fearing the "Yoke of Tyranny fixed on all the states, and the Chains Rivetted,"[8] initiated a pattern of rejection. Virginia then repealed its support of an impost, effectively ending Morris's and Hamilton's hopes for a stronger central government. When a major state rescinded its grant of a modest 5 percent to follow the leadership of the state most opposed to centralized government, prospects for the Union appeared dim. Such was the situation Hamilton encountered in the first six weeks in Philadelphia.

Confronting Mutiny

The inability of the Confederation to raise funds by import duties or by any other means produced interlocking domestic and foreign crises. The war was not yet terminated, and New York in particular was vulnerable as British forces remained in both New York City and the western part of the state. The first, and potentially the most serious, challenge involved unpaid soldiers, officers and men alike. The threat to the stability of a fragile new nation from disgruntled men in arms should have been obvious; a military coup could have terminated the life of the Confederation and exposed the Republic to domestic and foreign designs on its unity. Soldiers demanded their deferred pay and veterans their pensions. Presumably, an impost would have raised sufficient funds to satisfy their claims.

Nationalists in Congress recognized that the military could be exploited to pressure their opponents into accepting federal taxes and, with them, the payment of the public debt. Morris and Hamilton acted on this assumption. They sought to channel the military's discontent into constructive actions by employing Washington's prestige at the head of the army in Newburgh to end the crisis to the advantage of those who sought a stronger government.

Delegated to approach the hero of the Revolution, Hamilton warned Washington of the difficulties of keeping "*a complaining and suffering* army within the bounds of moderation," and reported rumors to the effect that the commander in chief was not espousing the soldiers' interests "with sufficient warmth." Washington, in turn, sensed "something very misterious [*sic*] in this business,"[9] suspecting army leaders were collaborating with public creditors to redress their grievances, even to the point of encouraging them not to disband until their demands were met.

What Hamilton and Washington were responding to specifically was the démarche that General Alexander McDougall, an early patron of Hamilton, had made toward Congress on behalf of the aggrieved army. If no action were taken, the implication was that the men would not fight in the event war continued, and would not disband should peace be won. It was to defuse the possibility of mutiny that Hamilton asked Washington to make it clear to army and country that he would make the dissidents' cause his own. A crisis seemed to have been brewing in early March when General Gates, Washington's old antagonist, and his aide, Major John Armstrong, used inflammatory rhetoric to inspire the army to resist disbandment until their concerns were met. To calm the emotions that these sentiments might raise, Washington addressed his troops at Newburgh on March 15 and urged them to avoid "any measure which viewed in the calm light of reason, will lessen the dignity and sully the glory you have hitherto maintained."[10]

The commander in chief's prestige once again upstaged Gates and minimized the danger of a military uprising against the civil government. The Confederation Congress responded by granting five years of full pay in lieu of pensions, but given the lack of funds, these payments took the form of federal securities. From the Hamiltonian perspective, this was not a satisfactory conclusion. It merely added burdens, as Ferguson observed, "to the growing body of the federal debt and join[ed] the officers with the other public creditors."[11] If the nationalists were attempting to use the army's discontent to intimidate Congress and push it into reforms that would give new powers to the central government, the Newburgh crisis failed to serve their purposes.

Was Hamilton's behavior indicative of a conspiracy of creditors and militant nationalists aiming to transform the Confederation? Historian Richard H. Kohn makes such a case in entitling his article, "The Inside History of the Newburgh Conspiracy: America and the Coup d'Etat." He credits Washington with making the Newburgh affair significant for what did not happen.[12] Kohn cites Hamilton as one of the conspirators. Although he was a close associate of Robert Morris, arguably the prime mover in the drive for a stronger government, evidence of his participation in a conspiracy was also circumstantial at best. There was no doubt of the colonel's sympathy with the army's cause, but there was also no question about his abhorrence of a military coup. This was the meaning of his asking Washington to take control of the situation. Associating Hamilton with dissidents such as Gates ignores a record of conflict between that controversial figure and the Schuyler family as well as with General Washington.

Hamilton's behavior a few months later when Pennsylvania soldiers marched on Philadelphia to claim their back pay was more revealing of his view of the military in the young Republic. Peace with Britain had been affirmed with the furloughing of troops without pay. After armed soldiers surrounded the congressional chambers in Philadelphia, the state government refused to disperse the mob. Hamilton, representing Congress, then denounced the "impropriety of such irregular proceedings, and the danger they will run by persisting in improper conduct."[13] The New Yorker's anger was directed as much against the behavior of the Supreme Executive Council of Pennsylvania as it was against the protesters. As a member of a committee that Congress had appointed to deal with the crisis, Hamilton was distressed by the unwillingness of Pennsylvania to call out the state militia to suppress the mutineers. The spectacle of unruly soldiers milling around the State House where Congress was sitting, holding the congressmen prisoners, was intolerable to him. Although the soldiers did not attack the legislators when they left the building, the disrespect with which they were treated rankled in Hamilton. Even more galling was the willingness of the weak Pennsylvania government to negotiate with mutineers and, in a sense, condone their actions.

In a lengthy letter to John Dickinson, president of the Supreme Executive Council of Pennsylvania, the New Yorker deplored the inability of Pennsylvania's militia to intervene and spoke of damaging consequences. He refused to consider the actions of the mutineers as "the disorderly riot of an unarmed mob," but saw them rather as "the deliberate mutiny of an incensed soldiery carried to the utmost point of outrage short of assassination. The licentiousness of an army is to be dreaded in every government, but in a republic it is more particularly to be restrained, and when directed against the civil authority to be checked with energy and punished with severity."[14] This was not the first time, nor would it be the last, that Hamilton spoke out against disorder. He understood and empathized with the grievances of the soldiers, but, before offering clemency, the authority of government had to be vindicated.

Once again, Hamilton directed most of his anger at the behavior of the Pennsylvania authorities. It was not enough to claim that the soldiers committed no acts of violence. Nor did he accept the decision to negotiate as a sensible way of handling the situation. What the soldiers witnessed was weakness on the part of the Council and the consequent impotence of Congress that forced its withdrawal from the city. Only when the mutineers' leaders feared the approach of Washington's troops, accompanied by a belated call for the Pennsylvania militia, did the mutiny dissolve. "They were reduced," he claimed, "by coertion [sic] not overcome by mildness."[15]

The Treaty of Paris

In the background was a consideration that frequently dominated Hamilton's thoughts about disorder in America: namely, its impact upon the nation's relations with the outside world. How would an ally such as France or an enemy such as Britain look upon a country that could not protect itself from internal disruption? Inability to defend itself could undermine the conduct of a successful foreign policy. Such was a potential consequence of the weakness of Congress. The problem, then, was more than an inability to raise funds for paying the nation's foreign and domestic debts. The flight of Congress to Princeton symbolized a fatal flaw that might have destroyed the Republic: the absence of means to sustain itself in the face of centripetal forces within the Confederation and external pressures from Europe anticipated the demise of the republican experiment.

It is important to observe that the war with Britain was still ongoing when Hamilton took his seat in Congress in November 1782. From his perspective, New York remained in peril. Britain occupied posts in the western part of the state, and British authority remained paramount in New York City until November 1783, three months after Hamilton left Congress and returned to Albany. Throughout this period, American relations with the British enemy were fractious. Granted that the fall of Lord North's ministry pointed toward termination of the war and American independence, his successors, Charles James Fox, the new foreign secretary, and Lord Shelburne, the colonial secretary, differed over the terms of independence. Fox, as the more radical figure, wanted a generous treaty, while Shelburne sought to link political independence for the United States to a dependent role in the British economic system.

Although peace negotiations had been initialed in Paris in November, news of this event took weeks to cross the Atlantic. Given the continued British occupation of much of New York, Hamilton had special reasons for concern. When he deplored Rhode Island's refusal to comply with the recommendation of Congress for a duty on imports, he had in mind not only the need for solidarity among the states but also the message that failure to raise funds would give comfort to the nation's enemies. In commenting on the negative report from the Speaker of the Rhode Island Assembly, he reminded his colleagues that "we have an enemy vigilant, intriguing, well acquainted with our defects and embarrassments. We may expect that he will make every effort to instill diffidences into individuals, and in the present posture of our internal affairs, he will have too plausible ground on which to tread."[16] Restoring confidence in the nation's public credit would be a signal to our enemy that his designs would fail.

Hamilton made these comments before Congress in December 1782, but they symbolized a pattern of thought that deemed American unity essential. While still in the New York legislature, he was credited with sponsoring a resolution calling for a convention to revise the Articles of Confederation. Among the many reasons for change was the disposition of "the present British Ministry . . . not less hostile than that of their Predecessors, taught by Experience to avoid their Errors, and assuming the Appearance of Moderation, are pursuing a Scheme calculated to conciliate in Europe, seduce in America." In brief, Hamilton, speaking through his father-in-law, distrusted Britain's putative steps toward ending the war, "while they direct all their Attention and Resources to the Augmentation of their Navy."[17] Both houses of the New York legislature passed the resolutions unanimously and sent them on to Congress. Nothing came of these efforts in 1782, but the section devoted to the British menace had more relevance for the New Yorker than the resolutions themselves.

France presented a different set of problems. Hamilton was depressed over France's naval defeat in 1782 and worried about its impact on continued support of the American cause. Withdrawal of the French army from the war would lead to a further drain on American finances. At a time when its minister in Philadelphia, Chevalier de la Luzerne, warned that France's reverses made it imperative for the Americans to exert greater effort, Hamilton had to admit to Lafayette that "these states are in no humour for continuing exertions; if the war lasts, it must be carried on by external succours. I make no apology for the inertness of this country. I detest it; but it exists . . .; I am sorry to see other resources diminished."[18] But it was not just the French military situation that disturbed Hamilton. He had enough information from Lafayette to suspect the steadfastness of France's commitment to American independence. He recognized its need to serve its own interests first, and with respect to its Spanish ally, those interests would not be identical with those of the United States. Considering the "duplicity and unsteadiness," he was writing, as late as January 1783, of his skepticism about the successful conclusion of peace negotiations.[19] The provisional peace treaty between the United States and Great Britain actually had been signed on November 30, 1782, but its terms were not known until March 12, 1783, when the ship carrying dispatches from the peace commissioners reached the United States.

Knowledge of the contents of the provisional articles resolved some of the questions that Hamilton and Congress had about future relations with the European powers. Certainly, there was relief that the war was ended and jubilation that the territory acquired was so extensive. There were some in Congress, along with Robert R. Livingston, the Confederation's secretary of foreign affairs, who were disturbed about the peace commissioners disobeying instructions to undertake no actions without the knowledge and concurrence of the French ally. Hamilton was not among them, trusting Jay's suspicions of France's behavior, as he did, and appreciative of the peace commissioners' independent initiative.

In speaking before Congress on the provisional peace treaty a week after the news reached America, however, he expressed mixed feelings about the behavior of the commissioners. Although Hamilton recognized France's selfish motives and had disapproved of the instructions to the American delegation in Paris, he also disapproved of their conduct in not showing the preliminary articles to the ally before they signed them. "This conduct," he speculated, "gave an advantage to the Enemy which they would not fail to improve for the purpose of inspiring France with indignation &

distrust of the U.S."[20] Not that he feared an Anglo-French combination against America; rather, he foresaw the end of mutual confidence between France and the United States because of the separate negotiations, and particularly because of the secret article on the Florida boundary. Nevertheless, in light of the "insincerity and duplicity of Lord Shelburn[e]," he proposed that the ministers be commended for their achievement.[21]

Looking at Anglophiles and Francophiles with equal distaste, he found "men in trust who have a hankering after a British connection. We have others whose confidence in France savours of credulity. The intrigues of the former and the incautiousness of the latter may be both, though in different degrees, injurious to the American interests; and make it difficult for prudent men to steer a proper course."[22] Hamilton's skepticism derived in part from the domestic obstacles to the nation's survival that army unrest and the inability of the Confederation to honor its debts had created. He was making his judgments, as he observed to Washington, at a moment of "ill-humours." He admitted that "there are good intentions in the Majority of Congress . . . even if there is not sufficient wisdom or decision."[23] He even recognized some progress on plans for funding all public debts including that of the army, and he had particular hope that New York would be evacuated in the spring.

It was clear that the quarrels of Europe could serve American interests, but only if the Republic was wary of the danger of being caught up in those quarrels. At the same time, Hamilton warned Governor Clinton not to disregard unwelcome provisions in the peace treaty. He was thinking particularly of Article 5, which stipulated that Congress should "earnestly recommend" that the state restore the properties of Loyalists who had not fought on the British side, and of Article 6, prohibiting future confiscation of Loyalist possessions. There was no hint of Anglophilia in his wish to honor the terms of the treaty. Rather, he feared that failure to do so would give Britain an excuse to violate its own obligations, which included withdrawal from parts of New York. As he observed, "we ought certainly to be cautious in what manner we act, especially when we in particular have so much at stake."[24]

Hamilton always recognized that no matter how malevolent the British government might appear, it was in the interest of the United States to restore a beneficial commercial relationship with the former mother country. He chaired a committee that recommended that the commissioners include provisions in the final peace treaty giving Americans the same access to Britain's imperial territories that its own subjects enjoyed. Much of the caution he expressed with respect to honoring treaty obligations to Britain derived from omissions in the agreement, the most prominent being the reconstruction of commercial relations. But the opening of British markets was not to be achieved under the Confederation. His fears proved prescient when the British denied the United States access to their markets and cited unfulfilled treaty commitments as part of their rationale.

Hamilton was also sensitive to the issue of national security. One way to achieve this security would be to place the sea and land forces exclusively under the control of the central government. As chairman of a committee reporting on a "Military Peace Establishment" in June 1783,[25] he emphasized the importance of having the army, navy, and militia under national control for political as well as military reasons. Familiar themes, such as the superiority of the federal government over state governments in military matters, characterized this report. The chairman revealed his experience as an artillery officer in his judgment that "there must be a corps of Artillery and Engineers kept on foot in time of peace, as the officers of this corps require science and long preliminary study, and cannot be formed on an emergency."[26]

The same sentiments may be found in his effort to give more powers to the secretary of foreign affairs. Neither Livingston nor his successor, John Jay, had been given sufficient leeway to meet on equal terms with European foreign ministers. He strongly urged the establishment of a "Department of Foreign Affairs," with its head empowered to control the nation's diplomatic establishment with minimal interference from Congress.[27] This was the direction in which Hamilton wanted to push Congress during his short time in that body. The discontents of the Continental Army at Newport and the potential mutiny in Pennsylvania gave an urgency to change that made failure all the more difficult to accept.

Discouraged by the lack of progress in reforms he thought vital to the future of the Republic, Hamilton left Philadelphia at the end of July 1783 with much the same sense of failure that he had harbored when quitting New York the year before. As he prepared to terminate his "short apprenticeship in Congress," he applauded Jay for his contributions to the nation as commissioner in Paris. He used the occasion to sum up the problems facing the Confederation but not without seeing a ray of hope for the future. "We have now happily concluded the great work of independence," he observed, "but much remains to be done to reach the fruits of it. Our prospects are not flattering. Every day proves the inefficacy of the present confederation, yet the common danger being removed, we are receding instead of advancing in a disposition to amend its effects."[28] His resolution to call for a convention to amend the Articles of Confederation, written in all likelihood in the same month, was an expression both of optimism and of depression. Knowing its certain fate, he did not submit the amendment. Yet he could also tell Jay with his hope "that when prejudice and folly have run themselves out of breath we may return to reason and correct our errors."[29] His urging Jay to continue his services abroad could be taken as an indication of his faith in the future.

Brief as his own service was, the New Yorker had made his mark in Congress. Whether it was his stance on the problems of the army or his persistent demands for more effective taxation or his understanding of the complexities inherent in the peace treaty, he exercised a leadership that was widely recognized if not always appreciated. As in the past, his forceful personality won devoted friends and determined enemies in his eight months in Philadelphia and Princeton. James McHenry, his colleague on Washington's staff and at this time a delegate from Maryland, reported that "the homilies you delivered in Congress are still recollected with pleasure. The impressions they made are in favor of your integrity; and no one but believes you a man of honour and republican principles. Were you ten years older and twenty thousand pounds richer, there is no doubt but that you might obtain the suffrages of Congress for the highest office in their gift."[30]

Defender of Tories

With a sense of depression over his experiences in Philadelphia, Hamilton was ready to practice law in New York, where he hoped to repair his fortunes—in the City itself, newly freed from British occupation, rather than in Albany. Although habitually in need of funds, he was almost always easily seduced into public service when a call came. But for a brief time in the mid-1780s, he was able to devote his talents to his profession. He quickly rose to its summit, achieving the kind of visibility he had won in the army and in Congress. Sometimes in competition and at other times in collaboration, his rivals in the growing metropolis included such luminaries as Aaron Burr, Rufus King, and his old friend Robert Troup. His success was immediate, helped not surprisingly by his connections with the Schuyler interests. But his preeminence at the bar owed much more to his quick mind and articulate tongue. Biographer and editor Jacob Cooke cited a distinguished judge whose long career permitted him to compare Hamilton with Daniel Webster: "In power of reasoning Hamilton was the equal of Webster; and more than this can be said of no man. In creative power Hamilton was infinitely Webster's superior."[31] This was high praise for a young man with such limited experience in the legal profession.

A primary source of his income derived from litigation over claims arising from war damages and from confiscation of Tory properties, The question of how those Loyalists who were prepared to transfer their allegiance to the new nation should be treated was a major issue of the day. New York had more than its share of Tories who had cheered British victories and, in many instances, profited from the plunder of patriot property. New York City alone had 50,000 Loyalists, many of them refugees from patriot vigilantes. This had been a major factor in delaying Britain's evacuation of the city until November 1783.

Their presence in such large numbers helps to account for the animus felt by many New Yorkers toward their former compatriots. The Tories were now beyond the pale, deserving of whatever fines, imprisonment, or confiscation of their property that the New York legislature could enact. Governor Clinton's assertion that he would "rather roast in hell to all eternity than . . . show mercy to a damned Tory" set the tone that dated from 1779, when a Confiscation Act had been passed for "the forfeiture and sale of the estates of persons who had adhered to the enemy."[32]

Hamilton was away on military service in 1779 and an appointee to the Continental Congress in July 1782, when the Assembly passed the Citation Act, relieving New York debtors of their obligations to Tory creditors. But there was no question about his feelings on the subject. His initial concern was exhibited in his support of Articles 5 and 6 of the peace treaty, which anticipated restoration of Loyalist properties and prohibition of future confiscation. As noted, he had pressed this issue to prevent the British from using American inaction as an excuse for avoiding their own obligations under the treaty. In a strongly worded letter to Clinton, he gave other reasons for treating Tories with consideration. They were potentially "useful citizens" who should not be driven out to "form settlements that will hereafter become our rivals animated with a hatred to us which will descend to their posterity." He warned that nothing "can be more unwise than to contribute as we are doing to people the shores and wilderness of Nova-Scotia, a colony which by its position will become a competitor with us among other things in that branch of commerce in which our navigation and fisheries and navy will essentially depend. I mean the fisheries in which I have no doubt the state of New York will hereafter have a considerable share."[33]

The newly settled New York City lawyer was not content to let the matter rest with a letter of protest to the state's governor. He fully recognized that his sense of the national interest was not shared by the dominant political forces in New York, led by Governor Clinton himself. In March 1783 the legislature had demonstrated how far it would go to punish New York's Tories. The Trespass Act gave any citizen whose property had been seized and turned over to a Tory under British auspices the right to sue the illegal occupant for damages. Hamilton's earlier fears seemed to be realized. The Trespass Act would accelerate emigration, and he foresaw the consequences; some violent papers sent into the city have determined many to depart, who hitherto have intended to remain. . . . Our state will feel for twenty years at least, the effects of the popular phrenzy."[34]

Was Hamilton revealing once again the streak of conservatism that he had displayed in 1775, when he helped to rescue his Tory teacher from an angry mob? Or was it simply an example of his foresight in realizing the folly of alienating a valuable portion of the state's population and making enemies of people who were now willing to stake their fortunes on the future of the new nation? Arguably, both considerations were in Hamilton's mind when he wrote a public letter in January 1784, under the name of Phocion, an enlightened Athenian general distinguished for his magnanimity toward his enemies. He castigated the New York legislature for violating Articles 5 and 6 of the peace treaty not only by refusing to restore confiscated Loyalist property but also by ignoring the prohibition against further confiscation. It was illegal, he asserted, to expel "a large number of their fellow-citizens, unheard, untried . . . in the face of the constitution, without the judgment of their peers, and contrary to the laws of the land."[35] Many former Loyalists, he asserted, were wealthy merchants with the capital that the state needed for its future prosperity.

Hamilton's concern embraced more than the special interests of Tories. The nation's future was at stake. Imprudent legislators "not only overleap the barriers of the constitution without remorse, but they advise us to become the scorn of nations, by violating the solemn engagements of the United States. They endeavor to mould

the Treaty with Great-Britain, into such form as pleases them, and
to make it mean any thing or nothing as suits their views. They tell
us, that all the stipulations, with respect to the Tories, are merely
what Congress will recommend, and the States may comply or not
as they please."[36] The young lawyer had not forgotten the warnings he had raised as a congressman about the necessity of respecting the treaty in order to win British compliance on such matters as
the evacuation of territory in western New York.

At the heart of his admonitions, the pamphleteer placed the
basic liberty of the individual for which the Revolution had been
fought. Every citizen could be affected "by letting into the government, principles and precedents which afterwards prove fatal to
themselves. Of this kind is the doctrine of disqualification, disen-
franchisement and banishment by acts of legislature . . . if it may
banish at discretion all those whom particular circumstances render obnoxious, without trial or hearing, no man can be safe, nor
know when he may be the innocent victim of a prevailing faction."[37]

Beyond Hamilton's florid rhetoric about ensuring the rights of
even the most unpopular individuals was a practical appreciation
of how the nation's relations with Europe would be affected. If the
actions of the New York legislature in the Trespass Act violated the
terms of the peace treaty, Britain would be given license to remain
in the West and to restrict American commercial opportunities. For
this reason, it was important that the central government be able
to prevent states from subverting such treaties. By drawing attention to the impact of a weak America facing a dangerous world,
Hamilton did more than urge respect for the provisions of the treaty
with Britain; he made this awareness an instrument in asking for a
stronger Congress. His polemics on the importance of elevating the
nation over the state were embodied in the assertion that states
should not be allowed to challenge the terms of a treaty.

The price Hamilton paid for defending Tories was defamation
at the hands of his enemies in the Clinton camp and among small
farmers and merchants who had suffered from the British occupation. At the same time, Hamilton's eloquence and skill as defender of Tory rights won him a comfortable living as a lawyer.
These rewards were necessary in light of his growing family. But
success at the bar was never his primary concern any more than
was the protection of Tory clients. Appreciative as he was of the
business that large landowners and prosperous merchants offered
him, Hamilton saw his service as defender of the liberties of all
citizens threatened by the emotions of an unthinking majority. And

to defend the nation that would protect these liberties, he always kept the need for a stronger national government uppermost in his consciousness.

The Bank of New York

In this context, Hamilton's interest in organizing a bank to provide credit for enterprising capitalists was part of the stabilization of society that he sought. He was influenced by the goals of Robert Morris's plans for a Bank of North America, centered in Philadelphia, that would hold government bonds, make loans to the central government, and discount its notes. Chartered by the Confederation, it would draw on private funds to strengthen the sinews of government, particularly as its circulating notes would become the national medium of exchange. By supplanting state currencies it would promote national solidarity. Morris was speaking Hamilton's language when he wrote to Jay about uniting "the several States more closely together in one general money connexion, and indissolubly . . . attach many powerful individuals to the cause of our country by the strong principle of self-love and the immediate sense of private interest."[38] Such were Morris's and Hamilton's hopes in 1783. As early as 1781, Hamilton had stated flatly that a national bank was vital to securing public credit: "There is no other that can give to government . . . extensive and systematic credit."[39]

Although Morris's Bank of North America never became the nation's bank, it inspired emulation in New York. Sparked by the ambitions of his enterprising brother-in-law, John Barker Church, Hamilton supported its New York counterpart—the Bank of New York—for the strength its success might give the nation, although he remained aware of the riches it would bring merchants and businessmen. His advocacy became more strident when it appeared that Robert R. Livingston was proposing a land bank that would accept mortgages as collateral for lending money on the security of land. This bank, in Hamilton's eyes, was a threat to a free society. If government could devalue the property of creditors at the instigation of popular majorities, the Lockean linkage of property and liberty would be lost. As he observed, "If everything floats on the variable and vague opinions of the governing party, there can be no such thing as rights, property or liberty."[40] To prevent this diversion of funds from a "money bank" to a land bank, Hamilton led the organization of the Bank of New York and became a director and stockholder. It is worth noting that he owned only one share of stock when he resigned as director in 1788 and never benefited personally from his connection with the bank unlike his brother-in-law, for whom he had served as an agent.

His lack of acquisitiveness did not signify any lack of zeal for the institution's success. Hamilton drew up the bank's constitution in 1784 and was instrumental in expanding the voting rights of larger stockholders, but the key mission was winning a charter. He worked for seven years to achieve it in the face of hostility from Governor Clinton and from a public suspicious of money men. He went to considerable lengths to provide full explanations of the value such a bank would have for society at large, including farmers. Although not a state institution, it would receive deposits of state funds and would lend money to the state. And above all, its banknotes would serve as stable currency that would benefit all segments of society.

Hamilton's aspirations for the service that his bank would render to his state—and, by extension, to the nation—failed under the Confederation, as did the Bank of North America. Not until 1791 did the bank receive a charter, but it was from the Federal Union, in which Secretary of the Treasury Hamilton could at last have a national bank established. He justified his public advocacy for banks by the need for society to recognize how instrumental they were to the strength of the nation. A working banking system would be a major factor in helping the United States confront a hostile world beyond its borders.

Supporting Vermont

The nation would first have to bring order within its borders, and in the mid-1780s those prospects looked dim. The internal disorder in the Confederation appeared overwhelming. The absence of authority in the central government encouraged disunion among territories and denied the possibility of nationhood because of the excessively sovereign powers of the original members. For example, Kentucky and Tennessee, claimed by Virginia and North Carolina respectively, might move into Spain's orbit so that their products could find overseas markets, since the Confederation was powerless to force Spain to open New Orleans to American goods. The Gulf of Mexico would be open to Kentucky and Tennessee shippers only if they left the Union.

The vulnerability of the United States to the machinations of its European adversaries was exacerbated by the centrifugal forces within the nation. Nowhere was this more apparent than in New York and New Hampshire, where both states staked their claims to territory in Vermont, an aspiring state that had declared its independence in 1777. New York accused Vermonters of encroaching on its territory, but when the state appealed to Congress it was hardly surprising that no action resulted. Given the number of influential New York investors in Vermont lands, a movement arose in the New York legislature to dispatch troops to oust the intruders. This was one occasion on which Hamilton's aristocratic friends, such as Gouverneur Morris, shared the sentiments of Governor Clinton, the self-styled populist who was also a land speculator in Vermont.

Hamilton parted company with his friends over coercion, and indeed over efforts to keep Vermont out of the Union. While still a member of Congress in January 1783, he had advised Governor Clinton "to take up the affair of Vermont on the idea of a *compromise* with Massachusetts and New Hampshire," on the grounds that Congress was unlikely to act. He recognized that although New York would recover no part of "the revolted territory," the national interest offered no other alternative.[41] Citing rumors of a Vermont conspiracy to throw off the authority of the United States and join Britain, Clinton believed that a small military force could compel submission. Although tales of toasts to King George may have been apocryphal in 1783, there was no doubt that the Allen family, the most prominent land claimants in Vermont, explored the possibilities of an alliance with Britain before the decade had ended.

Hamilton continued to advise caution. Military action would only inflame the Vermonters and probably win over other New Englanders to their cause. Whatever concerns he may have had for the investments of leading New Yorkers and however much he deplored infringements on property rights by Vermonters, his primary concern was with the nation and its precarious position vis-à-vis foreign adversaries. By 1787, as a member of the New York legislature, Hamilton urged his colleagues to accept the reality of an independent Vermont and minimize the threat of an alienated neighbor's seeking help against American pressure. And that help, he recognized, would come from the British in Canada, whether or not the impulse came from selfish speculators like Ethan and Ira Allen or from angry citizens frustrated over being denied membership in the Union.

Consequently, in 1787, Hamilton submitted a bill in the New York legislature directing the state's delegates in Congress to acknowledge and confirm the independence of Vermont and to pursue admission of the territory into the Confederation with the proviso that claims to lands in Vermont granted by New York in its colonial status would be respected. Hamilton's benevolence was motivated by fear that Vermont would pursue connections with Britain. He worried that Vermonters, "confederated with a foreign nation," would be "ready upon any rupture" to throw their weight "into an opposite scale."[42] For the sake of America's future, it was vital that the state be attached to the United States. Hamilton did recognize the possibility of Vermont's rejecting the terms of independence: "Her refusal would be a conclusive evidence of determined predilection to a foreign connection; and it would shew [*sic*] the United States the absolute necessity of combining their efforts to subvert an independence, so hostile to their safety."[43]

There was nothing new in his conviction that the survival of the nation was paramount and had to be the prerequisite for the enjoyment of all other rights. In the Vermont context, his reference to subverting Vermont's independence was intentionally misleading. His premise was that such an achievement would be possible only if the states combined their efforts, and "if they should find themselves unequal to the undertaking, it must operate as a new inducement to the several states to strengthen the union."[44] Here he was using New York's case against Vermont to remind his fellow New Yorkers of the importance of national power to cope with regional affairs. Only a stronger nation could win over Vermont to the Confederation and deny Britain the opportunity to take advantage of the schisms within the United States.

Whether his adversaries caught all the nuances of Hamilton's arguments was immaterial. The bill he introduced in 1787 passed the state's Assembly but failed in the Senate. The implications for America's relations with Britain in the disposition of the Vermont issue were lost as the concerns of speculators, that odd combination of Governor Clinton's and Hamilton's natural constituencies, emerged predominant. As in the past, when his ideas did not initially prevail, Hamilton continued his battle and ultimately won. In 1789, Vermonters and New Yorkers under the rubric of the new Federal Union accepted a Hamiltonian settlement whereby Vermont provided a cash settlement to New York claimants. Moroeover, further compensation in the form of land grants in western New York appeased the claimants. When Vermont entered the Union in 1791 with New York's approval, Hamilton deserved a considerable share of the credit.

From Annapolis to Philadelphia

The young lawyer's preoccupation with the supremacy of the nation over the state, displayed elliptically in his plea for Vermont independence, characterized his life under the Confederation. He had an opportunity in his law practice to make his fortune, even without the patronage of his father-in-law. His successes in the years 1784 to 1786, when he was not encumbered with public responsibilities, suggest that he could have provided well for his growing family—ultimately eight children—had accumulation of personal wealth been his goal. But the challenges of public service were irresistible. His retirement from the Confederation Congress in 1784 was relatively short-lived. In the spring of 1786, Hamilton won fourth place among sixteen candidates in securing one of the eight Assembly seats representing the City and County of New York. He was back again as gadfly to the Clintonians who controlled the legislature in 1787, as they had in 1783 when Hamilton served as receiver of continental taxes for the State of New York.

Hamilton's mission in the Assembly was not to exploit public office for private gain, or in any special way to promote the financial welfare of the Schuyler clan or of the class to which they belonged. Rather, it was primarily to promote the cause of a stronger central government that would keep the fragile young nation safe from its foreign enemies and lay the foundations for a prosperity that a weak Confederation could not supply. If the measures he advocated increased the value of the properties and investments of the seaboard merchants and great landowners, they would also strengthen the central government. In New York the Clintonians, the champions of state power and the debtor farmer, controlled the Assembly. Hope for change rested with the Schuylers and Van Rensselaers and Livingstons of the state Senate.

The means were familiar. The prospects of an interstate commercial convention to meet in Annapolis seemed to hold more promise than the customs duties that he had backed so vigorously earlier in the decade. The inability of Congress to control interstate commerce rendered meaningless the authority it had to make commercial treaties with foreign nations on a basis of reciprocity. There was no machinery in place to force a state to respect such treaties, nor could Congress prevent a state from imposing its own duties.

These deficiencies facilitated disregard for any mutual commercial relationship. Britain could deny entry into any of its ports without fear of retribution by the United States. Should one state impose a tariff on British imports, another would undercut its neighbor's actions by admitting the same goods without duties.

The nation resented Britain's hostility in denying America a commercial treaty as well as refusing to evacuate the Northwest posts or to compensate American slaveholders for those slaves emancipated by the British army. This resentment fueled sentiment for granting Congress power to control commerce. Hamilton had emphasized the importance of creating an American navigation system while he was still in the army, and in this respect Anglophobia had fostered his program. But Britain was his target only because it was the most dangerous European power in this period, not because it was governed by a system alien to American values. In fact, he continued to admire many elements of the British imperial system, and he was uncomfortable with those Americans who placed compensation for freed slaves at the head of their list of grievances. Hamilton himself was a sponsor in 1785 of the New York Society for the Manumission of Slaves.

Virginia's James Madison took the leadership in calling a convention to redress problems with interstate commerce, and Hamilton managed to have himself appointed a New York delegate through the efforts of Robert Troup in the Assembly and Philip Schuyler in the state Senate. The precedent of Virginia and Maryland working out an agreement to share the navigation of the Potomac in 1785 had inspired the broader aims of the Annapolis Convention. But no one recognized more clearly than Hamilton how limited those aims still were, or understood how slight were the possibilities of success for those gathered. Only five states were represented, and there were no accomplishments to report. But then little has been anticipated. As he wrote to Betsy, he expected to be in Annapolis "eight or ten days perhaps a fortnight."[45] He was right; there were only three more meetings before adjournment. In that last meeting on September 14, Hamilton pointed the way to a more comprehensive convention that would address "the important defects in the system of the Foederal Government." He recommended that the states appoint commissioners to meet in Philadelphia in 1787 "to devise such further provisions as shall appear to them necessary to render the constitution of the Foederal Government adequate to the exigencies of the Union."[46]

The path was open to change, but some skeptics questioned whether it could be effected through constitutional means. James Monroe in Virginia suspected a conspiracy afoot in Annapolis on the part of the eastern financiers, as did Stephen Higginson of Massachusetts. In declining to attend that convention, Higginson confided to John Adams, "I am strongly inclined to think political Objects are intended to be combined with commercial if they do not principally engross their Attention."[47] In fact, Hamilton had to tone down his report and make his recommendations more elliptical than he would have liked. What was plain, however, was the proposed date in Philadelphia, the second Monday in May.

The Constitutional Convention

The meeting of delegates in Philadelphia should have been the fruition of Hamilton's hopes for a central government strong enough to ensure both the survival of the Republic and its future prosperity. The Massachusetts rebellion of debtor farmers led by Revolutionary war veteran Daniel Shays, a protest against bank foreclosures and heavy state taxes, took place only two weeks after the end of the Annapolis meeting and added a note of urgency to the new prospective revisions of the Articles of Confederation. Hamilton won appointment on the first day to a committee for establishing rules and order for the convention, an initiative that suggested not only his energies at work but his expectations as well. But the first day might also have been the last as far as his optimism was concerned.

For the New Yorker, the proceedings in Philadelphia from May 25 through September 27 were filled with disappointment. His voice was rarely heard, and in fact he was rarely to be found in his seat; he was absent throughout July and most of August. Part of his problem was the continuing hostility of Governor Clinton. In New York's delegation, Hamilton was outnumbered by Clintonians John Lansing and Robert Yates, whose presence guaranteed that Hamilton's positions would be nullified. But the problem was more than an inability to swing the New York vote. There was none of Madison's suppleness in his view of the proceedings. When Hamilton did speak out, it was in opposition to the two major plans—of New Jersey and Virginia—both of which failed to grant the central government sufficient executive authority to safeguard the Republic.

In a major speech on June 18, Hamilton expounded his views in extravagant language that labeled him a monarchist and Anglophile in his enemies' eyes. His notoriety rested first on his recommendation of a supreme executive authority and a senate to be elected to serve indefinitely—during good behavior. Second, it was his admission that states were an impediment to the governance he envisaged. Robert Yates reported Hamilton's saying that "I did not intend yesterday a total extinguishment of state governments; but my meaning was, that a national government ought to be able to support itself without the aid or interference of the state governments. . . . Even with corporate rights the states will be dangerous to the national government, and ought to be extinguished, new modified, or reduced to a smaller scale."[48]

His praise for the "English model" was the most incendiary issue in this commentary. He asserted, "In his private opinion he had no scruple in declaring . . . that the British Govt. was the best in the world; and that he doubted much that anything short of it would do in America."[49] Shays and the accompanying popular passions triggered this observation and, in the New Yorker's mind, should have alerted representatives from the New England states to the wisdom of having a long-term tenure in his proposed senate. As for the executive, the virtue of a monarchy was its being "placed above the danger of being corrupted from abroad." He emphasized that "one of the weak sides of Republics was their being liable to foreign influence & corruption."[50]

Hamilton was to pay for these remarks, as he would for other hyperbolic outbursts in the course of his public life over the next decade. His admiration for the British system, however, was not based on a wish for a return to British rule, or even a replication of the monarchy. His proposals rested on the strength needed by the new nation to survive, which only a powerful executive could supply. As he informed his apparently shocked fellow delegates, only a chief executive with lifetime tenure would be a safe repository of power. "If this Executive Magistrate wd. be a monarch for life—the other propd. by the Report from the Comtte of the whole, wd. Be a monarch for seven years. The circumstances of being elective was also applicable to both."[51] Arguably, the key component of this discourse was the element of election. There would be no hereditary system in place, nor would there be a denial of a social contract; the people remained the source of power. In this context, the Virginia plan did not go far enough to ensure a balance between liberty and order.

Recognizing that he was out of step with even the Madisonian planners of a stronger union as well with the dissidents in the states' rights camp, Hamilton quit Philadelphia at the end of June with a sense of failure, but not without firing a few parting shots. His impatience with the reaction he encountered originated in the continuing fears of the dissolution of the new nation. The fragility of the United States was uppermost in his mind. He scoffed at the professed object of republican government as "domestic tranquility & happiness. This was an ideal distinction. No Governmt. could give us tranquility & happiness at home, which did not possess sufficient stability and strength to make us respectable abroad." His forebodings included alliances of fractured states "with different rival & hostile nations of Europe, who will foment disturbances among ourselves, and make us parties to all their own quarrels. Foreign Nations having American dominions are & must be jealous of us."[52] As Great Britain logically was among those European nations with designs on the United States, Hamilton's Anglophilia requires discriminating evaluation.

His jab at the role of the states was a reflection of his isolated position in the convention. But although he left Philadelphia, he made a point of telling Washington on July 3 that he would return if his attendance "will not be mere waste of time." Washington in turn urged him to come back to oppose "narrow minded politicians . . . under the influence of local views."[53] Among these politicians, of course, were Governor Clinton, whom Hamilton accused in a letter to the *New York Daily Advertiser* of denigrating the convention, and the Clintonian delegates who departed Philadelphia on July 10, leaving New York without any representation. Despite these obstacles, Hamilton returned to the fray in September, resumed offering substantive recommendations, and ultimately signed the finished document despite all his earlier reservations.

The Federalist Papers

The New York nationalist did far more than simply sign on to the Constitution. He was the driving force behind the series of papers, some eighty-five in all, identified as *The Federalist*, or *The New Constitution*, and published under the name of "Publius" over a period from the end of October 1787 to the end of May 1788. Knowing that New York would be a crucial state in ratifying the Constitution, Hamilton collaborated with his old ally and patron, John Jay, and his new ally, the Virginia nationalist James Madison, to present New

York newspapers with powerful arguments for the new Union in opposition to the entrenched interests of the Clintonian adminis- tration and assembly. Although there have been questions about the writers of individual papers since Hamilton revealed the au- thorship of the essays in 1804, there is no question about Hamilton's responsibility for most of them. It may be that the most significant of the papers was Madison's No. 10, and that the one most relevant to foreign relations came from the pen of John Jay, the Confederation's secretary of foreign affairs. Nevertheless, Hamilton wrote at least two-thirds of the essays, and did so in a restrained style that made his contribution almost identical with that of Madi- son. Unlike so many of his extravagant polemics over the 1780s, he defended the new Constitution with restraint as well as with elo- quence while he celebrated the virtues of an energetic central gov- ernment. In doing so, he subsumed his own reservations about the document on the principle that, despite its defects, it was both a workable instrument of governance and the best that could be se- cured under the circumstances of the time. Hamilton's objective of securing a stable Republic may have been his greatest gift to his country, much as Publius Valerius had served Rome in its crisis.

Although he expressed his views on foreign relations more cau- tiously than his two colleagues, Hamilton was always aware of the position of Europe in America's future, not only as a negative role model but also as a continuing threat to American sovereignty. In *Federalist* No. 17, he compared, as he did in many of the essays, America's experience with Europe's, exploiting the latter as case studies of what should be avoided by the United States. More seri- ous than the failure of Old World confederacies was the feudal sys- tem of Western Europe in which "each principal vassal was a kind of sovereign within his particular demesne. The consequences of this situation were a continual opposition to authority of the sov- ereign, and frequent wars between the great barons. . . . The power of the head of the nation was commonly too weak, either to pre- serve public peace, or to protect the people against the oppressions of their immediate lords." A strong leader was needed to resolve these problems, and in the new Constitution presidential power was the instrument. Although there was no question that Hamilton would have preferred a life term for the chief executive, as he had argued at the Constitutional Convention, failing that, he accepted and supported eligibility for reelection of the president.

For proper governance the nation must have the coercive power to make and enforce laws, which in turn required such agencies as an army and police force. He assured his readers in *Federalist* No. 9 that "the utility of a confederacy, as well to suppress faction and to guard the internal tranquillity of States . . . is in reality not a new idea." But while he noted in *Federalist* No. 8 that there was no need of an extensive military establishment in a nation where "Europe is at a great distance from us," he warned that if the nation breaks down into "two or three confederacies, we should be, in a short course of time, in the predicament of the continental powers of Europe—our liberties would be a prey to the means of defending ourselves against the ambition and jealousy of each other."

Hamilton's attack on the states was indirect in this instance. But in many of the essays, notably *Federalist* No. 15, he condemned the Confederation for requiring the "concurrence of thirteen distinct sovereign wills" before any important measure could be enacted. "Each State," he judged, "yielding to the persuasive voice of immediate interest or convenience, has successively withdrawn its support, till the frail and tottering edifice seems ready to fall upon our heads, and to crush us beneath its ruins."

This denigration of the individual states under the Confederation was a running theme of the essays, but on occasion "Publius" acknowledged that the states did have a place in the new system. In *Federalist* No. 9, he ostensibly shifted his position when he patronized anti-Federalists by claiming that "the proposed Constitution, so far from implying an abolition of the State Governments, makes them constituent parts of the national sovereignty by allowing them a direct representation in the senate, and leaves in their possession certain exclusive and very important portions of sovereign power. This fully corresponds, in every rational import of the terms, with the idea of a Foederal Government."

In essence, it was not a "foederal" government that "Publius" was seeking. The use of the term was to keep alive the illusion of a confederation of states when the framers of the Constitution— Hamilton in particular—were trying to create a strong national government. The states had a place but an inferior one if the American experiment was to survive. Nowhere in the *The Federalist papers* was the Hamiltonian vision more clearly expressed than in No. 11. The America of the future would have "an active commerce, an extensive navigation, and a flourishing marine," but only if there was a "vigorous national government" to "baffle all the combinations of European jealousy to restrain our growth." No matter how much he admired aspects of its system, Britain was just one more European state that would stand in the way of an America that would be "superior to the control of all transatlantic force or influence, and able to dictate the terms of the connection between the old and the new world."

Political scientist Isaac Kramnick found these horizons "dazzling. His internationalism transcended the cosmopolitan vision of his fellow Federalists as it transcended the localism of the Antifederalists."[54] For Hamilton, the reward was not wealth for himself or his friends, nor even the salvation of the Republic he hoped to see realized. Rather, it was the fame and glory that would be attached to his name, an ambition that had animated him ever since he became a soldier more than a dozen years earlier. No matter how suspicious he was of the behavior of the common man and no matter how much importance he attached to the selfish motives of the entrepreneurial elite, his own motives held no taint of corruption.

Still, his task was not completed with the issuance of the Federalists' message to the "People of the State of New York." The state had to ratify the Constitution in the face of the general opposition of Governor Clinton and the particular hostility of Hamilton's fellow delegates Yates and Lansing, who unlike their colleague did not return to sign the document after they walked away from the convention. The opposition was formidable, all the more so because the logic of "Publius" went over the heads of most New Yorkers. If the Constitution had a chance of acceptance, it was only in part because of the barrage of arguments that Hamilton made before the New York ratifying convention, which met in Poughkeepsie, a Clinton stronghold, in June 1788. Clinton's willingness to accept a convention, and even to serve as its presiding officer, demonstrated his conviction that the Anti-Federalists held the upper hand. The Federalists were concentrated in the New York City area, and the governor intended to guarantee an Anti-Federalist majority by arranging that delegates be chosen by a broader suffrage than previously permitted. Small wonder that Hamilton could tell Madison in July that "our arguments confound, but do not convince."[55]

Nevertheless, Hamilton and his small band of distinguished Federalists, including John Jay and Robert Livingston, won the day. As New Hampshire and then Madison's Virginia approved the Constitution, New York was under pressure to follow suit. After New Hampshire became the ninth state to ratify, making the Constitution the law of the land, the Clintonians found themselves on the defensive. Although the governor reluctantly agreed to bring over his supporters, it was with the proviso that amendments be made to the document. Hamilton might have accepted these caveats had Madison not declared that "the Constitution requires an adoption *in toto* and *for ever*. . . . Any *condition* whatever must vitiate the ratification."[56] Equally subversive was the Anti-Federalist call for a second constitutional convention to consider their reservations.

Hamilton's arguments were largely reiterations of much of what he had presented as "Publius," but they were given with moderation amid professions of his loyalty to republicanism and respect for the rights of states. Whether or not they made a difference to Melancton Smith, the most articulate exponent of Antifederalism at the ratifying convention, Hamilton received the credit for converting Smith through the power of his eloquence. More likely, as historian Robin Brooks has concluded, "Smith's vote for unconditional ratification represented acceptance of objective necessities rather than 'conversion.' "[57] Smith was moved less by Hamilton's rhetoric than by the recognition that New York's rejection would not lead to support from other states. Rather, secession of New York City and its surrounding counties might result if the state did not enter the Union. As the only prominent New York City resident in the Anti-Federalist camp, he knew the mood of the city. On July 26, 1788, New York ratified the Constitution by a close vote of thirty to twenty-seven.

The accolades that the "little Lion" received from New Yorkers as the great protagonist of the Constitution were merited. Notwithstanding his reservations about that document, Hamilton's dedication to the new Union was identified and celebrated even as the debate continued in Poughkeepsie. Three days before ratification, New York shipyard workers constructed a replica of a ship called the *Hamilton* and had it pulled by ten horses in a parade down Broadway. No statesman among his contemporaries had come so far so fast. Hamilton, at the peak of his popularity among his compatriots in New York, was hailed by men from all walks of life.

Notes

1. Admission as Counsel before the New York Supreme Court, October 26, 1782, in Syrett and Cooke, 3:189.
2. AH to Lafayette, November 3, 1782, ibid., 192.
3. Ibid.
4. Robert Morris to AH, July 2, 1782, ibid., 98.
5. AH to Robert Morris, July 13, 1782, ibid., 108.
6. "The Continentalist" No. 6, July 4, 1782, ibid., 103.

7. E. James Ferguson, *The Power of the Purse: A History of American Public Finance, 1776–1790* (Chapel Hill: University of North Carolina Press, 1961), 146.

8. Ibid., 153.

9. AH to Washington, February 13, 1783, Syrett and Cooke, 3:254; Washington to AH, March 12, 1783, ibid., 286.

10. "To the Officers in the Army," March 15, 1783, in Fitzpatrick, ed., *Writings of George Washington*, 26:226.

11. Ferguson, *Power of the Purse*, 164.

12. Richard H. Kohn, "The Inside History of the Newburgh Conspiracy: America and the Coup d'Etat," 3d series, *William and Mary Quarterly* 27 (April 1970): 220.

13. AH to Major William Jackson, June 19, 1783, Syrett and Cooke, 3:397.

14. AH to John Dickinson, September 25–30, 1783, ibid., 451.

15. Ibid., 457.

16. Continental Congress—Report on a Letter from the Speaker of the Rhode Island Assembly, December 16, 1782, ibid., 217.

17. Resolution of the New York Legislature Calling for a Convention of the States to Revise and Amend the Articles of Confederation, July 30, 1782, ibid., 111–12.

18. Luzerne to Secretary for Foreign Affairs, December 31, 1782, *Journals of the Continental Congress, 1774–1789*, 24:5; AH to Lafayette, November 3, 1782, Syrett and Cooke, 3:192.

19. AH to George Clinton, January 12, 1783, Syrett and Cooke, 3:240.

20. Continental Congress—Remarks on the Provisional Peace Treaty, March 19, 1783, ibid., 295.

21. Ibid.; AH to Washington, March 17, 1783, ibid., 291.

22. Ibid.

23. Ibid., 291, 292.

24. AH to Clinton, June 1, 1783, ibid., 368.

25. Continental Congress—Report on a Military Peace Establishment, June 18, 1783, ibid., 382, 383.

26. Ibid., 382.

27. Gilbert L. Lycan, *Alexander Hamilton and American Foreign Policy* (Norman: University of Oklahoma Press, 1969), 68.

28. AH to Jay, July 25, 1783, Syrett and Cooke, 3:416.

29. Ibid., 417.

30. Quoted in Schachner, *Alexander Hamilton*, 172.

31. Quoted in Cooke, *Alexander Hamilton*, 38.

32. Quoted in Schachner, *Alexander Hamilton*, 173.

33. AH to Clinton, June 1, 1783, Syrett and Cooke, 3:371.

34. AH to Livingston, August 13, 1783, ibid., 431.

35. A Letter from Phocion to the Citizens of New York, January 1–27, 1784, ibid., 484.

36. Ibid., 486.

37. Ibid., 485–86.

38. Quoted in Ferguson, *Power of the Purse*, 123.

39. AH to Robert Morris, April 30, 1781, Syrett and Cooke, 2:617.

40. Miller, *Alexander Hamilton*, 123.

41. AH to Clinton, January 1, 1783, Syrett and Cooke, 3:236.

42. New York Assembly, Remarks on the Act Acknowledging the Independence of Vermont, March 28, 1787, ibid., 4:116.

43. Ibid., 137.

44. Ibid., 137–38.

45. AH to Elizabeth Hamilton, September 8, 1786, ibid., 684.

46. Annapolis Convention, Address of the Annapolis Convention, September 14, 1786, ibid., 3:688–89.

47. Quoted in Schachner, *Alexander Hamilton*, 188.

48. Constitutional Convention—Speech on a Plan of Government, June 18, 1787. Madison's version, Syrett and Cooke, 4:193; Robert Yates's version, ibid., 211 (footnote).

49. Madison's version, ibid., 192–93.

50. Ibid., 193.

51. Ibid., 194.

52. Constitutional Convention—Remarks on Equality of Representation of the States in the Congress, June 29, 1787, ibid., 221.

53. AH to George Washington, July 3, 1787, ibid., 225; Washington to AH, July 10, 1787, ibid., 225.

54. Isaac Kramnick, "The Great National Discussion: The Discourse of Politics in 1787," 3d series, *William and Mary Quarterly* 45 (January 1788): 28.

55. AH to Madison, July 2, 1788, Syrett and Cooke, 5:140.

56. Madison to AH, July 20, 1788, ibid., 184–85.

57. Robin Brooks, "Alexander Hamilton, Melancton Smith, and the Ratification of the Constitution in New York," 3d series, *William and Mary Quarterly* 24 (July 1967): 356.

4

Secretary of the Treasury

1789–1791

The first Washington administration is frequently and appropriately identified as the setting for the conflict between the Hamilton and Jefferson visions of America's relations with Europe. Although the depth of the conflict is too often exaggerated, as this chapter will suggest, there is another identification that is considerably wide of the mark: namely, the contrast between the seasoned, reserved older statesman, Thomas Jefferson, and the youthful, impetuous Alexander Hamilton.

Yet this image is misleading. Hamilton—thirty-four in 1789—was a year older than Jefferson when he was the principal author of the Declaration of Independence in 1776 at the age of thirty-three. Youth was no barrier to office and responsibility in this revolutionary period. More important, Hamilton's experience prior to his appointment as secretary of the treasury was no less impressive than his rival's, despite the twelve-year gap between their ages. For almost fifteen years, Hamilton had been in the public arena as polemicist, soldier, legislator, and—above all—thinker and doer in the creation of a new polity for a new world. There was an air of confidence, with a touch of arrogance, about his expectations for himself and his country. His reservations about the Constitution had long been put aside, as his role in *The Federalist Papers* made clear, and he was excited about the new government that would come into being in 1789, not least because he knew he would have, and would deserve, a prominent role in it.

The desire for fame, glory, and power were all part of the ambition that drove Hamilton. But they were informed by a vision of the new nation that was only peripherally connected to the Anglophilia that has been attached to his career. Although he had clearly identified a preference for a British model in the debates over the Constitution, Britain's role for the most part was just an instrument in achieving a great national destiny for his adopted country. At the risk of hyperbole, biographer Broadus Mitchell underscored the romantic element in asserting that "he was in love with the noble ideal of creating a vigorous, expanding nation. Nothing was too difficult or interfered too much with his private concerns. He exerted himself in this behalf not from a sense of duty, nor with an eye to his own fame, but from a consuming affection. This was his fulfillment."[1]

Setting the Scene

Still, his eye on the survival and prosperity of the nation did not prevent him from exulting in the influence he believed he had in the shaping of the new government, including that of his home state of New York. Although he failed in his efforts to unseat Governor Clinton in 1789, his party won both houses of the New York legislature and sent two Hamiltonians—Rufus King and Hamilton's father-in-law, Philip Schuyler—to the new United States Senate. But his primary attention was on the choice of president and vice president, under the auspices of an Electoral College, which he prized as his guarantee that men "preeminent in ability and virtue" would be selected for these high offices. The small number of electors chosen for their possession of "information and discernment requisite to such complicated investigations" would ensure that the nation's future would be in the proper hands.[2] The Electoral College was compensation for the failure of the Constitutional Convention to accept his other recommendations.

Hamilton was not one to leave the matter totally to chance. The presidency was not a problem, given the national consensus over George Washington. The only difficulty here was to persuade the general to accept the office. In August 1788, two weeks after New York had ratified the Constitution, Hamilton was pressing Washington in the name of national unity to do so: "I take it for granted, Sir, you have concluded to comply with what no doubt be the general call of your country in relation to the new government. You will permit me to say that it is indispensable you should lend yourself to its first operations."[3] In fact, the former aide did not take Washington's concurrence for granted. When the general seemed to hesitate to commit himself beyond saying that "it is my great and sole desire to live and die, in peace and retirement, on my own farm," Hamilton replied that he "would be deeply pained . . . if your scruples in regard to a certain station should be matured into a resolution to decline it." He insisted that "a citizen of so much consequence as yourself has no option but to lend his services if called for."[4]

Hamilton's presumptions succeeded, despite the general's assurance that he "should unfeignedly rejoice, in case the Electors, by giving their votes in favor of some other person, would save me from the dreaded Dilemma of being forced to accept or refuse."[5] Even before Washington had formally committed himself, Hamilton was turning to the problem of the vice presidency. He may have regarded the Electoral College as his handiwork, but he was aware that the Constitution did not make it clear which of the electors' votes were for the president and which for the vice president. John Adams of Massachusetts was ultimately his choice, largely because the prospect of a Clinton or Hancock winning the post was out of the question, from his perspective. But he did not trust the opinionated, independent-minded New Englander, who was as jealous of Washington's fame as he was of Benjamin Franklin's. The New Yorker granted Adams's "love for the public good" and his sound knowledge of the world as countervailing factors at the same time that he feared a cabal might elevate Adams above Washington in the Electoral College.[6] Hence, he pressed such an Adams supporter as James Wilson of Pennsylvania to throw away a few votes to minor candidates and thereby ensure Washington's primacy. Adams was not happy with these machinations, but he did not know that it was Hamilton who manipulated the results.

Hamilton's prominent part in forming the Washington presidency went beyond managing the process. Once the general took office, the young confidant gave advice on "the etiquette proper to be observed by the President." The object was to enhance the dignity of the presidency without arousing the discontent of republicans. His means would be a "levee day" once a week for receiving visits—"an hour to be fixed at which it shall be understood that he will appear and consequently that the visitors are previously to be assembled." The president would speak with selected visitors for half an hour but give formal entertainments only on special days, usually relating to events of the Revolution. Hamilton was less concerned with the American experience than with the practices of European courts, as he made clear in his recommendations.[7] This imitation of European royalty was exactly what republicans such as Senator William Maclay of Pennsylvania, after he attended one of the levees, objected to. Even worse, Maclay saw that Washington's popularity would permit him to escape the charge of being "anti-republican" despite his monarchical behavior: "This certainly escapes nobody. The royalists glory in it as a point gained. Republicans are borne down by fashion and a fear of being charged with a want of respect to General Washington."[8]

Given Hamilton's influence not only in fashioning the new government but also in his special relationship with its leader, it is understandable that he felt it his due to be considered the primary figure in the president's cabinet as well as in the ruling circles of the Federal Republic. Watching from the sidelines—but not very far from the center—he could observe with satisfaction the first major bill of the new Congress, the Judiciary Act, with the implied power of judicial review. Much as he had hoped for in his contribution to *The Federalist Papers*, the president offered him the secretaryship only one week after the Treasury Department was established on September 11, 1789. Although Robert Morris is reputed to deserve credit for recommending Hamilton for the position, there is no supporting evidence for this claim, as some of his biographers have observed.[9] But even if the Morris recommendation could be validated, would it have been necessary? There seemed to have been little doubt in Washington's mind about the person most suited to the position. With characteristic enthusiasm, Hamilton plunged into the duties of his post, many of them defined by himself, with the clear objective of exploiting opportunities to free the nation from the coils of the Old World. The advantages that may have accrued to Britain as a consequence of Hamilton's elevation were always incidental to his conception of the nation's interest.

If Hamilton was a prime mover in the creation of the federal government, he was not alone in the enterprise. His partner in *The Federalist Papers*, James Madison of Virginia, not only shared many of Hamilton's objectives but was also in a position as leader of the House of Representatives to shape the ways the new government would raise revenues. In April 1789, Madison proposed that import duties on foreign goods along with tonnage duties on foreign ships be the foundation of an American mercantilist system. It would yield benefits far beyond helping to solve the nation's financial problems, including the rebuilding of a merchant marine and shifting America's trade from Britain to France. The discriminatory duties would fall on British ships and manufactures, which could force Britain to respect America's sovereignty in the Northwest and elsewhere. Hamilton should have applauded this intention; it accorded with his position as "Publius" to use America's new unity to exclude British ships from its ports, thereby forcing Britain to open the West Indian ports to American shipping or face the prospect of ruining their trade with the United States.[10]

When the idea of reprisals against British behavior assumed concrete forms, Hamilton was taken aback by the potential consequences. It was not that the New Yorker was ready to charge Madison with a dangerous Anglophobia. In fact, he approved of the nationalist thrust of his approach. Southerners, after all, would be sacrificing their economic interests in the short run to support northern shipping by the disruption of their connections with Britain. But disruption was at the heart of Hamilton's concerns: a commercial war following from the Madison plan could destroy an economy based on British commerce and British credit. It is noteworthy that northern shipowners were equally worried over the immediate effects on their welfare. Madison's anticipation of economic independence from Britain was as visionary as his expectation of France's ability to replace Britain as an economic partner. Hamilton was relieved to see the Madison bill, which the House passed, fail in the Senate. Although American ships were charged lower duties than foreign ones, there was no discrimination against British vessels in the final Tariff and Tonnage Act of 1789.

As the new Congress went into operation, it was obvious that Hamilton was ready to use his influence at every opportunity, even as he was conducting a successful law practice. He observed with particular interest the debate over the shaping of a cabinet, a process not covered in the Constitution. And he had a special interest in the vital office of finance, given the most pressing problems of the new government and his awareness of his own qualifications. Madison was responsible for moving to elevate the Treasury post to the level of a department, comparable to the three other departments (Foreign Affairs, War, Attorney General). His success was not a foregone conclusion. Elbridge Gerry, concerned about "putting all this power into the hands of one great man, who is to be the head of the department," preferred a board of three commissioners to prevent the granting of power to a person who would enjoy "greater influence than the President of the United States has, and more than is proper for any person to have in a republican government."[11] Despite republican reservations, Madison was among the key congressmen to approve the position as originally presented.

First Steps

Hamilton was fully prepared to assume the responsibilities of a position that had demoralized Robert Morris, and he dispatched a circular letter to the collectors of customs asking for ideas for the more efficient collection of revenue. The immediate problem was that "the number of Ports in several of the States would conduce to great evasions of the duties. It is my wish to be informed how far experience has justified this apprehension, and what can be done to correct the Mischeifs [sic], which may have ensued."[12] This was only one of several communications to collectors of customs in Hamilton's first month in office. They were designed to ensure the Treasury Department's control of America's ports, something that the Confederation had conspicuously failed to do. The objective was not simply to collect funds more efficiently but also to send a message to the world that America was a nation that must be dealt with as an equal.

This message was apparent in his elevation of Britain over France as an economic partner for the new government. It was not that Hamilton dismissed France because of its Revolution. In a letter to Lafayette, his commander at Yorktown, he wished France well, but dreaded "the vehement character of your people," and, in particular, "the refractoriness of your nobles" and the "reveries of your Philosophic politicians who appear in the moment to have great influence and who being mere specularists may aim at more refinement than suits either human nature or the composition of your Nation." In brief, he had serious doubts about the future stability of the ally and of its utility to the expanding economy of the United States. At the same time he emphasized that "the debt due to France will be among the first objects of my attention."[13] Only the pressure of problems concerning navigation and tariffs had postponed temporarily the management of foreign and domestic debts.

There is little doubt that if there was to be a foreign partner, it should be Britain, the supplier of credit for American business, the market for American raw materials, and the producer of needed manufactures that America could not yet produce. This sentiment was clearly expressed in the secretary's informal conversations with Major George Beckwith, former aide-de-camp to Sir Guy Carleton (subsequently Lord Dorchester) during the Revolution and informal agent of William Grenville, Secretary of State for Foreign Affairs in William Pitt's cabinet. Beckwith had been dispatched to New York in the wake of the passage of the Tariff and Tonnage Act with its potential discrimination against British commerce. Hamilton was able to assure him of his own sympathies for a people who think in the same language and "have a similarity of prejudices, and of predilections."[14] With his customary impulsiveness, the secretary indiscreetly let Beckwith know that his government had nothing to fear in the new tariff act. Those who would raise the duties on British commerce represented a minority that was soundly defeated in Congress. The sober leaders of the nation, including President Washington, prevailed over such opponents as James Madison. Hamilton somewhat patronizingly noted that although he was "a clever man, he is very little Acquainted with the world. That he is Uncorrupted and incorruptible; he has the same End in view that I have. And so have those gentlemen, who Act with him, but their mode of attaining it is very different."[15]

Beckwith made no mistake in identifying Hamilton not only as a key figure in the Washington administration but also as an Anglophile who would be useful to British interests. But at this stage of the relationship, the secretary of the treasury was no blind adherent of a British cause, even as he opposed Madisonian discrimination against British commerce. As the foregoing commentary on Madison and his friends suggests, the secretary's eye was on America's advantage from a British connection. If his outlook also served Britain, this benefit did not arise out of any altruism on his part. Hamilton made a point of urging a commercial treaty that would be advantageous to both countries. "I do think we are, and shall be," he asserted, "great Consumers, and I am of [the] opinion, that it will be better for Great Britain to grant us admission into her Islands under certain limitations of size of vessels, so as merely to Enable us to Carry our produce there, and to bring from thence the productions of those Islands to our own ports."[16] These transactions could be made without interfering with Britain's carrying trade in Europe. The current situation promotes "a system of warfare in Commercial matters," from which France hopes to benefit. Britain should not be concerned about the tariff, since "I cannot recollect that there is Any thing in the Impost, which marks a preference to any other Foreign Power, when put into Competition with You."[17] Nor should Britain be concerned about its provinces in North America; expansion applied only to the navigation of the Mississippi, an issue to be settled with Spain, given the vital importance of that river to Westerners. Such was the combination of professions of friendship with an implied warning that Hamilton presented to the British agent in October 1789.

To make credible the air of confidence the secretary of the treasury conveyed to Lafayette and Beckwith, the financial health of
the nation had to be assured. This meant finding the means to meet
the nation's obligations in a manner that would win respect abroad.
Putting in order the collection of customs was just a first step. Only
ten days after Hamilton assumed office, the House of Representatives asked him to prepare a plan "as a matter of high importance
to the national honor and prosperity."[18] These words of instruction
were more than rhetoric to the secretary. "National honor" dictated
the repayment of debts, but the honoring of obligations to foreign
creditors would also be an instrument in manipulating future relations with those nations in the interest of "prosperity." Failure to
manage the finances of the Confederation had doomed that government. He believed that the fate of the nation hung on the successful outcome of his labors.

Report on Assumption of Public Debt

Over the next four months, Hamilton worked at breakneck speed
to produce a report that would serve to establish a foundation for
America's future expansion as well as for its immediate prosperity.
He was fully prepared to undertake the task single-handedly even
as he sought advice from Madison, particularly about which taxes
would be "*least* unpopular." Madison was not yet an opponent, although Hamilton might have gathered that he had reservations
from Madison's comment that "the domestic part is well known to
be viewed in different lights by different classes of people."[19] That
part of the debt amounted to over $40 million as compared to less
than $12 million owed to French and Dutch creditors. But while
the report recognized the question of whether a distinction should
be made between the original holders of public securities and their
present possessors, it rejected the idea that "the latter ought to receive no more than the cost to them, and the interest." Hamilton
was vehement in denying a distinction between foreign and domestic debts; both should be repaid at full value, or there would be
a breach of contract that violated the rights of a fair purchaser.[20]

That the speculator in securities might benefit from the repayment at par value of the debts of the Confederation was obvious,
because it would bind influential beneficiaries to the Federal Union.
But while he was counting on that support for his ambitious program, Hamilton also expected a level playing field for those who
would benefit from the funding of the public debt. His response to

Henry Lee of Virginia reflected his discomfort with those who asked for advance information on the terms for payment that he was drawing up in his report: "I am sure you are sincere when you say, you would not subject me to an impropriety. Nor do I know that there would be any in answering your queries. But you remember the saying with regard to Caesar's wife. . . . *Suspicion* is ever eagle eyed. And the most innocent things are apt to be misinterpreted."[21]

When the secretary presented his "Report Relative to the Provision for the Support of Public Credit" on January 14, 1790, less than four months after Congress had commissioned it, he conceived it as a major event in the construction of a viable nation. The emphasis was not on private gain, although that would be a byproduct of his program. Rather, it was on the centrality of public credit as the hallmark of a sound economy A country such as the United States, "with little monied capital," must be prepared to borrow when needed but also to repay when promised. "But when the credit of a country is in any degree questionable," he warned, "it never fails to give an extravagant premium, in one shape or another, upon all the loans it has occasion to make."[22] The troubles that the nation suffered under the Confederation had derived from the inability of that government to repay its debts. The survival of the Federal Union would depend on its ability to correct its fatal errors. Public credit, like private credit, could be maintained only "by good faith, by a punctual performance of contracts. States, like individuals, who observe their engagements, are respected and trusted, while the reverse is the fate of those who pursue an opposite conduct."[23]

A moral strain frequently surfaced in his report. At the same time that he was proclaiming the proper funding of the nation's debts to be "a national blessing," he would not accept the notion that public debts were public benefits, "a position inviting to prodigality, and liable to dangerous abuse." The "creation of debt should always be accompanied with the means of extinguishment."[24] This was not cant. Whatever potential there was for corruption in the process, Hamilton never sought to gain financial advantage himself from the opportunities he offered to others.

He envisioned benefits for all segments of society in the funding of foreign and domestic debts at par value. Repaying loans to European creditors would make possible new loans from Dutch bankers as well as the floating of new bonds of uniform value that would stimulate the U.S. economy. Hamilton foresaw advantages for every class in the nation. Securities would function as money, thereby increasing the supply of investment capital, while merchants would be able to operate on a larger scale. Nor would farmers be left behind; they would not only have more affluent markets but would have access to capital for expanding their investments. These factors meant expansion of foreign trade, promotion of manufactures, and the flourishing of agriculture. Hamilton's was a national vision that would include all segments of society. Granted that the financial elite would enjoy the more immediate benefits, their profits would then assure their loyalty to the strengthened Union.

The same consideration governed another aspect of his report on public credit; namely, assuming the debts that the states had accumulated in the course of the war. By the exercise of federal authority, the interstate quarrels that had characterized the Confederation would be defused, and an infrastructure for a uniform system of taxation would be in place. Moreover, the beneficent role of the federal government in assuming the financial obligations of the states would reduce the danger of separation that had always lurked in the background of the Confederation governments.

Hamilton recognized that there were differences in the amounts of debt owed by the states. Some states, such as Massachusetts and South Carolina, which had exerted themselves more than others in the Revolutionary War, had debts of over $4 million each, and so they would welcome the federal assumption. In fact, Aedamus Burke of South Carolina feared that his state would go bankrupt if no federal relief was offered, "for she was no more able to grapple with her enormous debt than a boy of twelve years of age is able to grapple with a giant."[25] Other states, particularly in the South, had limited borrowings and feared that they would now be taxed to pay for northerners who had purchased state bonds.

There was a simplicity, bordering on naïveté, that governed the secretary's justifications. His objective was a strong central government, able to cope with the challenges of a hostile world, and to do so while maintaining high moral standards. Hamilton never came to grips with the arguments of those who thought his plans pitted classes and geographic regions against one another or with those who felt left out of the prosperity he envisioned for the nation. Although his personal standard of financial morality remained high, too many of his associates profited from inside connections associated with his fiscal policies. That he left office in 1794 no richer than when he entered was a testament not only to his probity but also to the myopic single-mindedness of his vision for America.

Report on Banking

His activities in 1790, after all, did not stop with the restoration of public credit. Rather, that reinstatement was a point of departure for unveiling plans for utilizing the newfound public confidence to promote a central banking system and a program for the encouragement of manufactures. These were embodied in successive reports, first on a national bank in December 1790, and on manufactures a year later. It is revealing that the former was introduced as "the second report on the further provision for establishing public credit."[26] In a very real sense, the creation of the Bank of the United States was the final realization of hopes Hamilton had nourished when supporting piecemeal solutions through the Banks of New York and North America in the 1780s.

Dismissing charges that a central bank would encourage fraudulent trading or remove specie from the country, he enumerated the benefits the nation and the business community would derive from the establishment of a central bank. First and perhaps foremost, the bank would solve the shortage of specie—gold and silver—which had afflicted the nation since the Revolution. "Well constituted banks," he claimed, "favour the increase of precious metals. It has been shewn, that they augment in different ways, the active capital of the country. This, it is, which generates employment; which animates and expands labor and industry . . . by furnishing more materials for exportation conduces to a favourable balance of trade and consequently to the introduction and increase of gold and silver."[27] It would follow that a species of American mercantilism would give the country equality in the world markets and strength to stand up to European competitors.

There was a firm link to a British model in the secretary's calculations. Adam Smith's *Wealth of Nations* provided a model for the conversion of specie deposited in banks to productive capital through the use of the banks' notes. The Bank of England, too, was a logical precursor to the Bank of the United States, although a key difference in Hamilton's conception was that only three-fifths of the U.S. bank's total capital would consist of government securities, as opposed to the totality of the capital in the English model. Historians Stanley Elkins and Eric McKitrick identified Britain's prime minister, William Pitt, as the dominant influence.[28] When Pitt took office in 1783, the government was burdened with a debt that required two-thirds of the nation's tax income to pay the interest. His reforms offered more than new sources of revenue. They

instilled confidence in the future of the country. Rather than anticipating national bankruptcy, the prime minister lifted the country's
mood through a combination of measures that included suppress-
ing smuggling, initiating new taxes, and establishing a sinking fund
to repay the national debt.

There is no question that Hamilton was aware of Britain's revival. And he was equally aware that his position was not unlike
Pitt's. The title of prime minister had not yet been formalized; primacy was in the office of the Chancellor of the Exchequer, which
Hamilton could see as a counterpart to his own role in the American government. Just as Britain's economy was being turned around
and strengthened, so Hamilton's policies, if accepted, could "hold
the Nation high, in the opinion of the world." Such was the effect
of Pitt's policies, as Beckwith informed Hamilton.[29]

Report on Manufactures

The two reports of 1790 did not exhaust the secretary's imagina-
tive plans. The third report, intimately connected with those on
public credit and the Bank of the United States, devolved on the
future of manufacturing in America. Two years in the making, the
report on manufactures was submitted to Congress in December
1791. It ranged far beyond the mandate from Congress on January 15, 1790, to present a "proper plan or plans" to make the United
States "independent of other nations for essential, particularly for
military supplies."[30] The secretary of the treasury used this commission to conceive what John Miller called "the grand design by
which the United States became the greatest industrial power in
the world."[31]

The report was a fitting conclusion to the reports on public
credit and banks. Sound public credit and a strong central banking
structure were the building blocks for a manufacturing system that
would be what historian Milton Cantor identified as "a declaration of economic independence from the Old World."[32] If the United
States were to assume the place in the world Hamilton envisioned,
it would have to develop industries that would bring prosperity to
all segments of society. A self-sufficient America would not be dependent upon foreign products. Not should the wealth of the United
States be tied only to raw materials to be transferred to manufacturing centers abroad. His response was not original, at least not in
the sources he consulted. They were primarily British, and it was
Great Britain's success that inspired the Hamiltonian vision.

The emphasis of the "Report on Manufactures" on the importance of a protective tariff for promoting American industries at the expense of European competitors did not fit the image of Hamilton as an inveterate Anglophile. Although Beckwith appreciated Hamilton's sentiments in favor of Britain over France, the British agent was aware as well of the potential consequences of the secretary's ambitions for his country. Beckwith listened to Hamilton's observations that the United States "must be for years, rather an Agricultural, than a manufacturing people." But he had also heard the declaration that "we are a young and growing empire." Hamilton then added that consequently "our policy has had a tendency to suggest the Necessity of introducing manufactures," which has produced some results in Connecticut and Pennsylvania. There was an implied warning that the progress in the development of manufactures would be "proportioned to your Conduct."[33] In short, unless Britain modified its discriminatory behavior toward the United States, it faced the prospect of fostering a serious competitor in manufactures. Beckwith recorded these comments two years before the "Report on Manufactures" was produced.

Tension with Britain was inevitable in the shaping of Hamilton's America. France, in the early stages of its Revolution, was dismissed both as a partner and as a threat. It continued the pattern of the Ancien Régime in keeping the United States out of the West Indies, and its potential as a supplier of products needed in America was meager. Britain, on the other hand, was a constant irritant in its exclusion of the United States from its colonial ports and its refusal to make a commercial treaty. But these were long-term problems. In the short term, Britain was vital to America's economy as a source of credit and a source of income. These considerations were always high in the secretary's consciousness when he considered the implications of a commercial war with Britain.

Beckwith was sensitive enough to capture the essence of Hamilton's vision. He never doubted the secretary's preference for Britain over France, or the importance he attributed to close commercial relations with the former mother country, or the respect he had for the British government in the hands of William Pitt. What the agent perceived in his informal conversations in October 1789 was an objective clearly expressed in No. 24 of *The Federalist Papers*, namely, the establishment of a government capable of a military presence that would cope with the threat posed by British and Spanish colonies, separately or in "future concert." Hamilton stressed the importance of an army and navy so that the new nation should not "be exposed, in a naked and defenceless condition, to their insults and encroachments." In *Federalist* No. 11, the future secretary had anticipated the opposition a stronger America would arouse in Europe: "They seem to be apprehensive of our too great interference in that carrying trade, which is the support of their navigation and the foundation of their naval strength." The only European country that fit this description was Great Britain.

The "Report on Manufactures" carried a challenge to Britain one step farther, beyond ships and trade, to the production of finished goods, hitherto a relative monopoly in British hands. Hamilton no less than Jefferson deplored America's addiction to British imports. If the United States were to become an equal of any European competitor, it would have to do so ultimately in industry as well as in commerce. Such would be the means of securing independence, political as well as military, from the former mother country. The central government, which had intervened in the managing of the public debt and in the creation of a national bank, would also need to support infant industries. A prominent part of the report centered on the pirating of British technology and the encouraging of British immigrants who could put that technology to use in the United States. The message was clear. If potential entrepreneurs became aware of government support—"an exemption from the chief part of taxes, burthens, and restraints, which they endure in the old world"—they would "probably flock from Europe to the United States to pursue their own trades or professions, if they were once made sensible of the advantages they would enjoy."[34]

Much of the report was devoted to the benefits the agricultural sector would reap from the prosperity manufactures would generate. But the central thesis was the employment of federal power in aiding the growth of manufactures—through bounties for the acquisition of raw materials vital to the production of finished goods, through imposing duties on rival manufactures, and particularly through promotion of the emigration of skilled workmen from foreign countries. In no place in the report did Great Britain surface as an enemy to Hamilton's design. If that country was mentioned at all, it was in the context of the important service its government rendered to its domestic manufactures through "the amelioration of the public roads of that Kingdom, and the great progress which has been of late made in opening canals."[35] Yet the mercantilism he expounded is based on a zero-sum relationship. What benefits the United States will damage Britain. This was not a conscious expression of Anglophobia. Rather, it was Hamilton's recognition that America's future power rested on the development of manufactures. As long as the United States remained an almost wholly agrarian nation, it would be the victim of European economic policies, again, particularly those of Great Britain. Such was the long-range vision of America in relation to the most important nation of the Old World.

In one sense, Hamilton's America was a striking success. Public credit was established, the obligations of the old Confederation and of the individual states were redeemed by the federal government, and a national bank was established with the resulting expansion of congressional authority. Even the failure of the "Report on Manufactures" to win over Congress to a protective tariff and to the immediate development of a manufacturing society was in the short term. Had Hamilton's life extended to three score and ten, he would have seen the seeds he had planted sprout in the wake of the Embargo Act of 1807 and the War of 1812. Britain would remain as the economic rival and often the enemy of the United States throughout the next century. Hamilton's anticipation of British hostility was justified. But in the political climate of the Federalist era, this conflict was obscured by the dependence of the American economy on the former mother country and on the Anglo-French wars that divided the nation into bitterly opposing factions.

Hamilton's Opponents

While the secretary of the treasury was winning his objectives, he was also building opposition that grew exponentially from the first report to the third report. Two powerful political figures gradually arose to impede his goals. One of them was his erstwhile colleague and collaborator, James Madison, now leader of the House of Representatives. The other was Thomas Jefferson, signer of the Declaration of Independence and minister to France from 1784 until his recall in 1789 to become the secretary of state in the new Federal Union. Their opposition grew slowly, if only because of the shared urgency behind the need of the new government to pay its debts to creditors, particularly foreign creditors. There could be no question about the necessity of respecting the obligations to French and Dutch holders of securities issued by the Confederation. The new nation's ability to borrow in the future as well as its standing in the world hung on its success in meeting its debts. No statesman understood this more clearly than Jefferson, who knew firsthand in

France the embarrassment experienced by a nation that was unable to repay its creditors. From his exposed position in Paris, he proclaimed that "these debts must be paid, or our character stained with infamy among all nations and to all times."[36]

Madison and Jefferson viewed domestic creditors differently. They feared that the monies owed by the Confederation or by the states would be given to speculators who had bought up the promissory notes from impoverished farmers or war veterans and who now expected to be paid at par value. Opposition to this aspect of Hamilton's program was the beginning of Madison's alienation from his former colleague's camp. He was strongly supported by the new secretary of state, just returned from Paris; Jefferson was even more appalled at what he identified as seeds of a corruption that could destroy the fruits of the Constitution. What appealed to Hamilton—the attachment of an enterprising financial elite to the new government through catering to its self-interest—was precisely what repulsed the agrarian-minded Jefferson. In the critical eyes of Senator William Maclay, there was a conspiracy afoot. "It appears," he observed, "that a system of speculation for the engrossing certificates has been carrying on for some time."[37]

Beyond these moral considerations of Hamilton's opponents was a recognition that the major financial beneficiaries of funding the debts would be the northern states. This question became even more acute when the emphasis was on the federal government's assumption of state debts. The Virginians were well aware that the southern states had few outstanding loans, and that relieving the northern states of the debts they had incurred would be another service to northern speculators.

Hamilton's arguments that no distinction could appropriately be made between foreign and domestic creditors applied as well to the debts of all the states. Although the secretary of the treasury accepted the enrichment of the urban few, it was in the cause of strengthening the central government and laying the groundwork for a uniform system of taxation. His was a powerful argument, made all the more powerful by successful lobbying with Congress. He made the case that revenues would be found to pay for these new obligations in the form of "the present duties on imports and tonnage, with the additions, which without any possible disadvantages either to trade or agriculture, may be made on wines, spirits, including those distilled within the United States, teas and coffee." He made a particular virtue of taxing "ardent spirits" as a luxury— a "pernicious" luxury—without realizing or caring about the effect a whiskey tax would have on western farmers unable to market their grain in any other form.[38]

Hamilton's Advantages

Hamilton's ability to mobilize Congress frustrated the Virginians at every turn. The secretary of state was susceptible to the suspicions raised by Maclay and other enemies of the secretary of the treasury. Jefferson did not return home from France until the new government was in place and Hamilton's program was well under way. He was dismayed by the contrast between the adulation he received in Paris as the mentor to aspiring French reformers and the attitude he encountered among the Anglophilic ruling class in New York. At its center was the youthful Alexander Hamilton, who was leading America toward a too-powerful central government in thrall to urban speculators and mercantile interests and valuing a British connection above that of the nation's French ally. Arguably as important was Jefferson's discomfort with the special favor the less distinguished secretary of the treasury enjoyed with President Washington, despite the prestige attached to the office of secretary of state.

The secretary of the treasury continued his sway over the agrarian interests, particularly those in the South, despite the charges of corruption that accompanied his program. In fact, scandal over speculation in federal securities forced the resignation of William Duer, the assistant secretary of the treasury, in April 1790. It seemed, however, that no matter how offensive Hamilton's policies were to the southern states, to the debtor farmers, or to Republicans concerned with the nation's virtue, he was able to prevail over the opposition. Even the establishment of the Bank of the United States, with its expansion of federal powers and the obvious enrichment of insiders, did not shake his hold over the government. The scandals emboldened his adversaries and weakened his control of Congress, but they did not divert him from the course he had taken since assuming office.

Hamilton's successes in those critical years of the early 1790s were the product of fortuitous circumstances. Probably the most important—and the most debilitating for the opposition—was an understanding among the Jeffersonians that the restoration of public credit was vital to the success of the Republic. Discharging the debts to foreign creditors was a theme that Jefferson himself had urged from Paris in the previous decade. No matter how resentful they were over the benefits speculators would gain through funding the debt at full value, or how unfair the assumption of state debts was to the South, they could not repudiate the principle behind Hamilton's policies.

Scholars have debated the reasons as well as the wisdom of Jefferson's "bargain" that traded support of Hamilton's insistence on the federal government's assuming state obligations for a capital on the Potomac. But what may have been equally significant was Jefferson's advice to Monroe that unless the issues of assumption and a capital site "can be reconciled by some plan of compromise, there will be no funding bill agreed to, our credit (raised by the late prospects to be the first on the exchange in Amsterdam, where our paper is above par) will burst and vanish, and the states separate to take care everyone of itself." While he remained uncomfortable with Congress's assumption of the function of states, "in the present instance I see the necessity of yielding for this time to the cries of the creditors in certain parts of the union for the sake of the union, and to save us from the greatest of all calamities, the total extinction of our credit in Europe."[39] The common ground shared by Hamilton and Jefferson over public credit helps to account for the Hamiltonian victories in 1790 and 1791. Jefferson's claim of being duped by the wiles of his rival was made only after the division between the Hamiltonians and Jeffersonians had become final.

Hamilton derived a second advantage from his position in the Washington administration that nominally was inferior to the secretaryship of state, but only nominally. Jefferson was still in France in 1789. Since there were no clear boundaries to the duties of either office, Hamilton could stretch—with Washington's approval—the responsibility of the Treasury Department for consular affairs, which legitimately placed him in the arena of foreign affairs. It was this interference that agitated the secretary of state and sharpened the personality conflicts between the two men. It was understandable that the older man would harbor resentment over the access to the president enjoyed by the younger man.

Long before Jefferson was on the scene, the secretary of the treasury was engaged, as noted, in conversations with a British agent and was advising the president on the importance of improving relations with Britain. His was the most important voice in assigning Gouverneur Morris, then in Paris, the mission of sounding out the British on regularizing diplomatic relations. Hamilton and John Jay prevailed over Madison on this issue, as the Washington administration tried to make a treaty of commerce that John Adams had tried and failed to obtain under the Confederation. When Morris offended the British by associating with French minister Luzerne and Pitt's opponent, Charles James Fox, the secretary seemingly defended Morris, noting that his "intimacy" with Luzerne dated from the Frenchman's mission to the United States during the American Revolution. Moreover, he added, Fox's sympathy for the American cause during the Revolution was reason enough for Morris's nourishing a relationship with him in London. But Hamilton's support lacked conviction; it was accompanied by "some doubts about his prudence; this is the point in which he is deficient, for in other respects he is a man of great genius."[40]

This commentary is noteworthy for more than one reason. First, it reflected Hamilton's close involvement in foreign relations outside his jurisdiction, even if that jurisdiction had not been clearly defined. The secretary of the treasury ventured further into Jefferson's territory when in a confidential conversation with David Humphreys, then en route to Spain and Portugal for a secret diplomatic mission, he wanted the minister to correct any misrepresentations Morris may have left at Whitehall. Second, the remarks about Morris were made to Major Beckwith, who had returned to the United States in 1790. Although Washington had suggested that Hamilton speak informally with the British agent, his assessment of Morris's behavior was unnecessarily and undiplomatically candid. Was he sending a cryptic message to the British disavowing any Anglophobic views Morris may have been conveying? There was no doubt about Hamilton's zeal in securing a treaty with the British, but there was still an ambiguity implicit in his warning that the Francophile party in America might succeed unless Britain responded to the new nation's interests.

Notes

1. Broadus Mitchell, *Alexander Hamilton: National Adventure, 1788–1804* (New York: Macmillan, 1962), 206–7.

2. Carl Van Doren, ed., *The Federalist* (New York: Heritage Press, 1945), No. 68, 456.

3. AH to Washington, August 13, 1788, Syrett and Cooke, 5:201–2.

4. Washington to AH, ibid., 207; AH to Washington, September 22, 1788, ibid., 220.

5. Washington to AH, October 3, 1788, ibid., 223.

6. AH to Theodore Sedgwick, November 9, 1788, ibid., 231.

7. AH to Washington, May 5, 1789, ibid., 335–36.

8. Charles A. Beard, introduction, *The Journal of William Maclay, 1789–1791*, December 14, 1790 (New York: Frederick Ungar Co., 1965), 341.

9. Jacob Cooke, *Hamilton*, 252, observed that "the traditional view that Robert Morris recommended Hamilton's appointment is unsupported by documentary evidence."

10. *The Federalist*, No. 11, 64–65.

11. *Annals of Congress*, May 20, 1789, 1:403.

12. Treasury Department Circular to the Collectors of the Customs, October 20, 1789, Syrett and Cooke, 5:420.

13. AH to Lafayette, October 6, 1789, ibid., 426.

14. Conversation with George Beckwith, October 1789, ibid., 483.

15. Ibid., 488.

16. Ibid., 484.

17. Ibid., 489.

18. The House resolution is given in full in ibid., 6:66, n 99.

19. AH to Madison, October 12, 1789, ibid., 5:439; Madison to AH, November 19, 1789, ibid., 526.

20. Report on Public Credit, January 9, 1790, ibid., 6:73.

21. AH to Henry Lee, December 1, 1789, ibid., 1. According to tradition, Caesar's wife must be above suspicion.

22. Report on Public Credit, January 9, 1790, ibid., 67.

23. Ibid., 68.

24. Ibid., 106.

25. Quoted in Schachner, *Alexander Hamilton*, 257.

26. Report on a National Bank, December 13, 1790, Syrett and Cooke, 7:305.

27. Ibid., 317.

28. Stanley Elkins and Eric McKitrick, *The Age of Federalism* (New York: Oxford University Press, 1993), 227.

29. Ibid., 228.

30. Report on Manufactures, December 5, 1791, Syrett and Cooke, 10:230.

31. Miller, *Alexander Hamilton: Portrait in Paradox*, 289.

32. Milton Cantor, ed., *Hamilton* (Englewood Cliffs, NJ: Prentice-Hall, 1971), 76.

33. Conversation with George Beckwith, October 1789, Syrett and Cooke, 5:483.

34. Report on Manufactures, ibid., 10:254.

35. Ibid., 310.

36. Jefferson to Monroe, May 10, 1786, Boyd, ed., *Papers of Thomas Jefferson*, 9:501–2.

37. *Journal of William Maclay*, 173.

38. Report on Public Credit, Syrett and Cooke, 6:99.

39. Jefferson to Monroe, June 20, 1790, Boyd, ed., *Papers of Thomas Jefferson*, 16:532.

40. Conversation with George Beckwith, September 25–30, 1790, Syrett and Cooke, 7:72.

5

To the Jay Treaty

1790–1794

Such suspicions as Jefferson had about Hamilton's foreign policies did not rise to the surface in the secretary of state's first year in office. Hamilton's style annoyed him, as did many of the aristocratic pretensions Jefferson witnessed in President Washington's court. But at this time the two men shared the objective of extracting concessions from the British.

Nookta Sound

Their approaches differed, however, as the Nootka Sound crisis revealed in 1790. A dispute arose between Spain and Britain over Spain's seizure of three British vessels that had established a base at Nootka Sound on Vancouver Island to develop a fur trade on territory claimed by Spain. This was Prime Minister Pitt's opportunity to demonstrate British power not only to expand trade in northwestern America but also to undo the stain of Yorktown. France, he recognized, was weakened by a revolutionary tide that would prevent it from coming to the aid of its Bourbon ally. The British demanded that Spain release its captives, pay an indemnity, and agree to the continued presence of British traders on the Pacific Coast.

On the assumption that Spain would not concede to British demands, Whitehall was forced to pay more attention to American interests, particularly over diplomatic relations. Given American resentment of British occupation of the Northwest posts, there was some concern in London that the United States might join with Spain in any war that could grow out of the Nootka Sound dispute.

It was this concern that brought Beckwith back to the United States in the spring of 1790, with instructions from Lord Dorchester to talk informally about a possible Anglo–American alliance against Spain. There was no doubt that if war did come, British troops would have to be assured not only of the United States' neutrality vis-à-vis Spain but also that the Washington administration would not use war as an opportunity to seize the Northwest posts.

Once again, the American diplomat was Alexander Hamilton, and, once again, Hamilton placed himself in a compromising position. Jeffersonian scholar Julian Boyd devoted an entire book to the betrayal he perceived in Hamilton's encounters with Beckwith. Boyd's title, *Number 7: Alexander Hamilton's Secret Attempts to Control American Foreign Policy*, indicates the tone of the criticisms. "Number 7" was the number assigned to Hamilton in Beckwith's correspondence with Lord Dorchester and seemingly identified the secretary of the treasury as a British agent. But a number was assigned to every American figure whom Beckwith dealt with in the United States, and hence it was not a symbol of service to Whitehall. Nor was the relationship a "secret"; the president had commissioned Hamilton to extract as much information as he could from Beckwith about British intentions, and then report his findings without committing the government to any specific arrangement. The burden of Boyd's attack was that the secretary had falsely claimed Beckwith's initiative in proposing an Anglo–American alliance when, in fact, this was Hamilton's proposal.[1] Historian Gilbert Lycan found no distinction between "proposing an alliance" and urging joint action against Spanish America in the event of war. As for duplicity on Hamilton's part, "any student of diplomacy knows that wide variations customarily appear in reports of diplomats sitting on different sides of the conference table, with no necessary imputations of duplicity." Such was the likely explanation for discrepancies in the respective reports of Hamilton and Beckwith.[2]

Hamilton's indiscretions aside, his conversations with Beckwith never failed to recognize the primacy of American interests. If an alliance were ever to be consummated, it would have to be preceded by full satisfaction of American claims, from evacuation of western posts to a commercial treaty. But these were not the critical issues in the discussions. Although there "was no particular connection between Spain and the United States" over the Mississippi, Hamilton made a point, as he reported to Washington in July 1790, of hinting "cautiously our dislike of an enterprise on New

Orleans" in the event of war between Spain and Britain.[3] The secretary explained to Beckwith two months later that there should be no quarrel between Britain and the United States over ambitions "to possess any thing to the northward of our present boundaries as regulated by the peace; but the navigation of the river Mississippi we must have, and shortly, and I do not think that the bare navigation will be sufficient, we must be able to secure it by having a post at the mouth of the river, either at New Orleans, or somewhere near it."[4] War with Spain was not beyond consideration.

The secretary of state was privy to the substance of Hamilton's conversations with the British agent, if not to the asides that spoke of the power of the Francophile party. But even with these indiscretions, Hamilton was following a path that Jefferson could accept. The New Yorker sought consistently to apply pressure on Britain to accommodate American interests. When the president was worried in 1790 that "New Orleans and the Spanish Posts above it on the Mississippi" will be among the first objects of a British operation from Detroit, he asked the two secretaries, along with John Adams and John Jay, what "should be the answer of the Executive of the United States to Lord Dorchester, in case he should apply for permission to march Troops through the Territory of said States from Detroit to the Mississippi."[5] Where the two men differed in this period was not in ends but in means.

Although there was a distinct tonal difference in their replies, Hamilton and Jefferson came to substantially the same positions and expressed substantially the same concerns. Most immediate was the appropriate response to the president's request, and both agreed that, if asked, permission should be granted. Jefferson was more uncomfortable in his response than was his counterpart. He was fearful that Britain might use the crisis with Spain to seize Louisiana and the Floridas, and he considered war as an alternative to such an eventuality. But this was a passing consideration, just as were his hopes that Britain might yield concessions to the United States, particularly with respect to the Northwest posts, in return for American neutrality. His answer then was a reluctant acceptance if Britain made the request. The alternative in this instance most likely would be Britain's sending troops without bothering about permission.

Hamilton shared this view and, in a much longer response than the secretary of state had given, made it clear that "if the United States were in a condition to do it, without material hazard, there would be strong inducements to their adopting it as a general rule never to grant passage for a voluntary expedition of one power against another, unless obliged to it by treaty." Still, he saw little choice in light of the nation's weakness except to accompany consent "with a candid intimation that the expedition is not agreeable to us, but that thinking it expedient to avoid an occasion of controversy, it had been concluded not to withhold consent."[6]

Jefferson would certainly have agreed with Hamilton's judgment that "the acquisition of the Spanish territories, bordering upon the U States by Britain, would be dangerous to us."[7] It was the position of Spain and the Mississippi River that united the two statesmen at this moment. Both were convinced that Spain must yield to American demands for access to New Orleans at the very least, and Jefferson speculated that the Nootka Sound crisis might just provide the opportunity to press Spain for major concessions. He seemed willing to guarantee all its possessions west of the Mississippi in return for ceding all possessions east of the river. "In fine," he observed, "for a narrow slip of barren, detached, and expensive country, Spain secures the rest of her territory, and makes an Ally, where she might have a dangerous enemy."[8] Hamilton was as obsessed with the Mississippi issue as Jefferson, but apparently with a pro-British touch. If Spain continued its policy of barring Americans from the Mississippi, he foresaw war "at a period not very distant." The nation must have an outlet for its commodities, and if a war should bring France in on the side of its Bourbon ally, "we should naturally seek aid from Great Britain."[9]

Hamilton versus Jefferson

This projection may fit the Anglophilia that critics have charged, and confirm Boyd's argument that Hamilton's deep involvement with Beckwith, much of it unknown to Jefferson, had subverted the American position. Beckwith in this interpretation had communicated to his masters information from Hamilton that relieved British anxieties about any aggressive American reaction on the matter of the Northwest posts as well as to crossing American territory. Yet the text of his long and anguished response to the president reflects the secretary's wariness about British intentions, and asserts an American interest as profound as Jefferson's in keeping the British out of New Orleans. "By rendering New Orleans the emporium of products of the western Country," he warned, "Britain would, at a period not very distant, have very little occasion for supplies or provisions for their islands from the Atlantic States.

. . . Whence a great diminution of the motives to establish liberal terms of Commercial Intercourse with the United States."[10] Given sentiments of this nature, Hamilton's Anglophilia requires careful definition. His ambivalence also helps to explain why Britain finally appointed a minister to the United States, George Hammond, in 1791. Beckwith's dispatches indicated concern that failure to establish a legation in Philadelphia might result in legislation hostile to British interests.

A case can be made for the presence of a general consensus on foreign relations through most of the first Washington administration. Removal of the British from the Northwest posts, access to British West Indian ports, and pressure on Spain to open the Mississippi to Americans were objectives the two secretaries shared. This consensus did not produce intimate relations. There was Hamilton's concern about Jefferson's ties to Madison as well as Jefferson's reservations about Hamilton's ties to the urban elites of the north. But France was not an issue between the two cabinet officers until the radicalization of its revolution. While Jefferson looked with hope at the prospects of his acolytes in France, he was frustrated by the persistence of old mercantilist habits; French West Indian ports were no more open to Americans than were the British islands. And while Hamilton considered with equanimity in his reply to President Washington the possibility of terminating the French alliance, his personal relations with French ministers such as Jean-Baptiste Ternant were more amiable than the secretary of state's. Hamilton seemed to display more enthusiasm for a new commercial treaty with France than did the secretary of state. His informal talks with Ternant in 1791 reflected once again his interference in Jefferson's jurisdiction but no particular bias against France. In fact, the secretary of the treasury sought equally a treaty from both Paris and London and even assured Ternant that the United States regarded full admission of American shipping into the West Indies as a prerequisite to a new treaty of commerce. He anticipated equal concessions from France if a new treaty were negotiated.

Despite these areas of common interest, the consensus on foreign relations was fraying in 1791, even before the Anglo-French war began. Jefferson's caution with respect to Ternant was caused less by the minister's enjoyment of Hamilton's company than by suspicion that the secretary of the treasury was not serious about a French treaty and was pursuing it only as a pretext to make a treaty favorable to Britain. The contests over the public debt and particularly over the Bank of the United States had taken their toll on the fragile connections between the two men. That Hamilton's dominant position in the Washington administration would attract enemies was inevitable. As noted, he had also inherited some enemies from New York—Governor Clinton and the Livingston faction. But as he built his program, with the help of what would be identified as Federalists in Congress, he ran afoul of southern agrarians, northern republicans, and the formidable duo—Jefferson and Madison—who united the opposition under the rubric of Republicans or Jeffersonians. The French Revolution played no genuine part in the break. Rather, it was from fear of replicating the British model of a corrupt elite governing class that brought the friction into the open.

Arguably, from Jefferson's perspective, the last straw came at a dinner in April 1791, at which he hosted Adams and Knox as well as Hamilton, that convinced the secretary of state of Hamilton's subversive monarchical views. On the British Constitution, Adams claimed that if it were purged of its corruption, "it would be the most perfect constitution ever devised by the wit of man." Hamilton then divulged his true beliefs when he said that if it were purged of its corruption, "it would become an *impracticable* government: as it stands at present, with all its supposed defects, it is the most perfect government which ever existed."[11]

This riposte was the irrepressible streak in Hamilton emerging, showing off once again his way with words. It was not the first time, after all, that he had touted the virtues of the British government; he had done as much during the Constitutional Convention. For Jefferson, it was as good an occasion as any to mobilize opposition to Hamilton and his programs. Not far beneath the surface was the secretary's festering resentment not merely over Hamilton's control of Congress but also over his constant interference in matters properly belonging to the State Department.

The Republican response was to establish a newspaper under the poet Philip Freneau to counter the Hamiltonian bias of the *Gazette of the United States*. The Republican alliance, symbolized by Madison and Jefferson's scientific expedition up the Hudson River in the spring of 1791, fed fears among Hamilton's friends that a plot against the secretary of the treasury was being hatched. Their suspicions were seemingly confirmed by the appearance of Freneau's new journal, *The National Gazette*, in the fall of that year. Freneau, Madison's Princeton College classmate, was induced to move to Philadelphia and publish his paper with the help of a clerkship in Jefferson's office. The thrust of Freneau's reports clearly revealed the *Gazette*'s role in countering the pro-Hamiltonian sentiments of John Fenno's journal.

That Hamilton should have been stung by Freneau's diatribes might have been expected. He was not one to let broadsides go unchallenged. Yet the magnitude of his successes might have permitted much of the criticism to go unanswered, at least by him personally. By the end of 1791, the secretary of the treasury had realized most of his vision for America—from assumption of the public debts to the creation of a national bank to thwarting with regularity Madison's efforts to discriminate against British commerce. Granted, his plan for manufactures did not succeed and charges of corruption personified by the guilt of his aide, William Duer, opened him to attack. But did this require the kind of ad hominem assault on Freneau that he leveled? Writing in Fenno's gazette in August 1792, he laid bare all the Federalist accusations against the Jeffersonian faction. Freneau's was "a paper more devoted to the views of a certain party of which Mr. Jefferson is the head than any to be found in this City." Freneau was recruited in the course of Madison's and Jefferson's visit to New York. Hamilton mocked the independence of a journalist who owed his salary to the secretary of state. "Is it possible," he asked, "that Mr. Jefferson, the head of a principal department of the Government can be the Patron of a Paper, the evident object of which is to decry the Government and its measures?"[12]

The president was sufficiently agitated by the increasingly open conflict between the two most important members of his cabinet to make an effort to bridge the gap between them. Washington urged them in almost identical terms, in August 1792, to recall that internal dissension played into the hands of foreign enemies, and he warned them of the danger of the nation's losing "the fairest prospect of happiness and prosperity that ever was presented to man."[13] He intimated that the troubles they gave him inclined him toward retirement rather than seeking a second term in office.

The only common ground Hamilton and Jefferson shared in responding to the president was their concern over his possible departure from office. Beyond that, they indulged in reprising all the resentments that had accumulated since Jefferson's return from France. The secretary of state finally put on paper his indignation over Hamilton's infringement upon his office, from his private conversations with British and French representatives to his skewing American foreign policy toward service to his subversive ideology. The secretary of the treasury for his part provided a mirror image of his opponent's case, claiming to be "the deeply injured party" and finding hostility from Jefferson from the moment the latter arrived in New York from Paris. Hamilton portrayed Jefferson as a leader of a party determined to undermine the successful program he had put into place.[14] He did offer to resign if Jefferson would do the same. Neither man's reply satisfied the president, but he had no wish for either to resign from the cabinet.

The newspaper war continued, and it was intensified by the changing course of the French Revolution. The fall of 1792 witnessed the end of the monarchy and a coalition of European monarchs bent on restoration of the Ancien Régime. France was at war, and whatever prospect a more liberal commercial treaty had had in 1791 had disappeared by the end of 1792. The execution of the king in January 1793 and the successful defense of the nation against the combined monarchs energized a French Republic under the Girondists intent on liberating Europe from the yoke of monarchy. With the death of Louis XVI, Britain entered the war against France, an act nominally initiated by the Girondists but in fact welcomed by its traditional enemy. These seminal events forced the United States into decisions and positions that were not anticipated in the first years of the French Revolution.

For Hamilton, they came at a difficult personal time, when he was under attack for corruption in Congress by Jeffersonian William Giles and open to blackmail for an illicit affair with Maria Reynolds. The secretary surmounted both challenges. Speculators may have profited through Hamilton's policies, but Giles's public challenge concluded with the secretary's credible defense of his honor. The Reynolds affair was less honorable, although his excessively sympathetic behavior toward a seemingly abused wife was reminiscent of his susceptibility to the charms of Peggy Arnold during Benedict Arnold's treasonous action in the Revolutionary War. In both episodes, Hamilton was taken in by a scheming woman, even if the Arnold relationship was not sexual. No matter how badly he behaved toward his own wife during this period, he ultimately recognized the collusion between the two Reynoldses and publicly admitted his indiscretion in 1798. He remained, however, free of the taint of corruption.

The Genet Affair

These problems did not deter the secretary of the treasury from pursuing a foreign policy and engaging in foreign relations with even more vigor than in the past. After January 1793, the lines were more clearly drawn, and they demarcated, in Hamilton's judgment, a Britain standing firmly on the side of civilization against the forces of anarchy and atheism rampant in revolutionary France. Again, a mirror image appeared from Jefferson's perspective. His earlier doubts about France's capability to absorb rapid change when he was minister and his subsequent resentment when French economic policies were not liberal enough dissipated as the nation became a republic and took on the monarchies of the Old World. What appalled Hamilton thrilled Jefferson. For the latter, the survival of the French Republic, at war with Prussia, Austria, and then Britain, was interpreted to mean the survival of American republicanism as well. "The liberty of the whole earth," exclaimed Jefferson, "was depending on the issue of the contest."[15] Hamilton, by contrast, feared the extension to America of the French Revolution as he observed the enthusiasm newly formed Democratic societies displayed toward the overseas republic. Hamilton and Jefferson saw each other as the agent of a foreign cause.

Inevitably, the inflamed political atmosphere influenced the course of American foreign relations. There was initially the question of whether the United States should even recognize the legitimacy of the French alliance, let alone the the alliance that had bound the two nations since 1778. Even before the execution of the king, Hamilton had urged the president to reject Ternant's request for American payments to be used in the French colony of Saint-Domingue (now the Dominican Republic) on the grounds that "if a restoration of the King should take place, I am of [the] opinion, that no payment which might be made in the interval would be deemed regular or obligatory."[16] Moreover, Ternant represented the doomed monarchy; he would be replaced by a minister from the radical republic, Edmond Genet, whose impending arrival impelled Hamilton to question, as he observed to Jay, the validity of the French alliance: "Ought we not rather to refuse receiving or to receive with qualification—declaring that we receive the person as the representative of the Government *in fact* of the French nation reserving to ourselves a right to consider the applicability of the Treaties to the *actual situation* of the parties?"[17]

Actually, it was unlikely that Hamilton anticipated annulling the alliance in this fashion; both he and the president had agreed to accept a minister from the new republic even before the issue was raised in the cabinet. Consequently, the secretary of state did not meet genuine resistance when he established the principle that

a representative of a government that controls the nation and respects its foreign obligations would be accepted by the United
States. By making an issue of this question, the secretary of the treasury could increase his bargaining clout over more sensitive problems, such as maintaining American neutrality in the war between
Britain and France and limiting the obligations owed to the French
ally. Hamilton had the advantage in this contest, because Jefferson
had no more appetite for entering war on the side of France than
did his adversary. Both accepted the need to express America's
neutrality, but Jefferson preferred to avoid the term. The result of
President Washington's consultation with his cabinet on the subject was a compromise that proclaimed "neutrality" on April 23
without using that word.

The secretary of state had hoped the omission of the word
would appease France (even though the treaty of alliance did not
obligate the nation to join in a war that was declared formally by
the European ally) and induce Britain to pay for the de facto neutrality with concessions on neutral rights. This ploy was not different in kind from his hopes in the Nootka Sound crisis; the difference
was that the stakes were greater in 1793 than in 1790. Jefferson
wanted a neutrality that would serve the interests of France by
having American ships carry provisions necessary for its prosecu-
tion of the war to France and by excluding British ships and manufactures from all ports if Britain did not accept the American
interpretation of neutral rights on the high seas. And the secretary
had popular sentiment on his side. On the one hand, the spectacle
of a republic fighting for its life against dangerous monarchical
adversaries inspired not only Francophiles in Democratic clubs but
also those who saw in the Federalists the same monarchical forces
that could destroy the American Republic. On the other hand, the
British order-in-council of June 8, 1793, denying neutral vessels the
right to carry provisions to France and the continuing practice of
seizing sailors from American ships increased the level of
Anglophobia throughout the country. Freneau's directing these
passions against the Hamiltonians insinuated that Washington's
proclamation was part of a monarchical conspiracy against the republic.

Hamilton could not resist responding to his enemies, and he
did so with his customary vigor in a series of seven essays published in the *Gazette of the United States* in June and July 1793, under
the pen name of "Pacificus." In these broadsides, he demonstrated
effectively that the president had the duty to announce to the world

that the country would be legally bound to abide by the duties of a neutral nation. Alliance obligations would be respected, so long as they did not involve the nation in war. The constitutional authority of the president to issue a proclamation of neutrality was indisputable: "The power of determ[in]ing virtually in the case supposed upon the operation of national Treaties as a consequence." He noted that "the power to receive ambassadors and other public Ministers is an important instance of the right of the Executive to decide the obligations of the Nation with regard to foreign Nations."[18]

Arguably, Hamilton's counterarguments were gratuitous. The popularity of the French cause combined with the arrogance of the British position tended to obscure the basic weakness in the Jeffersonian arguments. Both secretaries wanted to keep the nation out of war, but Hamilton had none of the reservations that accompanied Jefferson's acceptance of neutrality. France, in his judgment, was not even worthy of neutrality in its war against European civilization. "Whatever partial[it]y may be entertained for the general object of the French Revolution," Hamilton asserted in "Pacificus No. II," "it is impossible for any well informed or soberminded man not to condemn the proceedings which have been stated; as repugnant to the general rights of Nations, to the true principles of liberty."[19] The "fair" neutrality that the secretary of state wanted was in his eyes—and in France's as well—a neutrality that served Paris's war aims.

This meant supporting France's intention of bringing British prizes into American ports, which led almost inevitably into a further expectation of outfitting prize ships as privateers. Beyond the maritime aid that France expected of its American ally, the hope of the expansionist revolutionary government was to use American territory and American volunteers to attack Spanish possessions in the West, now that Spain was an ally of Britain. Hamilton could only profit from the difficulties these aspirations raised for his adversary.

The foregoing problems were not theoretical. The arrival of an aggressive young minister, Edmond Genet, dispatched from Paris by the Girondist government, developed into an embarrassment to the secretary of state and an opportunity for the secretary of the treasury. Initially, Jefferson welcomed the new minister, who had been instructed to arrange a new commercial treaty that would open the West Indies to American shipping, a proposal that had had no chance of success under Ternant. The secretary of state even applauded the enthusiastic greetings from Francophile crowds as

Genet traveled slowly from Charleston to Philadelphia. Genet later claimed that he was encouraged to denounce Washington's right to proclaim neutrality on the private advice of the secretary of state. In any event, he was so carried away by his reception that he offended the public as well as the government by his brash assault on the president. Then, flouting the Neutrality Proclamation, Genet went on to outfit a captured British vessel as a privateer in Philadelphia and ignored Governor Thomas Mifflin's directive to keep the vessel in port.

Hamilton took full advantage of Genet's blunders to embarrass the secretary of state. But his position did not denote only pleasure over his opponent's discomfort. Although Jefferson opposed employing force to prevent the *Little Sarah* from putting out to sea, he ultimately shared Hamilton's and the secretary of war's judgment that "it is impossible to interpret such conduct into any thing else than a *regular plan to force the United States into the War.*"[20] Both men were upset over Genet's behavior, and Jefferson had no reservations about demanding the French minister's recall in accord with the cabinet's decision on August 1, 1793. Hamilton was as worried about the prospect of America's being dragged into the war as he was pleased with the opportunity to lecture the secretary of state, in "Pacificus No. VI," that the Genet affair "ought to teach us not to over-rate *foreign friendships*—to be upon our guard against *foreign attachments.* The former will generally be found hollow and delusive; the latter will have a natural tendency to lead us aside from our own true interest, and to make us dupes of foreign influence."[21]

The secretary of the treasury had France in mind when he issued his broadsides, but his apprehension about foreign influence extended to Britain as well. Even as he excoriated France as a threat to civilization and identified Britain as a bulwark against the destructive forces of revolution, he recognized that British behavior could threaten America's neutrality as much as France's. The British order-in-council of June 8 ordering all ships carrying provisions to France to be seized alarmed Hamilton as an infraction of American commercial rights as well as an incentive for war on the part of the Jeffersonians. George Hammond, Britain's minister to the United States since 1791, reported Hamilton's reactions with some alarm. Hammond had enjoyed the same intimacy with the secretary as Beckwith, but with more authority than his predecessor. He reported to Whitehall that Hamilton had regarded the order-in-council "as a very harsh and unprecedented measure, which not only militated against the principal branch of the present American exports, but . . . appeared to be peculiarly directed against the commerce and navigation of the United States." The minister concluded his report by noting that he had failed to satisfy Hamilton's objections.[22]

The secretary of the treasury's dread of a war with Britain certainly had its foundation in the advantages such a war would give to Britain's enemy. But there was always the calculation that the United States could not afford a war—with France or Britain—because of limited financial resources. Nor did the country have an army or navy to deal with Britain's ability to frustrate an invasion of Canada or Florida. A more credible scenario, he suspected, would be an invasion of the United States by an Anglo-Spanish force aided by hostile Indians. Yet, as he asserted in his "Americanus" essays in February 1794, the nation would survive once again a British assault on American territory; "she [Britain] would run by it greater risks of bankruptcy and Revolution than we of subjugation."[23]

None of his strictures against Britain signified any lessening of his dislike of France, or of his core belief that America had a stake in Britain's victory over the French revolutionary government. Jefferson, who held precisely the opposite view of the stakes in the European war, shared once again with his adversary the necessity for American abstention from the conflict. While the secretary of state was pressing hard for Genet's recall, the secretary of the treasury intensified his pamphlet war against the Francophile friends of Genet. He sought to reduce the anti-British sentiments by reminding the nation that France had violated the terms of the alliance by ordering the seizure of neutral vessels carrying provisions to British ports. Both secretaries might have relaxed for the moment had they known that the French government, under the Jacobin-led Directory, had recalled Genet, who, anticipating execution at the hands of the successors to the Girondists, had decided to remain in the United States, marry a daughter of Governor Clinton, and live happily ever afterward on a farm near Albany.

It had been a difficult year for Hamilton and Jefferson. In June, shortly before Genet's disgrace, Hamilton considered retirement. His successes in Washington's first administration had been won at the price of accumulating enemies of all sorts—Francophiles, agrarians, Jeffersonian liberals, and those envious of his leadership skills. The Giles resolutions had challenged his probity as a public servant, and his affair with Mrs. Reynolds had exposed his private frailties. Moreover, his financial condition, the result of his refusal to profit from his insider's position, made a return to his law practice in New York almost a necessity, to meet the needs of his large—and still growing—family. Jefferson, too, was exhausted by the constant struggle in an administration where his rival seemed to hold most of the advantages. Genet's folly undercut the promise of redressing the balance between his faction and the Hamiltonians. Despite the able leadership of James Madison in Congress, his vision for the nation seemed to be stymied at every turn. It was Jefferson, not Hamilton, who retired from office at the end of 1793.

British Provocations

Jefferson's departure did not mean that the Federalists had removed the threat of legislation that would undo Hamilton's commercial policies. Nor did it mean that Francophilia was permanently squelched by the reaction against Genet's overt interference in American politics. The Democratic clubs that had accompanied Genet's arrival still flourished, and well-wishers of the French Republic still drank toasts to its success in the European war. More significant was the continuing anger against British treatment of American shipping as well as against their exploitation of Indians in the effort to retain the Northwest posts. French violation of treaty obligations appeared minor irritants by comparison. Before leaving Philadelphia, the secretary of state issued what biographer Merrill Peterson called his own "farewell address" in the form of a fifth draft of a long-deferred report to Congress on commercial policy.[24] In this last hurrah in the Washington cabinet, he concluded that Britain's behavior far outweighed any danger to the nation from Genet's insolence. Jefferson had his last chance to rail against British control of the American economy. France, by contrast, was interested in liberalizing trade with the United States. All the more reason, he concluded, to reward those who shared America's objectives and punish those who discriminated against the nation.

Jefferson's report drew strength from the apparent French retreat under the Jacobins from the aggressive thrust of Girondist expansionism, symbolized by the Genet mission. France, approaching the apex of its revolutionary course, was too preoccupied with defense of its territory from external attack and with turmoil from internal divisions to challenge the United States in the winter of 1794 as it had in the spring of 1793. The new situation permitted hostility to Britain to simmer to the point where Madison believed that his anti-British policies at last could be realized. In this political environment, in early 1794, Madison reintroduced in Congress the resolutions that had failed in 1791. Whether or not his mood was more buoyant than the circumstances warranted, the secretary of the treasury was on the defensive.

Hamilton's problems were partly personal. He and his family had suffered from the epidemic of yellow fever that swept Philadelphia in the fall of 1793. His political associate, John Fenno, faced bankruptcy in November 1793, "ruined by his Patriotism," Hamilton asserted, as he asked well-placed friends for a loan to keep *The Gazette of the United States* afloat.[25] To make matters worse, the president followed Jefferson's rather than his advice in preparing his Annual Message to Congress in December. His address was far more "neutral" than the secretary of the treasury wanted.

In February 1794, Congress added to his troubles by naming a special committee to investigate his department, particularly the propriety of his depositing the proceeds of European loans in the Bank of the United States. Washington's tepid defense, noting that he could not recall all the details of the transactions, did nothing to lift Hamilton's spirits. He informed the president that he "cannot help entertaining and frankly expressing to you my apprehension, that false and insidious men, whom you may one day understand, taking advantage of the want of recollection, which is natural, where the mind is habitually occupied with a variety of important objects, having found means by artful suggestions to infuse doubts and distrusts very injurious to me."[26]

But the foregoing troubles paled in comparison with the dangers he anticipated from Madison's mischievous legislation. They were compounded by the impact of Britain's further order-in-council of November 6, 1793, empowering British ships to seize American vessels carrying goods to and from the French West Indian ports. News of this latest outrage reached the United States in March 1794 and contributed to the Anglophobic temper of Congress. Hamilton's immediate response to Washington sounded more Jeffersonian than Federalist in the measures he recommended: "The present situation of the United States is undoubtedly critical and demands measures vigorous though prudent. We ought to be in a respectable military posture, because war may come upon us, whether we choose it or not."[27] He went so far as to urge an embargo on exports of commodities, and consideration of a league of neutral powers for common defense against British abuses. With the president's approval, Congress imposed a thirty-day embargo on all ships bound for all European ports.

This action could have been a prelude to war with Britain, an action that would have nullified every aspect of Hamilton's foreign policy. Despite its arrogance, Britain was the defender of civilization against the advances of the French Revolution as well as the engine of America's economic prosperity. Not least among his considerations was the damage a war with Britain would do to the fortunes of his party. In this context, the secretary asked for a more vigorous approach to negotiations backed by military preparedness. And he was convinced that he would be the negotiator most appropriate for this task. But in light of the target his appointment would make for his enemies, he looked about for a suitable substitute and found him in Chief Justice John Jay, "the only man in whose qualifications for success there would be thorough confidence."[28]

The Jay Mission

In this situation, as in so many others in Washington's first administration, Hamilton seemed to act as the secretary of state, if not as de facto chief executive. Edmund Randolph, Jefferson's successor, played a minor role in dealing with the latest crisis. Jay was an old friend and ally who would adhere to Hamilton's program, and it was Hamilton who crafted the instructions Jay was to follow, even though Randolph included consultation with European maritime powers about the possibility of the United States' joining a new League for Armed Neutrals. Hamilton objected to this as a provocation, even though he had raised that possibility in a moment of anxiety over the latest order-in-council.

That the British minister, George Hammond, would turn to Hamilton as the agent to help Britain calm the Americans without granting them excessive concessions was only to be expected. Beckwith had laid the groundwork with the secretary of the treasury and had marked him as Britain's man, if not agent, in America. The British minister confirmed this relationship in his communications with Whitehall. When Genet appeared on the scene, Hammond informed the Foreign Office in March 1793 that "by an assurance of Mr. Hamilton," the Franco–American alliance "would not be enforced to such an extent as that the observance of them might involve the United States in any difficulties and disputes with other powers."[29] In short, Britain need have no worries about the United States's joining its ally in the Anglo-French war. In this same dispatch, Hammond congratulated himself on his ability to use the secretary of the treasury to Britain's advantage: "Notwithstanding the present appearance of this government, I shall continue to watch its future operation with the most unremitting attention. For this purpose, your Lordship will, I flatter myself that you approve my cultivation of Mr. Hamilton . . . all his interests political and personal are so implicated in the preservation of peace as to leave no doubt of his sincerity."[30] The secretary of state was a marginal figure in Hammond's presentation, whose hostility was countered by his adversary's friendship.

Given this setting, it is understandable that a historian of the distinction of Samuel Flagg Bemis would judge any agreement that would come out of Jay's Treaty as a Hamiltonian accomplishment—or a Hamiltonian blunder.[31] The instructions for Jay were based, as Hammond anticipated, on the essential empathy the Federalists had for the British cause, to a degree that could withstand the obstacles the British government placed before them. This conviction was driven by ideology, but also by a recognition that the nation was in no position to defeat Britain's naval power. As Hamilton advised the president, "Tis as great an error for a nation to overrate as to underrate itself. Presumption is as great a fault as timidity. Tis our error to overrate ourselves and underrate Great Britain."[32]

The instructions to Jay were essentially bipartisan in nature. Even if war could be avoided, the secretary recognized with the Jeffersonians that Britain must redress America's grievances. At the same time, he deplored the Francophiles who anticipated "a more complete and permanent alienation from Great Britain and a more close approximation to France."[33] He was firm in resisting war except "in the last extremity," especially since he was convinced that Britain had no intention of initiating it. As he observed, "There are two ideas of immense consequence to us in the event of War. The disunion of our enemies—the perfect union of our own citizens."[34] Neither was present in the current crisis. Thus, diplomacy was the only reasonable means of securing American interests.

Both Francophiles and Anglophiles could unite over goals that Hamilton presented to Washington on April 23, 1794, for Jay's mission. They included indemnification for the depredations on American commerce, a definition of contraband goods that would limit the excessively loose British construction, a similarly narrow conception of a blockade, and a stipulation against the sale of prizes in American ports. Beyond redress for past grievances he projected once again a treaty of commerce that would include the privilege to carry to and from "the West India Islands in our vessels of certain burthens (say not less than 60 tons nor more than Eighty Tons)" all articles now carried from the United States exclusively in British ships.[35]

His requirements, moreover, ranged beyond maritime issues. Surrender of British-held posts in the Northwest was vital as was a stipulation that in any war with Indian tribes, neither party would furnish supplies to the warring tribes beyond what had been furnished to them in times of peace. For its part, the United States would also fulfill the terms of the Treaty of Paris and take responsibility for compensation for obstructions to the collection of debts to British creditors. Almost pro forma was the indemnification for slaves carried away during the war, an issue sensitive to the South but embarrassing to Hamilton and Jay. If Britain would behave liberally with the United States, there could be a de facto alliance serving both parties.

These hopes were not to be fulfilled, and in the views of some historians it was the information that Hamilton conveyed through Hammond that limited Jay's options in his negotiations. This may have been the case with respect to Randolph's instruction to sound out representatives of Russia, Sweden, and Denmark about American involvement in the projected League of Armed Neutrals aimed at Britain. Although Randolph accepted most of Hamilton's recommendations, the secretary of the treasury had opposed that provision. The British were aware of Hamilton's views, as Hammond reported to the Foreign Office that the secretary, "with great seriousness and with every demonstration of sincerity assured me that there was no prospect of the United States participating in a European association of armed neutrals."[36]

Given the intimate conversations with Hammond, the question arises as to how many of the shortcomings of Jay's Treaty were the result of Hamilton's indiscretions. Did they consist of behavior that justified Richard Morris's charge that the secretary was a "treacherous collaborator," subverting Jay's negotiating position in London? Samuel Flagg Bemis was convinced that the possibility of inserting an article into the treaty protecting American seamen from impressment, a major object of Minister Thomas Pinckney's mission to Britain, might have been achieved if Grenville had not discovered that the United States had no intention of joining the Scandinavian countries and Russia in an anti-British armed neutrality.[37] Accusations of treachery and subversion were understandable from Jeffersonians convinced that Hamilton was plotting to impose monarchy upon America, terminate the Franco-American alliance, and make the nation subservient to the British Empire.

In light of the circumstances of 1794, these charges were excessive. Despite Hammond's communication of Hamilton's information on America's position on armed neutrality, historian Gerald Combs, in opposition to Bemis, judged that this dispatch had little effect on Jay's failure to move the British with a threat of member-ship.[38] Neither side harbored illusions on this subject. Nor was it likely that Hamilton's intervention was the reason for Britain's refusal to budge on impressment or to accept the American interpretation of neutral rights. In his advice to Jay, Hamilton observed "how unwise" it was of Britain "to remain exposed to the hazard of constant interruption & derangement by not fixing on the basis of a good Treaty the principles on which it should continue."[39] Hammond caught a note of exasperation the month before when he informed Grenville that "he was much surprized" by the secretary's cold reaction to the official British explanation of its maritime policies. Instead, Hamilton "entered into a pretty copious recital of the injuries which the commerce of this country had suffered from British cruisers, and into a defense of the consequent claim which the American citizens had on their government to vindicate their rights."[40]

Hamilton knew the limits of the nation's bargaining power and consequently adjusted his priorities accordingly. Although reparations for damages committed on the high seas were desirable, Hamilton recommended that these grievances "be more laxly dealt with if a truly beneficial treaty of Commerce (embracing privileges in the West India islands) can be established."[41] The control of Mississippi navigation was an equally important goal of the treaty, and at least the Anglo–American conflict over this issue was resolved by Jay's diplomacy. Navigation of that river, as the secretary of the treasury put it, "is to us an object of immense consequence. Besides other considerations connected with it, if the Government of the UStates can procure & secure the enjoyment of it to our Western Country, it will be an infinitely strong link between that Country & the Atlantic States."[42]

The Jay Treaty

The resulting treaty became a symbol in the eyes of Jeffersonians—and of many historians in later generations—of Hamiltonian subservience to British interests. It appeared to them that Jay was seduced by the flattery of his British hosts as well as by his friend Hamilton's intervention to give away the advantages the United

States should have enjoyed in the negotiations. After all, the Jay mission presumably forestalled punitive congressional measures against British commerce, American retaliation in the Northwest against the British–Indian alliance, and association with a new League of European Armed Neutrals.

None of those threats materialized. Instead, the British could raise duties on American vessels to equal those on British ships in American ports, although the United States was forbidden to raise its duties on British ships for twelve years. So much, then, for Madison's hopes to extract commercial concessions from Britain. As for the sensitive issues of neutral rights, they were essentially invisible. The question of the right of neutral ships to carry enemy goods was deferred for the future, which meant that the British could continue to confiscate enemy property on American ships and, at the same time, maintain their loose definition of contraband goods. On the admission of American ships to the West Indies, the inadequate 70-ton limit was further undercut by the denial to Americans of exportation from the United States of such West Indian products as sugar and molasses, whether or not they were procured from the British West Indies. This provision would end the reexportation of French West Indian products from American ports to Europe. Even more provocative was the provision granting Britain the same privileges that France had enjoyed since 1778 in bringing captured prizes into the United States, in direct contradiction to the Franco-American treaty of amity and commerce. Despite the stipulation in Jay's Treaty stating that nothing in the Anglo–American document would affect obligations already binding on the signatory powers, the contents made a mockery of the Franco-American alliance.

What advantages, then, did the treaty bring to the United States? Certainly, the most immediate benefit was the British surrender of their control of the Northwest posts. Hamilton's strong advocacy and Jay's own firmness on this issue were major factors. They succeeded in the face of pressure from Montreal fur traders who wanted to preserve their profitable relations with the Indians of the Northwest. And it ended, at least for a dozen years, British efforts to establish independent Indian nations with the help of their mediation. General Anthony Wayne's crucial victory at Fallen Timbers in northwestern Ohio in August 1794 undermined Lord Dorchester's encouragement of Indian hopes for recovering lost lands from the United States. The Foreign Office's subsequent rebuke to Dorchester and the governor-general's resignation from office were significant marks of Britain's receptivity to conciliation with the United States.

More questionable but still an achievement was the treaty of commerce that the secretary of the treasury had long wanted, which gave the nation relatively peaceful and profitable relations with the former mother country over the next ten years. The modification of the provocative order-in-council of November 1793 signified some softening of the British position on neutral rights, and the treaty reflected this change by allowing compensation for spoliations under the order of that council to be adjudicated by a mixed (U.S. and British) commission. The very concept of a "mixed commission" implied equality between the parties as well as a commitment to peace in the future. Mixed commissions leading to arbitration were a means often used to reduce tensions in Anglo–American relations in later years.

In retrospect, these were impressive achievements. Jay was much more than Hamilton's mouthpiece. He recognized the possibilities as well as the limits of diplomacy and made the most of them. Only Jay's adamancy about ceding any American territory prevented a new boundary from being drawn in the Northwest. If British creditors had had their way, arbitral commissions would not have been accepted. Grenville as well as Jay displayed firmness in resisting pressure from Montreal traders to postpone delivery of the Western posts for three years. Although the social success the American minister and his wife enjoyed in London raised suspicions about his adversaries' playing upon that worthy's vanity, the close personal bonds formed between Jay and Grenville in the course of negotiations appeared genuine. Historian A. L. Burt was convinced that, for their mutual efforts, "both the United States and the British Empire owe them a great debt of gratitude."[43] As for the treaty, John Miller compared it favorably with the Treaty of Ghent, and Bradford Perkins called it "the first proof that independent America was important enough to secure any concessions from a major power."[44]

Yet it was understandable that, in the context of the times, the shortcomings of the treaty would be the most visible. And from all sides, critics appeared. Southerners were unhappy with the failure to win compensation for the loss of slave property carried away by the British army during the war. Westerners were upset over Jay's apparent failure to gain a British commitment against meddling in Indian affairs in the Northwest. Anglophobes charged that Jay had accepted the British definition of neutral rights. Francophiles were incensed, even before they knew the specific terms of the treaty, over the strains it would put on America's ties with France. Nor was Hamilton himself pleased with all the results; his hopes for a treaty that would have accorded equality to American commerce were not realized. The limited admission of American ships into West Indian ports stipulated in Article XII was linked to full British privileges in American ports. In this context, he labeled Jay's handiwork as "execrable," made by "an old woman."[45]

The foregoing criticism does not include all the objections raised against the treaty. But the others were not in the public arena until the spring of 1795, after Hamilton left office. Some of the information he received through Randolph was disconcerting, particularly the absence of reciprocity in Grenville's projection of a commercial treaty. But Hamilton's disappointment was fleeting even after he learned of the details of the treaty. Jay was an old friend and former patron, and the secretary of the treasury shared his belief, as Jacob Cooke has pointed out, that no more favorable treaty could have been attainable at that time.[46]

What was attainable—and attained—was in large measure what Hamilton had been seeking since the end of the Revolution, namely, an arrangement with the source of America's credit and trade that would give the new nation time to mature in peace. Ideology and politics were factors, as they would favor Britain's struggle with France and frustrate his Republican enemies at home. His massive interference in the foreign affairs of the Washington administration merited criticism, but it was not a source of the failings in the final treaty. Hamilton had a vision of the future that discomfited his British confidants. His America would be independent of all foreign control—British or French—when it dominated the continent and challenged Europe on equal terms in commerce, manufacturing, and military power.

Jay's Treaty was signed on November 19, 1794, and Hamilton left office at the end of January 1795. The links were not coincidental. The secretary wanted to return to New York shortly after Jefferson had resigned, but he was persuaded to stay on to ensure that Madison's discriminatory bill against British commerce was defeated through the special mission to London. It was a sacrifice for him, given his financial needs that might have been met through a lucrative law practice. But the influence he could exert in office in aid of Jay and in the suppression of the rebellion in Pennsylvania against excise taxes on whisky in 1794 was sufficient to keep him in Philadelphia. By the end of the year, the treaty was completed and the rebels defeated.

Two weeks before his departure from office, Hamilton tried to sum up, as Jefferson did before him, the essence of his contribution in a farewell address. In this "valedictory," as Madison called it,[47] he returned to the keystone of his major reports, the vital need of Congress to guard the nation's credit: "There can be no time, no state of things, in which Credit is not essential to a Nation, especially as long as nations in general continue to use it, as a resource in war. It is impossible for a Country to contend on equal terms, or to be secure against the enterprises of other nations without being able equally with them to avail itself of this important resource."[48]

Notes

1. Julian P. Boyd, *Number 7: Alexander Hamilton's Secret Attempts to Control American Foreign Policy* (Princeton: Princeton University Press, 1964).
2. Gilbert L. Lycan, *Alexander Hamilton and American Foreign Policy: A Design for Greatness* (Norman: University of Oklahoma Press, 1969), 123.
3. AH to Washington, July 15, 1790, Syrett and Cooke, 6:494–95.
4. Conversation with George Beckwith, September 26–30, 1790, ibid., 7: 73.
5. Washington to AH, August 17, 1790, ibid., 6:572–73.
6. AH to Washington, September 15, 1790, ibid., 7:37–38, 56.
7. Ibid., 54.
8. Secretary of State to William Carmichael, enclosing "outline of Policy on the Mississippi Question," August 2, 1790, in Boyd, ed, *Papers of Thomas Jefferson*, 17:116.
9. AH to Washington, September 15, 1790, Syrett and Cooke, 7:53.
10. Ibid., 46
11. Quoted in Richard Brookhiser, *Alexander Hamilton: American* (New York: Free Press, 1999), 104
12. "An American," August 4, 1792, Syrett and Cooke, 12:158–59.
13. Washington to AH, August 26, 1792, ibid., 276.
14. AH to Washington, September 9, 1792, ibid., 347–49.
15. Jefferson to William Short, January 3, 1793, in Boyd, ed., *Papers of Thomas Jefferson*, 25:14.
16. AH to Washington, November 19, 1792, Syrett and Cooke, 12:170.
17. AH to Jay, April 9, 1793, ibid., 14:298.
18. "Pacificus No. I," June 29, 1793, ibid., 15:41.
19. "Pacificus No. II," July 3, 1793, ibid., 62.
20. Reasons for the Opinions of the Secretary of Treasury and the Secretary at War Respecting the Brigantine "Little Sarah," July 8, 1793, ibid., 75.
21. "Pacificus No. VI," July 17, 1793, ibid., 106.

22. Conversation with George Hammond, August 21–30, 1793, ibid., 257.

23. "Americanus No. II," February 7, 1794, ibid., 16:17.

24. Merrill D. Peterson, "Thomas Jefferson and Commercial Policy, 1783–1793," *William and Mary Quarterly* 22 (October 1965): 609.

25. AH to John Kean, November 29, 1793, Syrett and Cooke, 15:418.

26. AH to Washington, April 8, 1794, ibid., 16:252.

27. AH to Washington, March 8, 1794, ibid., 134–36.

28. AH to Washington, April 14, 1794, ibid., 278–79.

29. Hammond to Foreign Office, March 3, 1793, Public Records Office (PRO), FO 55/5-1.

30. Ibid.

31. Bemis, in fact, called it "Hamilton's Treaty," in Samuel F. Bemis, *Jay's Treaty: A Study in Commerce and Diplomacy* (New Haven: Yale University Press, 1962), 373.

32. AH to Washington, April 14, 1794, Syrett and Cooke, 16:276.

33. Ibid., 268.

34. Ibid., 276.

35. "Points to be Considered in the Instructions to Mr. Jay, Envoy Extraordinary to G B," an enclosure in AH to Washington, April 23, 1794, ibid., 322.

36. Hammond to Foreign Office, August 3, 1794, PRO, FO 5/5-5.

37. Bemis, *Jay's Treaty*, 358–59.

38. Gerald Combs, *The Jay Treaty: Political Battleground of the Founding Fathers* (Berkeley: University of California Press, 1970), 157.

39. AH to Jay, May 6, 1794, Syrett and Cooke, 16:383.

40. Conversation with George Hammond, April 15–16, 1794, ibid., 281.

41. AH to Jay, May 6, 1794, ibid., 382.

42. Ibid., 284–385.

43. A. L. Burt, *The United States, Great Britain, and British North America* (New Haven: Yale University Press, 1940), 156.

44. John C. Miller, *The Federalist Era, 1789–1801* (New York: Harper, 1960), 178; Bradford Perkins, *The First Rapprochement: England and the United States, 1795–1805* (Berkeley: University of California Press, 1967), 5.

45. Albert H. Bowman, "Jefferson, Hamilton, and American Foreign Policy," *Political Science Quarterly* 61 (Spring 1956): 36.

46. Cooke, *Alexander Hamilton*, 144.

47. Quoted in Mary-Jo Kline, ed., *Alexander Hamilton: A Biography in His Own Words* (New York: Harper, 1973), 330.

48. Report on a Plan for the Further Support of Public Credit, January 16, 1795, Syrett and Cooke, 18:125.

6

Behind the Scenes

1795–1798

O ut of office but not out of power at the end of 1794,
Hamilton served as a "gray eminence" to the Federalist Party despite his relative youth. In some respects
these next years would be anticlimactic. His apex of power
was reached as the shaper of economic and, by extension,
of foreign policy as Washington's secretary of the treasury. In nominal retirement, he remained a confidant and
adviser to President Washington and was equally influential with the Adams cabinet. Hamilton always attracted
enemies as well as allies, and in President John Adams
he encountered an implacable adversary whom he managed to outmaneuver throughout his administration. But
not entirely. Although he was instrumental in denying
the president a second term, Adams also sabotaged
Hamilton's most cherished dream: leading the nation in
arms against its enemies in the uniform of a commanding general. His romantic ambitions undercut the common ground that he shared with Adams. Both statesmen
sought to protect the nation from the grip of Britain or
France, but in his passion for glory, Hamilton lost his own
grip on reality. Again, not entirely. His voice was vital in
enabling Jefferson, not Aaron Burr, to succeed Adams.

These events were all in the future, of course, as Hamilton left Philadelphia for New York, intending to resume
his law practice and earn a living for his large family. Despite the accusations of his enemies and despite the insiders' advantages some of those connected with the
Treasury Department had taken, the secretary himself did
not profit from his government service. He was not exaggerating when he told his sister-in-law, "I go to take a

little care of my own: which need my care not a little."[1] His debts
when he left office were greater than his assets, but he was still not
tempted to follow the advice of his college friend Robert Troup and
speculate in Western lands as a means of building his fortune. When
he opened his practice in New York in June 1795, his immediate
success could have been translated into considerably more wealth
than he actually earned.

If he did not become a rich man, it was in part because the lure
of public life remained strong. As William Bradford wrote in 1795,
"It is in vain to kick against the pricks. You were made for a Statesman, & politics will never come out of your head."[2] Even if his
powers of resistance had been stronger, it is difficult to see how he
could have refused the responsibilities thrust upon him. It was not
just that President Washington needed his counsel on political appointments: those chores were easy enough to perform. What made
his involvement imperative shortly after his departure from Philadelphia was the fate of two of the most important issues of his term
as secretary of the treasury.

The Public Credit

First—and the more emotional issue—was the protection of public
credit, the most sacred vessel of the fragile Republic, which was in
possible jeopardy through the inattention of Congress. Hamilton's
farewell address in January, after all, was not concerned with the
specifics of any one policy but with the all-consuming importance
of credit in confronting a hostile world. As he exclaimed, "Credit is
an *intire thing*. Every part of it has the nicest sympathy with every
other part. Wound one limb, and the whole Tree shrinks and de-
cays. The security of each creditor is inseparable from the security
of all Creditors. The boundary between foreigner and Citizen would
not be deemed a sufficient barrier against extending the precedent
of an invasion of the rights of the former to the latter. . . . Hence the
Government, by sequestering the property of foreign citizens in
the public funds at the commencement of a war, would impair at
least if not destroy that Credit, which is the best resource in war."[3]

It seemed as if the House of Representatives was not paying
attention to his advices. The House jeopardized America's standing with foreign creditors by rejecting debt arrangements that had
given confidence to Dutch bankers in the solidity of the U.S.
economy. Little more than a month after Hamilton gave his final
speech, he was bemoaning to his friend Rufus King the "unneces-

sary, capricious & abominable assassination of the National honor by the rejection of the propositions respecting the unsubscribed debt in the House of Representatives." The former secretary indulged in hyperbole to express his dismay: "To see the character of the Government and the country so sported with, exposed to so indelible a blot puts my heart to the Torture. Am I then more of an American than those who drew their first breath on American Ground?"[4] He calmed down when the Senate reversed the House action.

While asserting that it was always more important to protect the nation's credit at home, given the damage failure would wreak on "our whole internal economy," he was insistent in his advice to the new secretary of the treasury, Oliver Wolcott Jr., on preserving external credit. To pay such creditors as the Dutch house of Willink, Van Staphorst, and Hubbard, he urged that "our Creditors must not be paid, without a *reasonable indemnification*, in depreciated paper," and recommended ways in which ordinarily suspect notes, French *assignats*, might be used when there was no choice so long as the commissioners secured "a premium of exchange equal to the depreciation."[5] His advices amounted to instructions, with full details designed to minimize the disruptions caused by war. Hamilton was no longer secretary of the treasury, but his concerns over financial relations with European creditors were fully articulated and eagerly accepted by his successor.

Impact of the Jay Treaty

The Jay treaty was a more serious challenge. The document itself did not arrive in Philadelphia until March 1795, although rumors abounded as early as January. Assuming the worst, the Jeffersonian *Aurora* of Philadelphia noted that John Jay had visited Bath immediately after signing the treaty: "No wonder he should be short breathed, and have such palpitations as to need the Bath waters to restore him after subscribing to so dishonourable a treaty as that said to have been concluded."[6] Although the editors did not know its contents, they were laying the groundwork for defeating what the Republicans considered to be an anti-French capitulation to British interests on the part of Federalist Anglophiles. When, after a series of mishaps on the high seas, the treaty was received in March, the president and secretary of state tried to keep the terms secret during the Senate's deliberations. The Federalists diverted criticisms for the moment by agreeing with the Republicans to remove the unacceptable Article XII, which limited the size of

American ships trading with the British West Indies and forbade reexportation of West Indian produce brought into the United States. Hamilton was uncomfortable with the Federalist efforts to prevent senators from allowing copies to be made and correctly recognized that they would only fuel Republican flames when the terms were leaked, as they promptly were.

The flames became literal when a Boston mob confused a British vessel docked in the harbor with a privateer preying on American ships and burned it down. Jay himself was burned in effigy. When Hamilton attempted to defend the treaty in New York, he drew shouts and stones. One of the stones struck him on the forehead. In withdrawing, he was said to have remarked, "If you use such knock-down arguments, I must retire."[7] Hamilton was not unfamiliar with mobs; he had confronted them in the past with some success. As his response suggests, his encounter in New York did not affect his composure or his sense of humor, although, as always, he was quick to respond when he felt any affront to his sense of honor. When Maturin Livingston later alleged that he had displayed "a want of spirit" in leaving the scene, Hamilton would have challenged him to a duel if Livingston had not denied making the remark.[8]

There was actually a possibility of a duel in July 1795, after Hamilton had challenged Commodore James Nicholson for presumably accusing him of being an "Abettor of Tories."[9] This was not the first or last time that the sensitive Hamilton would seek this remedy to keep his reputation unsullied. Fortunately, for the fate of the Jay treaty, their seconds worked out a face-saving understanding at the very time Hamilton was mounting his formidable defense of the treaty. As noted in the previous chapter, he had reservations about Jay's product, but when he considered the implications of its rejection, he resumed his role as polemicist with his customary vigor.

Hamilton's intervention came at a critical moment. Fierce criticism arose from Republican quarters when the treaty was submitted to the Senate, even after that body had followed Hamilton's recommendation by deleting the controversial Article XII from the text. The treaty was ratified by a bare two-thirds majority on June 24. The timing was unfortunate for the pact's proponents. The British order-in-council of April 25, 1795, authorized seizure of neutral ships bound for France that identified grain as contraband. The president, conscious of the public reaction to these new British captures of American ships, hesitated to sign the agreement. He first invited his former secretary of the treasury to comment dispassionately on the merits of the treaty, "because I believe that your late employment under the General government afforded you more opportunities of deriving knowledge therein than most of them who had not studied and practiced it scientifically, upon a large & comprehensive scale."[10]

Washington's protégé did not disappoint. Within a week he dispatched detailed commentaries on each of the articles. He rested his case on the vital importance of peace to the future of the nation: "the more or less of commercial advantages which we may acquire by particular treaties are of far less moment. With peace, the force of circumstances will enable us to make our way sufficiently fast in Trade." He worried that "war at this time would give a serious wound to our growth and prosperity."[11] It is worth noting that it was war with Britain that most concerned him, even as his opponents railed against the treaty as an occasion for French retribution for putative violation of the Franco-American alliance. Hamilton's eye was on the future when the nation would be strong enough to cope with threats from any European belligerent.

Hamilton countered all the anticipated objections to the treaty, concluding that the advantages of ratification far outweighed its disadvantages. He asserted that those who faulted Article XI for allowing too much time to elapse before repossessing the posts should recognize that the British would need time to establish new posts to be prepared "without prejudice to their Traders for the future course of their business."[12] Hamilton was equally dispassionate in discussing the discarded Article XII, as he tried to "do justice to Mr. Jay's reasoning on the subject. He thought rightly that the reexportation of the articles in ordinary times was a matter of little consequence to this country and that it was of importance by a formal Treaty to establish the precedent of a breach in the navigation system of Great Britain which might be successfully widened. These reasons were not light ones, but they are in my judgment outweighed by the other considerations."[13]

Similarly, he offered a cold assessment of the impact of the treaty on relations with France. He was unhappy with the loose interpretation of contraband in Article XVIII not only because it might be abused by Britain but might also become the subject of legitimate complaint on the part of France. He "should have liked the Treaty better without it. . . . I think this article the worst in the Treaty except the 12th—though not defective enough to be an objection to adoption."[14] There was no inflammatory rhetoric in his advices to

Washington. In commenting on opening American ports to British prizes, he underlined the *"express proviso"* that nothing in the treaty should be construed to conflict with obligations to *"former* & existing public *Treaties with other sovereigns or States."* Hamilton closed his remarks with the hope that in their own interest the French would not take umbrage over the terms of the treaty.[15]

The foregoing judgments were delivered privately to the president, unlike the public assault on the Jeffersonian opposition that Hamilton unleashed under the pen name of "Camillus." As biographer John C. Miller has observed, Hamilton did not choose his classical pseudonyms haphazardly; like his Roman model, the American statesman would save his Rome from the modern Gauls.[16] He turned to such legal philosophers as Pufendorf and Vattel to belabor his opponents, a familiar array of authorities he had used in the past. And his language was hyperbolic, as he asked his readers "to consult the history of nations to perceive, that every country, at all times, is cursed by the existence of men, who actuated by an irregular ambition, scruple nothing which they imagine will contribute to their own advancement and importance." And what these men wanted was nothing less than "to make the United States a party in the present European war by advocating all those measures which would broaden the breach between us and Great Britain."[17] Such was his introduction in the first "Camillus" essay on July 22 to the character of those who dared to oppose the treaty and to the ends that their hostility would achieve. The tone in this essay was very different from the careful dissection of the articles that he had offered to the president earlier in the month.

Of the thirty-eight essays published in the *New York Argus* in the summer of 1795, Hamilton wrote all but the ten contributed by Rufus King. He glossed over the shortcomings of the treaty, which he had clearly pointed out to Washington, and concentrated on the dangers of falling victim to Anglophobia. Because France had claims on American sympathy, the nation should be on guard against regarding Britain as some form of devil seeking to destroy American sovereignty by its defensive actions on the high seas. If freedom of the seas was a victim in the European war, it was not the consequence of the Jay treaty. Hamilton made sure that his readers understood that France, too, was violating neutral rights, even though it was bound by the treaty of 1778 to respect them. In brief, the "Camillus" essays were less reasoned arguments in favor of the treaty than they were diatribes against its enemies. Yet despite his extravagant language, Hamilton was not advocating an alliance with Britain. He remained consistent in his advocacy of his nation's freedom from all foreign control as far as it was possible. In the long run he predicted that the free trade with Canada deriving from the Jay treaty would open up "an immense field of future enterprise," at which time American manufactures would displace those of Britain in both Canada and the United States.[18]

The effectiveness of the Camillus attacks was open to question. Certainly, Jefferson was worried enough to urge Madison to respond in kind. Hamilton loomed in his eyes as a "colossus to the antirepublican party. Without numbers he is an host within himself."[19] Madison, however, did not take up his pen, as Jefferson had hoped, and for the moment a response was not necessary. Camillus was too erudite, too legalistic, and, above all, too long-winded to whip up the emotions Jefferson had feared. No votes were changed as a result of these essays, and Washington finally signed the treaty on August 14, 1795.

The treaty's problems did not end with ratification. Republican leaders believed that they had the country behind them in their opposition to the British treaty. Even as Jefferson bemoaned the presence of the Hamiltonian colossus, he felt that the Federalists "have got themselves into a defile, where they might be finished" before Hamilton's talents and "indefatigableness" could extricate them.[20] Given a sense that the nation was behind them, the Republicans sought to block implementation of the treaty by defeating funding in the House of Representatives as a viable means of denying victory to the Federalists. The Republican-dominated House could undo the damage in the arbitration commissions established by the treaty. This was precisely the object of Edward Livingston's motion on March 2, 1796, asking the president to submit copies of all documents relating to Jay's mission. If the president complied with the request, it could reveal details of the negotiations that would embarrass the Anglophile party. If he refused, the administration would be exposed to charges of a cover-up, which would be equally embarrassing to the Federalists.

Although Washington was convinced that submitting to the Republican initiative would be an unconstitutional diminution of executive authority, he felt the need of support from his cabinet, and particularly from the most influential Federalist, Alexander Hamilton. It was not a theoretical issue. Congress approved Livingston's motion, and an immediate response was needed. Initially, Hamilton advised caution in a letter to Rufus King: "a too preemptory and unqualified refusal might be liable to just criticism." But he made it clear in his correspondence with the president that compliance with the congressional request could be "fatal to the negotiating power of the government." On further reflection, he recommended a total rejection of Livingston's motion, asserting that compliance would form "a very dangerous precedent."[21]

The controversies over the Jay treaty did not end in the spring of 1796. Instead, the treaty poisoned an already troubled relationship with the French ally. James Monroe, the Francophile minister in Paris, exacerbated the problem by assuring the French that the treaty would contain nothing detrimental to their interests. When the provisions were finally revealed to him, he intimated to his French friends that the majority of the country was pro-French and that a new administration succeeding Washington's would remove the Anglophiles and restore good relations between France and the United States. This may have been the most damaging of the many indiscretions Monroe committed in Paris. By convincing the new Directory of the validity of his predictions, he warded off the government's plan to break the alliance. At the same time, by exaggerating the Francophile sentiments in America, he tempted French agents to interfere in the new presidential election in support of the Republican candidates.

The Farewell Address

In the shadow of French disapproval, Washington prepared to take his leave. This provided an opportunity for the former secretary of the treasury to continue his role as shaper of American foreign policy. It was hardly a surprise that the president would ask his confidant to revise the Farewell Address that Madison had prepared for him in 1792, at a time when the party lines had not fully separated Washington from Madison. Four years later, much had changed. The vitriolic attacks on Washington in his second term confirmed his decision to retire from office and altered the tone of the address. The New Yorker offered the president both his own new draft on July 30, and a revised version of the 1792 Madison-Washington draft on August 10. The final address, printed on September 19, was Hamilton's, and it became the subject of some controversy when the Hamilton family, after his death, maintained that their paterfamilias was the sole author. Whatever the merits of this claim, the tensions of 1796—the Jay treaty ratification, the rising anger in France, and the successful Pinckney treaty opening access to New Orleans—figured prominently in the making of the address. In short, foreign relations occupied a place that it did not have in 1792.

Hamilton's role was prefigured in points he prepared in the late spring or early summer of 1796. The language was not precisely that of the final version, but the sentiment was. The former secretary of the treasury emphasized advice on foreign relations that became the touchstone of American nonentanglement over the next century and a half: namely, that "the greater rule of our foreign policies ought to be to have as little connection as possible with foreign Nations." This judgment was expanded to include a recognition that "our separation from Europe renders standing alliances inexpedient." This was obviously aimed at France, particularly when he added a specific reference to the neutrality proclamation of 1793 as "the key to my plan . . . uninfluenced by & regardless of the Complaints & attempts of any powers at War or their partizans to change them."[22] He did exempt "existing engagements" from the warning against standing alliances, but added that they should not be extended.

Although only France had such a relationship and only France and its American friends were worrying both Hamilton and Washington as the address was being written, there is nothing in Hamilton's advice or in Washington's final address that would exempt Britain from these strictures against alliances. By July, the language of the address was smoother, but the message was the same: "The great rule of conduct for us in regard to foreign nations ought to be to have as little political connections with them as possible— so far as we have already formed engagements let them be fulfilled—with circumspection indeed but with perfect good faith. Here let us stop."[23]

Historians are still debating whether the Farewell Address was a partisan shot aimed at a hostile France and its American sympathizers. Certainly the temper of the times could support this interpretation; the passions aroused over Jay's Treaty were still alive. Yet there is a Hamiltonian theme in the address that he had articulated many times in the past: namely, that the nation must stay clear of all alliances so that it might grow strong enough to be independent of the Old World. The internecine battles of Europe should not entangle the United States. This was the instruction implied in the question: "Why by interweaving our destiny with any part of Europe should we intangle our prosperity and peace in the nets of European Ambition, rivalship or merest Caprice?" Hamilton answered the question by claiming that "if we remain a united people under an efficient Government the period is not distant when we may defy material injury from external annoyance."[24] Here was a challenge that was not directed only to Francophiles and that provides an explanation for the special place that Washington's Farewell Address occupies in the development of American isolationism.

Election of 1796

Immediate problems with France inevitably took precedence over hopes for the future as the nation proceeded to elect a new president. It was not surprising that Hamilton's voice would be heard in the process of selecting Washington's successor. He favored Thomas Pinckney, then minister to Britain, and a redoubtable Federalist from South Carolina. The alternatives were Vice President Adams, whose independent spirit Hamilton distrusted, and Thomas Jefferson, the candidate of the Republican opposition. Although Adams won with a three-vote margin in the Electoral College, he never forgave the New Yorker for his behind-the-scenes machinations against him. But it was not domestic politics that preoccupied Hamilton in 1796; it was the threat of French intervention on Jefferson's behalf, implied in the Farewell Address and expressed through France's minister, Pierre Adet.

The temptation to intervene became irresistible to Adet as the fevers of campaign oratory rose in the summer of 1796, and after the last hope of preventing the implementation of Jay's Treaty died with the House of Representatives' appropriations. On the eve of the election, Adet proclaimed the Directory's decree of July 2, 1796, that France would treat American vessels exactly as the British did; he charged that the Jay treaty created a virtual alliance with Britain by allowing the sale of British prizes in American ports; and, finally, he asserted that the de facto nullification of the Franco–American alliance required suspension of his functions as minister to the United States. This uncertain state of affairs would "last until the Government of the United States returns to sentiments, and to measures, more conformable to the interests of the alliance, and the sworn friendship between the two nations."[25] Published on November 2, 1796, in the Republican journal *Aurora*, Adet's broadside left little doubt that he sought to influence the presidential election and acted with the approval of influential Jeffersonians. Madison recognized that French intervention would cause the party embarrassment, even though Adet's involvement came too late to influence the choice of presidential electors in most states.

Not surprisingly, Hamilton was compelled to comment on Adet's message. In his letter of November 11 responding to Washington's request for advice, he expressed regret that Secretary of State Timothy Pickering had not responded immediately to Adet's conduct, even though he, along with Jay, had advised against this response a week earlier on the grounds that it "would countenance & imitate the irregularity & would not be dignified." But, on reflection, he recognized that "silence commonly carries with it the appearance of *hauteur* & *contempt.*"[26] Silence, he felt, should be employed only if a break with the minister was intended. His revised advice was to distinguish between Adet and his government, framing a reply that would reflect the nation's effort to keep calm and repair relations between the two countries.

Hamilton's measured tone took into account the spirit of moderation that accompanied the French minister's blast against the Washington administration. Citing the "sweet emotions" that the name of America evoked, Adet made a point of adding that "the executive directory wish not to break with a people whom they love to salute with the appellation of friend." Adet also prefaced his notification with the statement that "the Government of the United States, and the American people, are not to regard the suspension of his functions as a rupture between France and the United States, but as a mark of just discontent."[27]

Secretary Pickering prepared a reply in the week following the French minister's message. But again, not surprisingly, Hamilton felt the need to contribute his own refutation of Adet's charges, which he did on December 8 in the New York *Minerva*. He was especially anxious to challenge the assumption that the United States had violated its treaty with France, a familiar refrain of the French after they learned the terms of Jay's Treaty. That the minister repeated and exaggerated the canard was bad enough; what made it worse was his failure to couch the complaint "*in the language of friendship.*" Hamilton chided Adet for using menacing language to influence timid Americans in the election of their president and vice president. He purposely employed a moderate tone in painstakingly examining such complaints as the illegal arrests of French privateers, a subject he had disposed of in 1793 when he referred to France's receiving "a doubtful privilege, to which she was not entitled by treaty," namely, selling prizes from captured British ships in American ports. Yet in concluding that "our government has acted with consistency, firmness, and moderation, in repelling the unjust pretensions of the belligerent powers," he was pointing his finger at Britain's abuses as well as at its enemy's.[28]

Rapprochement with France

What Hamilton was signaling in his response to Adet was not a call to arms, but rather an appeal for some sort of rapprochement with France. "You need not be told," he informed Rufus King, "that every exertion, not degrading to us, will be made to preserve peace with France." But there were limits to the nation's forbearance. He made it clear to Theodore Sedgwick that France should not be allowed to dictate terms to America and that, if its conduct did not change, armed vessels would convoy merchant ships "to protect our commerce & save our honor."[29]

It is worth noting that he likened the troubles with Paris to those with London before the Jay mission and suggested that "something like a similar plan ought to be pursued." This was not an aside. Settling relations with the ally was almost as important as coming to an accommodation with Britain. As he told Washington in January 1797, "I have reflected as maturely as time permitted on the idea of an extraordinary mission to France, and notwithstanding the objections, I rather incline to it under some shape or other."[30] And he had a clear vision of the shape he would like to see. Rather than have a single envoy in Paris, he recommended a three-man commission that would include a Jeffersonian spokesman. The South Carolina Federalist, Charles Cotesworth Pinckney, had already been appointed to succeed Francophile James Monroe. To appease French sensibilities, he felt that the appointment of Madison would send a message that the Directory would appreciate. And since both Madison and Pinckney were Southerners, he named George Cabot of Massachusetts as an appropriate third member, not to negate Madison but to solidify the national character of the mission.

Hamilton understood Washington's reluctance to take this step for fear of offending Pinckney. But "cogent motives of public utility must prevail," the New Yorker claimed, "over personal considerations. Mr. Pinckney may be told in a private letter from you that this is an unavoidable concession to the pressure of public exigency & the state of *internal parties*."[31] Despite this advice, Washington did not appoint the commissioners his former aide had advocated. This lapse on the part of the lame-duck president did not signify Hamilton's loss of influence in the government. The tenor of his communications with Washington's and later Adams's cabinet as well as his relations with the Federalist Congress attested to the power that he continued to wield in Philadelphia. He was confident that his words were wise and that his correspondents would heed them. He may have operated for the most part behind the scenes, but the psychic distance between his law office in New York and the seat of government in Philadelphia was minuscule.

The source of much of his influence lay in his connections with key members of the Washington cabinet who remained in office almost to the end of the Adams administration. They were part of a Hamilton coterie, although the ties between each of them and the leader were not uniform. Secretary of State Pickering was a stalwart and stiff-necked Federalist, attentive to the New Yorker's views but not subservient. Secretary of the Treasury Wolcott had served as comptroller in the Treasury Department under Hamilton, and he appreciated the guidance of the former secretary throughout the Adams administration. The least able of the three and the most dependent was Hamilton's good-natured friend, Secretary of War Dr. James McHenry. Given these loyal allies, Hamilton maintained a position of power behind the scenes almost to the end of the Adams presidency.

In light of the election of two able and persistent opponents—President John Adams and Vice President Thomas Jefferson—Hamilton's initial optimism over the prospects of the nation's foreign relations seemed surprising. "Opponents" may not be a strong-enough term. By 1793, Jefferson and Hamilton each had identified the other as a dangerous ideologue, dedicated to subversion of American liberties and devoted to the interests of a foreign power, France and Britain respectively. As for Hamilton and Adams, there was bad blood between them. The New Yorker was distrustful of Adams's independence. As far back as 1788, he had supported Adams for vice president only because John Hancock would have been an even less acceptable choice. In 1796, as the jockeying for office went into high gear, Hamilton did his best to place Thomas Pinckney as Washington's successor. The thin-skinned Adams, always a prey to paranoia, did not know the details of Hamilton's machinations, but there was no question about his feelings regarding the former secretary's personality. President Adams from the outset had no intention of soliciting Hamilton's advice.

In spite of this history, Hamilton perceived an opportunity for the new president to furnish the French government "a bridge to retreat over." The president, he thought, might have an opportunity to restore calmer relations with the Directory simply by being the new man in office. "Were I Mr. Adams," he wrote, "I should begin my Presidency by naming an extraordinary Commission to the French Republic." Even before the presidential inauguration, Hamilton revived the prospect of the commission's being composed of Madison, Pinckney, and Cabot. He elaborated on reasons for his selections by noting that he "would have a man as influential with the French as Mr. Madison yet I would not trust him alone lest his Gallicism should work amiss."[32] Hamilton's conviction that the nation required peace with both European belligerents outweighed his biases against Adams and the Jeffersonians

Even as he was promoting a peace mission, he remained concerned about the nation's honor. He was upset at the extent of France's depredations upon American trade with the West Indies. Secretary of State Pickering's report to Congress on June 21, 1797, condemned the French capture of American merchant ships in the West Indies as a "monstrous abuse in judicial proceedings . . . as well as flimsy and shameless pretexts" for profiting from their war with Britain.[33] The "ally's" behavior was unconscionable given the terms of the treaty of amity and commerce of 1778, and the damage to present and future American commerce would exceed anything that Britain had done prior to Jay's Treaty.

But it was the imperialistic thrust of the Directory's military policies that was especially disturbing. The fact that France was "intrinsically the most powerful nation of Europe" seemed to give it license to reduce smaller states to servitude, as he wrote for the *Gazette of the United States*.[34] The case of Genoa, he said, should serve as a warning for the United States. What bothered Hamilton as much as the arrogance of French demands was the failure of the attempts of Genoa to maintain neutrality in the European conflict. "How fruitful . . . of instruction to us," he exclaimed, "is this painful example!" He concluded with the assertion that "the honor of a nation is its life. . . . The Nation which can prefer disgrace to danger is prepared for a Master and deserves one."[35]

These concerns notwithstanding, Hamilton was still prepared to urge the dispatch of a mission to Paris. In fact, France's refusal to accept General C. C. Pinckney as Monroe's successor until its grievances had been addressed only made the appointment of a commission all the more urgent. Since Adams retained Washington's cabinet, the New York lawyer was able to maintain the influence he had enjoyed in the Washington years. In the following letter, he appeared to give Pickering his marching orders with the full expectation that they would be carried out: "It is now ascertained that Mr Pinckney has been refused and with circumstances of indignity. What is to be done? The share I had in the public administration added to my interest as a Citizen make me extremely anxious that at this delicate Crisis a course of conduct exactly proper may be adopted."[36]

This "Citizen" then proceeded to lay out a program that the administration should follow. It included a day of "humiliation and prayer," the summoning of Congress as quickly as possible, and then the appointment of Jefferson or Madison along with Cabot to join Pinckney. This essentially was the proposal he had made two months earlier in Washington's last weeks in office, and for the same reasons he had offered then. What was added were alternatives to rapprochement—defensive measures that would include creation of a naval force to convoy American merchant ships, commissions to arm those ships in self-defense, and the building of a twenty-five-thousand-strong provisional army. As he looked at the plight of Europe, he saw an isolated Britain facing an expanding France ready to seek revenge against the United States. And while the Adams administration should continue to pursue possibilities of peace, he thought that "we shall best guarantee ourselves against calamity by preparing for the worst."[37]

Pickering was unreceptive to the idea of an extraordinary commission. It was President Adams, who shared Hamilton's views on this critical issue, who welcomed the concept without crediting Hamilton's authorship. Its route to Adams was circuitous but effective. Secretary of War McHenry submitted the president's request for opinions to his friend, and promptly delivered Hamilton's suggestions to Adams without divulging his source. Ultimately, neither Jefferson nor Madison accepted Adams's invitation. Jefferson professed a disinclination to return to Europe, which may have been one of his ways of expressing suspicion of the president's motives. He suspected that the administration's reason for calling Congress into extraordinary session was simply to evaluate the depth of support he could expect in confronting France.

Adams completed his list of commissioners when he chose John Marshall, a Virginia Federalist, and Elbridge Gerry, a lukewarm Federalist but a close friend, to represent the United States in Paris in 1797. And Hamilton seemed content for the moment to "believe there is no danger or want of firmness in the Executive. If he is not ill-advised he will not want prudence. I mean that I believe that he is himself disposed to a prudently firm course."[38]

While the idea of an extraordinary mission, composed of putative Francophiles, continued to preoccupy Hamilton as a way out
of the ally's rejection of Pinckney's ministry, his imprudent affair
with Maria Reynolds took precedence, by the summer of 1797, over
all matters of state as well as his own law practice. This was not a
new problem. James Monroe, along with other congressmen, had
learned in 1792 of the blackmail her supposedly cuckolded husband had demanded. Hamilton had confessed his indiscretions to
them, and they agreed to pursue the issue no further. But five years
later, a muckraking journalist, James Callender, had exposed the
liaison, with the additional charge of colluding with the husband,
James Reynolds, in illegal speculation. In a 28,000-word pamphlet,
Hamilton admitted his infidelity but also denied any financial im-
proprieties. Much of the summer of 1797 was devoted to clearing
his name of illegal financial activities, and to do so he was willing
to expose his dalliance with Mrs. Reynolds. He would rather risk
the embarrassment of an illicit affair than have his name unfairly
tainted by accusations of corruption, as Callender alleged. Conceivably, he took this course in the knowledge that his devoted family, particularly his wife, would forgive him, as did his circle of
friends.

In any event, the Reynolds affair diverted his attention in the
short run from his concerns about the nation's relations with France.
The scandal did have consequences. It confirmed Adams's hostility by adding moral turpitude to the reasons for the president's
dislike of the former secretary of the treasury. If Hamilton ever expected to become an adviser to Adams as he had been to Washington, these expectations should have been dissolved by the summer
of 1797. Yet there was an asymmetry in the attitudes of the two
statesmen; Adams was the more passionate in his feelings. Had he
known of Hamilton's role as secret adviser to his cabinet, those
negative feelings would have been exacerbated. Hamilton may have
had reservations about the president's manner but he recognized
his essential probity and, in the early days of the administration,
agreed with his views on questions of war, military preparations,
and relations with France.

Failure of the Pinckney Mission

France's attempt to extort funds from the American commissioners as a precondition for official acceptance of their credentials became known as the XYZ Affair, when news of Foreign Minister

Charles-Maurice de Talleyrand's behavior reached Philadelphia in March 1798. But even before that news had arrived, Hamilton was ready with answers to Secretary of War McHenry's request for advice on the administration's reactions in the event that the joint mission should fail.

His advice emerged more as instructions than recommendations: "The measures to be taken by the Executive will therefore be to communicate to Congress the failure of the mission with *manly* but *calm* and *sedate* firmness & without strut." Without abandoning hope of ultimate accommodation, he should take measures to ensure the protection of commerce on the high seas and to ensure "ultimate security" if an open rupture occurred.[39] In brief, Hamilton seemingly returned to the military option that he had earlier made secondary to the diplomatic one.

Still, he was not advocating war, in part because too many Americans retained some attachment to the alliance. In the background was his awareness of the deep divisions within the country, and particularly in the summer of 1797, when Republican anger was fueled by Monroe's attack on Washington over his recall from Paris. The need to allay suspicions about Anglophile intentions was a factor in favor of moderation. Formal war with France should be avoided, if only because "there is nothing to be gained. Trade she has none—and as to territory, if we could make acquisitions they are not desirable." And it was very close to the course the president followed when the XYZ crisis broke in 1798. Hamilton even anticipated the future by advocating, in the event of continuing French rejection of the American envoys, that one or more of "our Commissioners remain in Europe . . . (say in Holland) to have the air of still being disposed to meet any opening to accommodation."[40] This hope for some accommodation was understandably vague.

Far more specific were Hamilton's recommendations for defense measures, in January 1798, that would include arming merchant vessels and preparing "as fast as possible a number of *Sloops of War*, say Twenty of from 10 to 20 guns each." He went on to outline defense plans closer to his heart: "a substantial regular Force of 20,000 men" and an auxiliary army of some 30,000. Given the real possibilities of American armed vessels capturing French privateers hovering near U.S. shores, he would set in motion the suspension of the treaties of alliance and commerce between the United States and France. Although a declaration of war, and hostilities themselves, should be avoided if possible, he was confident that America could cope with French power should all peace gestures fail.[41] As he grandly pointed out in the press on March 30, 1798, "With an immense ocean rolling between the United States and France—with ample materials for shipbuilding, and a body of hardy seamen more numerous and more expert than France can boast,"[42] America had nothing to fear from French hostility.

These advices did not include an alliance with Britain to secure the nation's objectives. Like a declaration of war against France, that move would be against the national interest. With cold objectivity, he asserted to McHenry that "mutual interest will command as much from her as [a] Treaty. . . . Should we make a Treaty with her & observe it we take all the chances of her fall. . . . 'Twill be best not to be entangled."[43] Behind the bravado of his rhetoric was a recognition that France seemed well on its way to subjugating all of Europe. In a subsequent article for the New York *Commercial Advertiser*, Hamilton paid special attention to the hypocrisy of the French Revolution that professed to be the "champion of universal liberty," while "exerting every faculty, by force and fraud, to accomplish the very conquest and aggrandizement which she insidiously disavowed."[44] Genoa and Venice and Switzerland were witnesses to the role that the United States was to play in the French empire.

Ironically, his Virginia adversaries essentially agreed with him about French ambitions and their impact on the United States. Hamilton could share Madison's speculations about the threat of a vengeful France conspiring with Spain to disturb navigation on the Mississippi and could echo Jefferson's gloomy prediction that there will be "new neighbors in Louisiana (probably the present French armies when disbanded)," who would join "the enemies on that side where [we] are most vulnerable."[45] Where the Virginians differed from the New Yorker was over the means to cope with the French challenge.

Notes

1. AH to Angelica Church, December 8, 1794, Syrett and Cooke, 17:428–29.
2. William Bradford to AH, July 2, 1795, ibid., 18:397.
3. Report on Public Credit, January 16, 1795, ibid., 127–28.
4. AH to Rufus King, February 21, 1795, ibid., 278.
5. AH to Wolcott, April 10, 1795, ibid., 326.
6. Perkins, *The First Rapprochement*, 30.
7. Quoted in Schachner, *Alexander Hamilton*, 350.

8. Quoted in Miller, *Alexander Hamilton: Portrait in Paradox*, 424.

9. Draft of Apology Required of James Nicholson, July 25–26, 1795, Syrett and Cooke, 18:501.

10. Washington to AH, July 3, 1795, ibid., 399.

11. Remarks on the Treaty of Amity, Commerce and Navigation Lately Made between the United States and Great Britain, July 9–11, 1795, ibid., 452.

12. Ibid., 405.

13. Ibid., 432.

14. Ibid., 443.

15. Ibid., 449, 454.

16. Miller, *Alexander Hamilton: Portrait in Paradox*, 427.

17. "The Defence, No. 1," July 22, 1795, Syrett and Cooke, 18:480–81.

18. Quoted in Miller, *Alexander Hamilton: Portrait in Paradox*, 428.

19. Jefferson to Madison, September 21, 1795, in Andrew A. Lipscomb and Albert E. Bergh, eds., *The Writings of Thomas Jefferson*, 20 vols. (Washington, DC: Thomas Jefferson Memorial Association, 1903-04), 9:309–10.

20. Ibid., 310.

21. AH to King, March 16, 1796, Syrett and Cooke, 20:76–77; AH to Washington, March 7, 1796, ibid., 68–69.

22. Abstract of Points to Form an Address, May 16–July 1796, ibid., 182.

23. AH to Washington, June 30, 1796, enclosing draft of Washington's Farewell Address, ibid., 284.

24. Ibid., 285.

25. Adet to Pickering, November 15, 1796, in Walter Lowrie and Matthew Clark, eds., *American State Papers, Foreign Relations* 1, vol. 1 (Washington, DC: Gale and Seaton, 1832), 583.

26. AH to Washington, November 4, 1796, Syrett and Cooke, 20:373; November 11, 1796, ibid., 389.

27. Adet to Pickering, November 15, 1796, *American State Papers, Foreign Relations*, 582–83.

28. "The Answer," New York *Minerva*, December 8, 1796, Syrett and Cooke, 20:433–34.

29. AH to King, December 16, 1796, ibid., 445; AH to Theodore Sedgwick, January 20, 1797, ibid., 474.

30. AH to Washington, January 25–31, 1797, ibid., 480.

31. Ibid., 481.

32. AH to Sedgwick, February 26, 1797, ibid., 522.

33. Report of the Secretary of State respecting the Depredations Committed on the Commerce of the United States since the 1st of October 1796, June 21, 1797, in *American State Papers, Foreign Relations*, 2:29.

34. "The Warning, No. II," February 7, 1797, Syrett and Cooke, 20:509.

35. "The Warning, No. III," February 21, 1797, ibid., 518, 520.

36. AH to Pickering, March 22, 1797, ibid., 545.

37. Ibid., 545–46.

38. AH to King, April 8, 1797, ibid., 21:26.

39. AH to James McHenry, January 27–February 11, 1798, ibid., 344.

40. Ibid., 342.

41. Ibid., 342–43.

42. "The Stand, No. I," in New York *Commercial Advertiser*, March 30. 1798, ibid., 385.

43. AH to McHenry, January 27–February 11, 1798, ibid., 345.
44. "The Stand, No. III," April 7, 1798, ibid., 405.
45. Madison to Col. James Madison, November 27, 1796, in J. C. A. Stagg et al., eds., *The Papers of James Madison*, 16:417; Jefferson to Thomas Pinckney, May 29, 1797, in Lipscomb and Bergh, eds., *Writings of Thomas Jefferson*, 9:389.

7

General Manqué

1798–1800

The XYZ Affair

There were distinct limits to any consensus with the Jeffersonians. After President Adams's announcement on March 19, 1798, of France's rejection of the American commissioners, Hamilton unleashed a vitriolic attack on French behavior in the hyperbolic language he had often employed in the past. He denounced the "most flagitious, despotic and vindictive government that ever disgraced the annals of mankind" in a series of broadsides in late March and early April 1798. He accused "the despots of France [of] waging war against us. Intoxicated with success and the inordinate love of power, they actually threaten our independence." To maintain the nation's sovereignty in the face of this powerful challenge was "the most sacred of duties, the most glorious of tasks."[1] Such was the tenor of Hamilton's rhetoric when the news broke about the shabby treatment given the American envoys. It was his counterpart to the cry of "Millions for defense, not one cent for tribute," the widely circulated, if inaccurate, response of Charles Cotesworth Pinckney to Talleyrand's demands for bribes and loans before the Americans would be received.

While Pickering's reaction was to declare war immediately, Hamilton's private advice was more measured and also much more temperate than his intemperate public broadsides. In fact, it mirrored once again Adams's own response. Upon receiving the news, Hamilton recommended to the secretary of state that the president

calmly present the facts to Congress, review the history of relations with France, with special reference to the January 1798 decree allowing seizure of any American vessel carrying British
merchandise, and then, after "a day of humiliation and prayer,"
urge Congress to put into effect those defense measures—arming
merchant ships, building more frigates, and increasing the military establishment—which he had been pressing on McHenry and
Sedgwick in the six weeks prior to the receipt of the dispatches
from Paris. In his view, "bold language and bold measures are indispensable. . . . 'Tis vain to talk of peace with a Power with which
we are actually in hostility." It is worth noting, however, that his
final point—suspending the treaties with France—differed in an
important particular from his earlier advice to McHenry, namely,
that the treaties be suspended "till a basis of connection shall [be]
reestablished by Treaty."[2] In this respect his recommendations were
milder than the ones he had offered in February.

This flicker of hope for peaceful resolution went unnoticed by
Jeffersonians. They saw in the Federalist response to France's de-
crees subjecting to confiscation American ships carrying anything
of British manufacture an excuse to wage war on behalf of belea-
guered Britain. Their suspicions that Hamilton and his friends were
using France's behavior as an excuse to justify their own acts of
aggression were displayed before the contents of the commissioners' dispatches had been disclosed. Adams would have preferred
to preserve their confidentiality, but he bowed to Republican pressure for their release. When the French insults were finally revealed,
they only added to the war fever and further discredited the Republican opposition and the dwindling number of friends of France.
The names of the figures who sought to bribe the American negotiators, while no secret, were identified as X, Y, and Z, which added
a sense of mystery and intrigue to the proceedings. There was no
mystery in Jefferson's eyes. The vice president saw the XYZ Affair
as a "dish cooked up by Marshall where the swindlers are made to
appear as the French government."[3]

Adams himself was carried away by the sudden and unexpected
popularity he now earned in standing up to France. There followed
a flurry of anti-French laws passed with presidential support by
triumphant Federalist congressmen. If war was not declared, it was
primarily because a state of war, as Hamilton had put it earlier,
was already in place as a consequence of France's depredations
against American commerce. It was only a matter of form when
Congress unilaterally abrogated the Franco–American alliance of

1778 in the summer of 1798. High Federalists, and even John Adams, anticipated a declaration of war at this juncture to quicken military preparations and further demonize the Republican opposition. But there was sufficient opposition on the part of moderate Federalists and Republicans to hold back from full-scale war and let the French make the first move. The war remained undeclared.

The Alien and Sedition Acts

The martial spirit aroused by France's action was expressed in the passage of the Alien, Sedition, and Naturalization laws in the heated atmosphere of the summer of 1798. They were intended to prevent the subversion of the government by both foreign and domestic enemies and were clearly aimed at Jeffersonians and immigrants supportive of the Republicans or of France. The supporters were primarily French aliens but included some Irish veterans of the failed revolt against Britain who presumably would be predisposed against the Anglophile Federalists. This was the object of the three alien laws. To further reduce the dangerous political impact of aliens, Congress required fourteen years rather than five before citizenship could be granted. And for domestic enemies, the Sedition Act would punish conspiracies against the government and make defaming members of Congress or the administration a crime. These measures, designed to stifle dissent, posed a challenge to civil liberties.

Hamilton's attitude toward the Alien and Sedition laws is unclear. He exulted over the "spirit of patriotism, kindling everywhere." In a letter in June to Rufus King, he wrote: "And you will not be sorry to know that it is my opinion that there will shortly be *national unanimity* as far as that idea can ever exist. Many of the leaders of the Faction will persist and take ultimately a station in public estimation like that of the *Tories* of our Revolution."[4] Congressional measures against France not only would foster national unity but also confound his enemies. Actually, he appeared to be more wary than Adams about the implications of the acts. His sparse comments on them suggest a level of discomfort with the severity of the Alien Enemy bill, which was soon to be enacted, when he wrote to Pickering that "if an Alien Bill passes I should like to know what policy in execution is likely to govern the Executive." There should be "guarded exceptions," he felt, for those who would suffer from the consequences and whose behavior has been "unexceptionable. Let us not be cruel or violent."[5]

The New York lawyer had even less to say about the Sedition Act. In the one letter he apparently wrote on the subject, he did express concern about provisions that might strengthen the Republicans in their opposition, and perhaps even lead to civil war: "Let us not establish a tyranny. Energy is a very different thing from violence."[6] Biographer Jacob Cooke concluded, from the absence of the extensive commentary that Hamilton would ordinarily give to a controversial subject, that he essentially accepted the laws, despite a few minor qualms.[7] But one might also conclude that if he had supported the Alien or Sedition laws, he would have written with some passion and considerable more prolixity about their virtues.

A case may also be made that he regarded this repressive legislation as the price the nation would hope to pay for its defense against a dangerous enemy. His fear of France was genuine. Yet even at the height of Francophobic tensions, Hamilton was ready to criticize Britain for its resumption in 1798 of seizures of American vessels carrying goods from France, Spain, or the Dutch West Indies to any part of Europe, a practice that had presumably been abandoned in 1794. He wondered at the folly of Britain's taking actions against the United States contrary to that nation's own interests. The effect would be to blur distinctions between France and Britain, "who it will be said are equally disposed to plunder and oppress. . . . Why are weapons to be furnished to our Jacobins?"[8] Even though Hamilton did not equate the malevolence of the two powers and wrote in sorrow as much as in anger, he made it clear to Pickering that "it is of the true policy of our Government to act with spirit and energy as well towards G Britain as France. I would *meet* [sic] the same measure to both of them." Nevertheless, he was hopeful that a "pointed call on the British Minister here . . . may have a good effect."[9] This was the Hamiltonian stance in the wake of the XYZ humiliations. In public his attacks against France were harsh, but in his correspondence he was no demagogue. He wanted neither war with France nor dependence upon Britain.

Inspector General

Hamilton's sangfroid was to undergo severe challenges over the next two years, and its root cause rested on the implications of the defense measures that had most appealed to him as a response to the French challenge. The undeclared war was an opportunity to take the measures he believed vital for the nation's security. It was also an opportunity for him to gratify a passion that had always been a critical factor in his psychic makeup: a thirst for military glory wrapped in a romantic mantle. To realize this goal, he was willing to neglect his law practice, separate himself from his large and devoted family, and demonize the enemy in a way that his more rational self would not have found sensible. To be a general in command of all the American forces, even if Washington was nominally the leader, was worth almost any sacrifice.

The conditions for his leap back into public service, this time in uniform, were all in place in the summer of 1798. Rebellion at home, invasion from abroad, fears of defeat of Britain and of French control of Louisiana were sufficient incentives in the wake of the XYZ humiliation for Congress to pass legislation that Hamilton had campaigned for so ardently earlier in the year. Frigates were built, merchant ships armed, and, most important, a provisional army was raised.

These measures were not quite all Hamilton wanted. Only 10,000 men, not 20,000, were to form a provisional army, to be activated only if war were declared, or if the country were invaded or in imminent danger of being invaded. Popular hostility to a standing army never disappeared during the undeclared war with France. Colonel Hamilton was impatient with this sentiment, which was not confined to Republicans, and questioned in April 1798 whether the militia could manage an invasion on its own. "Can it be doubted," he asked, "that a rapid and formidable progress would in the first instance be made by the invader? . . . To have a good army on foot will be best of all precautions to prevent as well as to repel invasion."[10]

Although the provisional army seemed inadequate, a subsequent bill augmenting the regular army by twelve new regiments and six troops of dragoons awakened prospects of command in Hamilton. If war did come, there would be an opportunity to win once again the glory that he had enjoyed too briefly at the end of the Revolutionary War. This time, he would have a rank commensurate with his abilities as well as with his ambitions. Small wonder that he perceived himself "bound once more to sacrifice the interest of my family to public call."[11] The "call" had a specific direction. He turned down Governor Jay's suggestion that he take an unexpired New York seat in the Senate and Robert Harper's that he replace McHenry as secretary of war. Hamilton wanted more; and, given his influence with officials in high places, he expected to win at least a de facto supreme command.

Recognizing that de jure command was impossible, he turned to his old patron, George Washington, and appealed to him in the name of patriotism to accept the president's appointment as commander in chief. Adams made the nomination on July 2, 1798, in accordance with the article in the act authorizing the president to raise a provisional army, and the Senate unanimously confirmed it the following day. Hamilton was well aware that when Congress subsequently augmented the regular army, it also authorized the appointment of two major generals and an inspector general with the rank of major general. Washington was prepared to make his former aide-de-camp second in command with the title of inspector general. Generals Henry Knox and Charles Cotesworth Pinckney would serve under Hamilton.

Washington's preference triggered a three-month squabble initiated by President Adams, who disliked Washington's choice and had earlier dismissed Hamilton's proposal of a 50,000-man army as "one of the wildest extravagances of a knight-errant." This was one of his milder descriptions of "a proud, spirited, conceited aspiring Mortal," as he informed his wife in 1797. "I shall take no notice of his Puppy head but retain the same opinion . . . and maintain the same conduct towards him I always did, that is to keep him at a distance."[12] Until the issue of an army and its leaders arose, Hamilton had not been aware of the intensity of Adams's feelings toward him. When Washington supported the New Yorker's candidacy for second in command, the reaction was explosive. "Oh no!" the president exclaimed to Pickering, "It is not his turn by a great deal. I would sooner appoint Gates, or Lincoln, or Morgan," although, as the secretary of state tried to point out, none of them was equal to the responsibilities of the position.[13]

Adams was discomfited by Washington's pressure to have Hamilton as his second in command, an arrangement with which the former colonel was in full agreement. Given the old general's age and his reluctance to return to service, Hamilton knew that the reins of power would fall to him. The president did his best to frustrate this expectation. He preferred Henry Knox, who had been a major general in the Revolution and later secretary of war under Washington, or Charles Cotesworth Pinckney, who had retired from the war as a brigadier general and was en route home from his unsuccessful mission to France. Both outranked Hamilton, and Knox in particular was conscious of his seniority. Hamilton was insistent, however, on rejecting the "principle that every officer of higher rank in the late army who may be appointed is to be above me."[14] He believed that public opinion would support him. In any event, he told Pickering that "few have made as many sacrifices as myself—to few would a change of situation for a military appointment be so injurious as to myself—if with this sacrifice, I am to be degraded below my just claim in public opinion. Ought I to acquiesce?"[15]

It was obvious that the prospect of command with the patronage of Washington and the cheers of his cabinet followers had gone to Hamilton's head. His sacrifices, whether of his law practice or his duties to his family, were freely chosen. It was ambition that drove him once again, and once again he succeeded. Reluctantly, Adams conceded to Washington's ultimatum and appointed him Inspector General and Major General on July 19, with Pinckney and Knox of equal rank but in inferior positions.

Once the appointment was made the new Inspector General claimed, in a letter to Washington, "that were I convinced of injustice being done to others in my favour, I should not hesitate even to volunteer a correction of it." But since the great majority of Federalists believed that "in the event of your declining the command of the army, it ought to devolve upon me, and that in case of your acceptance, which everybody ardently desired, place of second in command ought to be mine."[16] Such was Hamilton's rationalization for usurping, as General Knox saw it, a post that rightfully should have been his. An angry Knox refused his appointment.

General Hamilton immediately went to work in his customarily efficient fashion, submitting to McHenry a long list of candidates for army appointments under his command, from field grade officers to lowly subalterns. Many were friends and relatives, and as many as possible were certified Federalists. The fear of a French invasion was now matched by fear of French subversion through their Republican allies, although the new major general was willing to give youthful Republicans an opportunity to join the lower grades if they were malleable enough to accept Federalist leadership. Biographer John Miller concluded that these efforts demonstrated Hamilton's nationalist sensibilities as he sought to avoid making his army too partisan.[17]

But another reading of his policy would find a narrowing of his definition of patriotism. The common ground that connected him to those who worried about both French and British ambitions had collapsed. His army was directed against the French menace, and consequently he abandoned the nuanced judgments he had made about the Republican opposition in the past. It is unlikely that, in 1798, he would have considered Jefferson or Madison as a suitable envoy to France. He had no comment about Congress's unilateral abrogation of the Franco–American alliance on July 7, 1798. Nor did he have, as noted, more than feeble objections to aspects of the Alien and Sedition laws. France was clearly the enemy, and its adherents in the United States were inherently traitors.

The new Inspector General was in his element. All his energies were devoted to building his army, attending to the most minute details in the process. In many ways he was at the height of his influence in this new role. The president, forced to accept the New Yorker against his better judgment, spent as little time in Philadelphia as he could manage, and went home to Quincy at the earliest opportunity. Adams left the cabinet to its own devices as the army was being mobilized, and the cabinet in turn took its instructions from Hamilton with fewer reservations than ever before. It was not necessary for Washington to ask him to "give, without delay, your *full* aid to the Sec'y of War."[18] He would have done so without being asked. McHenry was totally unprepared to fulfill his responsibilities and turned to his old friend for guidance.

Hamilton did more than just guide McHenry. He was, in effect, the secretary of war as well as de facto commanding general. He wrote the guidelines for the army buildup, supervised recruitment of new troops, laid plans for reforming the army supply system, and then drafted legislation for the secretary to present to the House. Such qualms as Hamilton had about exercising authority were largely centered on the financial sacrifices he was making as "a man past 40 with a wife and six Children, and a very *small* property beforehand."[19] This concern, never to be resolved, did not prevent him from delineating for the secretary of war the division of authority between him and the other major general, C. C. Pinckney, or from taking on the many obligations that raising an army involved. While he complained frequently about McHenry's incompetence, it was the absence of civilian leadership that permitted General Hamilton the freedom to engage in projects that otherwise might have been denied him.

Hamilton's influence with McHenry was reinforced by Washington's transmission of letters drafted by the Inspector General and forwarded to the secretary of war. They answered questions that covered quartermaster contracts and locations of new arsenals. Coping with the enemy took relatively little space in these communications, but the dangers of an invasion were never far from the general's mind, even though Admiral Horatio Nelson's victory at the Battle of the Nile might make the "prospect of invasion by France, less probable or more remote. Yet duly considering the rapid vicissitudes, at all times, of political and military events . . . it can never be wise to vary our measures of security with the continually varying aspect of European affairs." Consequently, he emphasized the need for "prudence to cultivate a spirit of self-dependence. . . . Standing, as it were, in the midst of falling empires, it should be our aim to assume a station and attitude which will preserve us from being overwhelmed in their ruins."[20]

The Miranda Temptation

Important as the imperative of a strong defense posture was, Hamilton's estimate of Britain's potential for survival in its contest with Bonaparte's France was more positive than negative. Britain's partnership at this time was also critically important for Hamilton's military plans. By the end of 1798, he wanted nothing less than a French declaration of war to implement his designs on Louisiana and Spanish South America. Talleyrand, France's foreign minister and prime mover in the XYZ Affair, had no wish for war and, indeed, disclaimed any responsibility for X, Y, and Z and for the depredations upon U.S. shipping. But a new outbreak of French hostility was not necessary. For the moment—the winter of 1799—Hamilton had found an informal ally in Britain willing to join the United States in action against France's ally, Spain.

If there was no glory to be won in repelling a French invasion of the American mainland, there could be much in westward expansion. Hamilton's visions were no longer defensive; they embraced a new American empire, justified by the necessity of "frustrating hostile designs of France, either directly or *indirectly through any of her Allies.*" There was no hidden message in these words. In the same letter to Massachusetts Congressman Harrison Gray Otis, he emphasized the importance of "taking possession of those countries for ourselves, to obviate the mischief of their falling into the hands of an Active foreign power, and at the same time to secure to the United States the advantage of keeping the key of the Western Country." He could rationalize an expedition against Spanish Louisiana as a means of preventing France from regaining its lost empire. But his rationalizations extended beyond North America: "If universal empire is still to be the pursuit of France, what can tend to defeat the purpose better than to detach South

America from Spain, which is the only Channel, though [*sic*] which the riches of *Mexico* and *Peru* are conveyed to France."[21]

Converting these dreams into reality was quite another matter. Hamilton's days as effective commander in chief ended in failure and disillusion for reasons largely beyond his control. His imperial adventure collapsed in part through his collaboration with two unreliable adventurers, both of whom he had known since the Revolution. One was General James Wilkinson, an ambitious and unscrupulous officer who betrayed his colleagues throughout his career yet was in charge of the Western army while collecting a pension from Spain. Hamilton's single-minded goal at this point blinded him to Wilkinson's character despite warnings from his friends. The other was Francisco de Miranda, the Venezuelan patriot and inveterate schemer who had sought for years to enlist British and American support for the liberation of Spanish America.

Miranda was not unknown to Hamilton. As an officer in the Spanish army, he had participated in the capture of Pensacola from the British, but, alienated by the arrogance of the Spaniards, he returned to America in 1784 with a plan to detach Spanish America from the mother country with the help of Britain and as many Americans as he could enlist. Hamilton was one of those whom he visited, and while the New York lawyer was supportive, to the extent of supplying the Venezuelan with lists of potential officers, he had other priorities in the 1780s. When Miranda tried again to secure U.S. backing in 1790, the Nootka Sound controversy allowed little space for the emancipation of South America. But at the end of that decade, Miranda's schemes coincided with the ambitions of the newly appointed Inspector General. Together the two leaders, with the important assistance of Britain, could achieve glory and fame. Miranda would be the liberator of his homeland, and Hamilton would win for his adopted homeland an empire freed from Spanish or French intrigue. It was Miranda's vision that encouraged Hamilton to look beyond Louisiana to South America, and to the time when the United States would be able, as he wrote in *Federalist* No. 11, "erelong, to become the arbiter of Europe in America."

Hamilton's ambivalence toward Britain had to be suppressed, at least until victory had been won. If he had been given more time to look closely at the British role in this plan, he would have recognized that the British ally might have a different view on who should be the "arbiter" in America. As it was, he balked at a formal alliance, even as Pickering would have welcomed it. The Foreign Office was intrigued with the idea, as minister Rufus King reported from London, of an Anglo–American collaboration to free Spanish America. According to King, "As England is ready she will furnish a fleet and military stores and we should furnish the army."[22]

Did Britain intend for the American army to be the agent for U.S. domination of the hemisphere? This would be an unlikely scenario. Spain, since 1796, had been a satellite of the Directory, and in its war effort Britain was interested in ensuring that the United States would leave the control of Saint-Domingue to the British in exchange for whatever results the Miranda operation might yield. Should the Americans succeed, it was unlikely this division would endure. Britain's' long-term objective was the penetration of Latin American markets. Its achievement would make Britain, not the United States, the arbiter of the New World's economy and polity.

Hamilton's dream of becoming the hero of the Western Hemisphere was not to be realized. But as the quasi-war with France on the seas developed in 1798, it seemed possible. He knew the Venezuelan soldier of fortune to be "an intriguing adventurer,"[23] but the prospects Miranda laid out, if not his flattering description of the role the New Yorker would play, pushed aside his reservations. Hamilton informed King of his correspondence with General Miranda endorsing his enterprise: "I wish it much to be undertaken but I should be glad that the principal agency was in the United States—they to furnish the whole land force necessary." What made the plan so attractive was an assumption that "the command in this case would very naturally fall upon me—and I hope I should disappoint no favourable anticipation." It seemed to be a source of satisfaction to him that "Great Britain cannot alone ensure the accomplishment of the object."[24] While there remained a trace of discomfort with the British role, there was none with respect to Wilkinson's whom he had entrusted with moving against Spain from Natchez, once either Spain provided a casus belli or France ventured to occupy Louisiana and the Floridas. Like most of his contemporaries, Hamilton never recognized Wilkinson's duplicity.

Given the combination of dependence on an adventurer and a traitor, it is hardly surprising that the grand enterprise never took place. It was not for Hamilton's lack of trying. He did everything within his power to see to the raising of troops, selecting their leaders, supplying their equipment, planning tactics, arranging maneuvers and field exercises, and in general preparing his army for a war against France. Gone was the time (six months earlier) when he had urged his party's hawks to wait for France to declare war. But if France would not, he wanted Adams to announce a state of war in place of the informal naval conflict; he needed an excuse to put into place the invasion plans that would bring Louisiana and Florida under U.S. control.

The European scene had changed. In 1798, it looked as if Britain was in danger of defeat, and a defeated Britain could not shield America from French aggression. In 1799, as France appeared vulnerable in the wake of Nelson's victory in Egypt, Hamilton was anxious for the United States to enter the war before Britain took too much credit and probably too much territory from France. There never was a formal declaration. The Franco–American conflict remained a "quasi-war," and Hamilton in a sense remained a general manqué.

If General Hamilton failed to recapture the glory that he had won only partially in the Revolution, it was not only because of the unreliability of Wilkinson or Miranda or because of France's retreat from open warfare with the United States. Nor was it a national revulsion against his military ambitions that might be translated into a Napoleonic dictatorship. Although it was understandable that Jefferson could see in his rival a counterpart to the thirty-year-old Bonaparte, whose coup d'état in 1799 made him the de facto ruler of France, the link to Hamilton was inappropriate. The American general may have been a potential man on horseback, but his goal was not personal power but fame and acclaim. Ultimately, he had to be satisfied with his military successes in the Revolution and with his contributions to the nation's economy as secretary of the treasury.

The least of the many obstacles in his past was one that occupied much of his time, namely, securing the means to effect his administration of the new army. Throughout much of 1799, General Hamilton had had to assume the functions of the secretary of war and act as quartermaster and paymaster as well. He was constantly annoyed by McHenry's incompetence. He admonished the secretary in no uncertain terms: "It is one thing for business to drag on—another for it to go well. The business of supply in all its branches (except as to provisions) proceeds heavily and without order or punctuality—in a manner equally adapted to economy— on a large scale as to efficiency and the contentment of the army. It is painful to observe how disjointed and peace-meal [*sic*] a business it is."[25] In September 1799, a month later, he warned McHenry that "symptoms bordering on mutiny for want of pay have been reported to me." Payroll forms prescribed by the Treasury Department had not been filled out or submitted, a situation that he found deplorable. "Are the soldiery to suffer a privation of pay for several months," he asked, "because these forms never prescribed have not been fulfilled?"[26]

With McHenry's mismanagement of the military aside, the root cause inhibiting the mobilization of an army was financial. Economic historian Herbert Sloan observed that "the conditions under which the Adams administration attempted to finance the maritime contest with France probably would have taxed even Hamilton's capacities."[27] They were certainly beyond Oliver Wolcott's ability to secure funds for the navy, let alone the army. Borrowing from Dutch bankers, as was done in the past, was out of the question after France had taken over the Netherlands. Loans from domestic sources were no more likely to be found than they had been earlier. And to resort to excise taxes once again evoked memories of the Whiskey Rebellion at a time when Republican opposition was rising in the wake of the Alien and Sedition Acts. The solution was to enact direct taxes on land, houses, and slaves, but it met with limited success. It helped to stoke a rebellion against tax collectors among Germans in Pennsylvania under a militia officer, John Fries, that was all too reminiscent of the Shays and Whiskey rebellions.

Rebellion in Pennsylvania did bring out the army, and for a moment even united Adams with Hamilton, but Fries was pardoned and Hamilton was perceived as overreacting to a nonexistent threat when he led his army in pursuit of the tax resisters. Nor was he able to make the Virginia and Kentucky resolutions against the Alien and Sedition Acts into "an attempt to change the Government."[28] Such challenges to the federal government were the general's justifications for a professional army even without external dangers. "Happy it would be," he mused, "if a clause would be added to the constitution" that would redress the anarchic path the nation was following. If only laws could be passed "restraining and punishing incendiary and seditious practices." But he asked, "What avail laws which are not executed? Renegade Aliens conduct more than one of the most incendiary presses in the Ustates. . . . Why are they not sent away? Are laws of this kind passed merely to excite odium and remain a dead letter?"[29] Hamilton reproached the president for lack of vigor.

The Murray Mission

When the president did act, it was not in a manner Hamilton would have wanted. He was a general without power. After reaching the pinnacle of his aspirations, his achievements turned to ashes. President Adams in particular was his nemesis. Even Washington, who had loyally seen to his elevation as Inspector General against Adams's wishes, failed him. As commander in chief he stood in the way of any offensive operations against Spanish territory prior to a declaration of war. But it was the president who stopped Hamilton's plans in their tracks when he decided to send another commission to Paris without consulting his cabinet. Resentful over Washington's demand to make Hamilton his second in command and always suspicious of the objectives of the newly raised general, Adams was open to information from reliable sources that France would welcome new negotiations.

His friend, Elbridge Gerry, one of the three victims of the XYZ Affair, had remained in Paris when his colleagues returned home to inflame the nation, and he was convinced that Talleyrand was sincere in his wish for a rapprochement. Gerry's optimism was confirmed by reports from William Vans Murray, U.S. minister to the Netherlands, and particularly from Adams's son, John Quincy, minister to Prussia. Adams's failure to include a recommendation for a declaration of war against France in his December 1798 Message to Congress prefigured the steps he would take in 1799.

Hamilton still held some hopes from the president's insistence that France assure the American envoys a proper reception before any further steps were taken. Adams's message did emphasize continued preparations for war in case France's overtures proved to be illusory. In this context, Hamilton advised Harrison Gray Otis, chairman of the House Committee on Defense, to empower the president, "at his discretion, in case a negotiation between the United States and France should not be on foot by the first of August next . . . to declare that a state of war exists between the two Countries, and thereupon to employ the Land and Naval forces of the United States" to prevent and frustrate France's hostile designs. His fantasy of a war that would inhibit France from taking the Floridas and Louisiana and "at the same time secure to the United States the advantage of keeping the key of the Western Country" was not yet extinguished.[30]

Biographer Jacob Cooke noted the irony of the double standard that historians apply to Hamilton and Jefferson with respect to their common interest in acquiring Louisiana for the United States.[31] Jefferson's successful purchase of that territory marked the summit of his presidency, although Hamilton's eye on Louisiana marked him as a potential Bonaparte lusting for conquest. Both men would have gone to war if access to the Mississippi had been denied them. The difference lay in their characters rather than in their objectives. Hamilton envisioned glory in a war that would achieve this goal and accepted France's peace overtures reluctantly. Always seeking alternatives to war, Jefferson welcomed France's initiatives.

The question of war became moot when Adams nominated William Vans Murray as Minister Plenipotentiary on February 18, 1799, thereby following the recommendations of his son and of Gerry. The president's action came as a shock to Hamilton and to Adams's cabinet. In the course of a lengthy diatribe in October 1800 against Adams's reelection Hamilton revealed his unhappiness over the appointment of Murray "without previous consultation with any of his ministers. The nomination itself was to each of them, even to the Secretary of State, his Constitutional Counsellor, in similar affairs, the first notice of the project. Thus was the measure wrong, both as to mode and substance."[32]

The Murray appointment ultimately led to the Convention of Mortefontaine over a year and a half later, terminating the Franco–American alliance. But even though considerable time elapsed before peace was arranged, Adams's unilateral action doomed the limited prospect Hamilton had to lead his nation to battle and nullified the need for the kind of army he had been working to build. The decision to dispatch a new mission to Paris followed closely congressional legislation to add 30,000 men to the new army. This was essentially the work of Hamilton, who basically shoved aside the incompetent McHenry as he drafted the legislation and plotted congressional strategy. The committee chairmen accepted his advice, in essence adopting virtually all of Hamilton's proposals.

The general and his cabinet acolytes then managed to delay implementation of the mission by having the number of envoys increased to three, including Chief Justice Oliver Ellsworth and North Carolina's Governor William R. Davie, who presumably were more resolute Federalists than Murray. Hamilton's intentions were clear enough. Delay in sending the envoys might permit the volatile condition of the European war to offer excuses for ending the mission before it ever left American soil. And for a time the ploy seemed to be succeeding. The coup of 30 Prairial in June 1799 that removed Talleyrand from the Foreign Ministry and the rise of a

new anti-French coalition provided the occasion to justify postpone-
ment of sailing until affairs in Paris were more settled. In fact, a
second coup, on 18 Brumaire in November 1799, should have made
the mission all the more vulnerable, because it marked the overthrow of the Directory and the installation of the Consulate, led by
the young general, Napoleon Bonaparte.

Even before First Consul Bonaparte assumed power, Hamilton's
plans began to fall apart. Arguably, his meeting with the president
in October at Trenton, when Adams arrived unexpectedly to find
Hamilton consulting with Ellsworth and Pickering, sealed the fate
of his intention to subvert the president's initiatives. Turmoil or
not in Europe, Adams was convinced of a Hamiltonian plot against
him, which made him determined to have Davie and Ellsworth
depart immediately. This move effectively ended any possibility of
military action against France. Moreover, the death of George Washington in December 1799 left Hamilton without the patron who had
been his most devoted supporter for two decades. No one was more
aware of the effect Washington's passing would have on his career
than Hamilton himself. As he noted to Charles Cotesworth
Pinckney, "perhaps no friend of his has more cause to lament, on
personal account, than myself. The public misfortune is one which
all the friends of our Government will view in the same light. I will
not dwell on the subject. My Imagination is gloomy and my heart
sad."[33]

The general had good reason for his gloomy outlook, particularly over the military establishment he had worked so hard to form,
at the expense of both his law practice and his family. When he
raised the rhetorical question with Rufus King over "who is to be
the Commander in Chief?" he knew it would "not [be] the next in
Command. The appointment will probably be deferred."[34] In reality, it would never be made, as he rightly sensed. With a new daughter in the family as of October 1799, his eighth child, he had reason
enough for reviving his practice.

Acceptance of failure did not come easily. President Adams
seemed relentless in undoing both Hamilton's army and his foreign policy. There would be no war with France or invasion of Spanish territories. With the American negotiators in place, military
preparations were suspended. The president signed two congressional acts in the spring of 1800, the first halting enlistments in the
Additional Army and the second disbanding it. Adams had public
opinion on his side. With negotiations in progress and the absence

of a French presence in America, few citizens were interested in joining the army.

Adams's ostensible objection was its cost; the president exclaimed that "this damned army will be the ruin of this country." He placed the blame on the "Creole" who "knew no more of the sentiments and feeling of the people of America, than he did of those of the inhabitants of one of the planets."[35] To underscore his rejection of the Inspector General, Adams in May 1800 removed Hamilton's two friends, Pickering and McHenry, from the cabinet. Upon dismissing McHenry, the president unleashed his accumulated bitterness when he reproached the secretary of war for subservience to Hamilton: "It was you who biassed General Washington's mind (who hesitated) and induced him to place Hamilton on the List of Major Generals, before the Generals Knox and Pinckney."[36]

The Election of 1800

Recognizing that his own hopes were shattered beyond repair, Hamilton devoted his time and energy in 1800 to denying Adams reelection by supporting General Pinckney for president. This goal seemed all the more difficult when even Federalist New England appeared to welcome Adams's peace overtures. Renewed British assaults on American commerce and pride further undermined Hamilton's campaign on behalf of Pinckney. With considerable annoyance, he reported that a sea captain from Jamaica claimed "that the British capture all American vessels that afford the slightest pretext for condemnation, and impress all their seamen without discrimination."[37] Once again, Britain's arrogance revived Hamilton's determination to be as free from British as from French influence.

His putative role as a British agent, however, was among the many charges that Adams was directing against the disappointed general in the summer of 1800. He was, according to Adams, leader of a British faction, a group "more inimical to the Country than the worst Democrats or Jacobins."[38] Hamilton professed shock over this calumny, and echoes of it appeared in his notorious ad hominem broadside against the president a few months later. He dismissed the notion of his being a "leader of a British Faction," asserting that he "never advised any connection with Great Britain, other

than a commercial one, and in this I never advocated the giving to
her of any privilege or advantage which was not to be imparted to
other nations." In fact, he insisted that "her pretensions as a belligerent power in relation to neutrals, my opinions, while in the administration, to the best of my recollection, coincided with those of
MR. JEFFERSON."[39]

Hamilton overstated his case, as he recognized in a footnote to
his remarks: "I mean a lasting connection. From what I recollect of
the train of my ideas, it is possible I may at some time have suggested a *temporary* connection for the purpose of co-operating
against France in the event of a definitive rupture."[40] Suspicion of
and independence from Britain always coexisted with admiration
for its institutions and with opportunities the British connection
might have for his country as well as for his career. At the height of
the quasi-war, when he might have been a leader in a fight for glory
and American expansion, he was as carried away by his emotions
as Jefferson had been when he seemed to welcome a French invasion of England in 1795. The Virginian was tempted, or so he said,
to leave his "clover for a while," to dine with General Charles
Pichegru in London, where he could join his French friends in hail-
ing "the dawn of liberty and republicanism in that island."[41]

As the presidential election of 1800 grew closer, the schism between Hamilton and Jefferson narrowed. It was not that any rapprochement between the two statesmen was imminent. When the
Federalists lost the New York legislature in April 1800, Hamilton
had urged Governor Jay to recall the lame-duck Federalist legislature to prevent the victorious Republicans from controlling the New
York electoral vote. He justified this request, which he knew to be
unethical if not illegal, by invoking the dangers of a Jeffersonian
presidency. Admitting "weighty objections" to his proposal, he
feared sacrificing "substantial interests of society by a strict adher-
ence to ordinary rules." The alternative was the probability of a
Republican legislature, secured through Aaron Burr's machinations,
that would give "an *Atheist* in Religion and a *Fanatic* in politics . . .
possession of the helm of the state."[42] At this point, at least,
Jefferson, not Adams, was his target.

Jay refused to take the steps his old friend had urged, but the
loss of New York to the Republicans quickly became of less
concern to Hamilton than the possibility of Adams's winning reelection. Only three days after his proposal to Jay, he not only disparaged Adams's fitness for the presidency but also went on to say
that he "will never more be responsible for him by my direct sup-

port—even though the consequence should be the election of *Jefferson.*"[43] This statement was hardly a ringing endorsement of the Republican adversary, but that he would even consider preferring Jefferson to Adams was a measure of the depth of his feelings against the president. His alternative remained Charles Cotesworth Pinckney, whom the Federalists had designated as Adams's vice presidential running mate.

The relations between Hamilton and Adams grew even more strained when McHenry recorded that the president called Jefferson "an infinitely better man; a wiser one, I am sure, and if President, will act wisely. I know it, and would rather be Vice President under him, or even Minister Resident at the Hague, than indebted to such a being as Hamilton for the Presidency."[44] Until the firing of McHenry and Pickering, Hamilton's commentaries on Adams had been more restrained than Adams's on Hamilton. But the New Yorker more than compensated for his earlier restraint by his long, angry broadside in October 1800, condemning Adams's character and conduct with a vitriol that damaged his own standing with Federalist leaders. It became obvious that his campaign to elevate Pinckney was inspired more by his hopes of destroying Adams's candidacy than by concerns for Pinckney's prospects.

Hamilton's campaign succeeded in denying the presidency to both Federalists. He anticipated that the Federalist-dominated House of Representatives would resolve a tie between Adams and Pinckney in the latter's favor since, until the Eleventh Amendment to the Constitution, no distinction was made between the two offices. The presidential candidate with fewer votes would become vice president. Hamilton misjudged the result. Instead, the tie was between Jefferson and his prospective vice president, Aaron Burr. Consequently, Hamilton had to use his waning influence to prevent Federalist congressmen from making a deal with a man who was even less acceptable than Adams or Jefferson.

Hamilton, having failed to remove Adams in favor of Pinckney, preferred Jefferson to Burr; his distrust of Burr was deeper than his contempt for Adams. Writing to his loyal friend Oliver Wolcott, who remained a disloyal member of Adams's cabinet, he worried that some Federalist congressmen would support Burr over Jefferson. But, "upon every virtuous and prudent calculation," Hamilton insisted, "Jefferson is to be preferred. He is by far not so dangerous a man and he has pretensions to character." Jefferson then seemed to have been the lesser of two evils. If he was a threat to the Federalist Party, he was not a threat to the nation, particularly, as

Hamilton told Gouverneur Morris, if he maintains "the cardinal points of public Credit, a *Navy, Neutrality*."[45]

The Convention of 1800

"Neutrality" may have been the most important element in Hamilton's acceptance of Jefferson, and arguably it was more credible than the new president's position on public credit. The presidential campaign's fiery rhetoric with its resort to character assassination obscured the common ground Jefferson and Hamilton had always occupied despite radical deviations from time to time on both sides. Historians understandably have concentrated on and deplored Hamilton's passionate denunciations of Jefferson and his party. These diatribes helped to demarcate the differences between Federalism and Republicanism in the crucial decade of the 1790s. Scholars generally have paid more attention and allocated more criticism to the Hamiltonian role in this relationship than to the responsibility of Jeffersonians for the schism between the two parties and two men. Yet in the vital area of foreign relations, the divisions between Jefferson and Hamilton were always more apparent than real. When the polemics from both sides are removed, what is left is a shared understanding that the survival and prosperity of the United States rested on independence from the great powers of Europe.

While there was never a doubt on ideological grounds about Hamilton's partiality for Britain, or Jefferson's for France, their sympathies were reinforced by the practical benefits Anglophilia or Francophilia would yield to their personal advantage as well as foster their respective conceptions of the national interest. For Hamilton, Britain would be the bulwark protecting America from the wave of anarchy and atheism overwhelming Europe as well as a wellspring of America's economic welfare. For Jefferson, France served as an exemplar inspired by the American Revolution and as a barrier against the return of monarchy as well as a potential counterweight to British control of the American economy. Each regarded his political opponents as agents of a foreign power.

But there were always limits to Hamilton's or Jefferson's faith in their putative allies, grounded as they were in resentment of their arrogant behavior and in potential exploitation of their services to the United States. Jefferson opposed unilateral abrogation of the Franco–American alliance, but he was under no illusions about any fraternal bonds between the two countries in 1798. Hamilton was anxious for British collaboration in his military plans against Spanish Louisiana in the same year, and yet he had no wish for too intimate a connection with a British cobelligerent. In the long run, General Hamilton, like Secretary of the Treasury Hamilton, anticipated rivalry with Great Britain when the New World secured economic independence from the Old World.

President Adams's acceptance of the Convention of 1800, with France terminating the alliance of 1778, provided an occasion for the convergence between Hamilton's and Jefferson's views on the appropriate direction of America's foreign policy, although neither statesman was prepared to grant Adams credit for this consensus. The convention, signed at Joseph Bonaparte's estate at Mortefontaine on September 30, 1800, was the final product of Commissioners Murray, Davie, and Ellsworth. It was a de facto peace treaty that tacitly detached the United States from its entangling alliance with France at the price of claims for damages to American shipping since 1793. Claims for indemnities were deferred.

It was a high price, and Hamilton, among other Federalists, was uncomfortable with it. On balance, though, he was convinced that the Senate should accept it, as he recommended to Gouverneur Morris. He recognized that Britain would be unhappy with provisions of the convention that included the principle of free ships making free goods, but he asserted that "we had a right to make these stipulations, and as they may be fairly *supposed* to be advantageous to us—they are not in fact indications of enmity—they give no real cause of umbrage." And while France should have been made to pay for its spoliations, the public would not want the end of the alliance jeopardized by rejection on this ground. He recommended then that "on the whole the least evil is to ratify." Two days later, he coupled this recommendation with his preference for Jefferson over Burr "*on the same ground.*"[46]

This was Hamilton's judgment in the midst of the bitter contest over the presidency. Whatever his personal feelings toward Jefferson and Adams were, they did not prevent him from seeing the nation's interest in ending the war with France despite potential reverberations in Britain. He would rather "close the Subject *so far* than leave all open to the next administration."[47] The critical point of the convention was to make the French alliance inoperative, to be revived only with the consent of the United States. Ultimately, this was Jefferson's conclusion as well. But at the very time that Hamilton was downplaying British reaction and minimizing the omission of spoliations, Jefferson was complaining to Madison that it was not a real treaty without limitation of time. He worried that "its disagreeable features . . . will endanger the [*sic*] compromising us with Great Britain." In brief, he deplored "a bungling negotiation."[48] Ironically enough, it was Jefferson rather than Hamilton who had qualms about a British reaction.

If there was a consensus between Hamilton and Jefferson in the beginning of the 1790s, there was also a consensus at the end of the decade, and over the same issue: America's relations with Europe. The Convention of 1800 was a source of dissatisfaction for both men, but neither perceived any reasonable alternative to its acceptance. Although there was no meeting of the minds or a gracious reconciliation between the two adversaries, Jefferson's Inaugural Address emphasizing the links between Federalists and Republicans was based on a consensual assumption about the necessity for abstention from entanglement with Europe. Without abandoning his doubts about the future under a Republican administration, Hamilton arguably had more confidence in Jefferson's understanding of the national interest than Jefferson had in Hamilton's.

The Federalist statesman prepared to return to private life after attending President Jefferson's inauguration and finding "the speech in political substance better than *we* expected; and not answerable to the expectations of the Partizans of the other side." While Hamilton speculated that "it is not at all improbable that under the change of circumstances Jefferson's Gallicism has considerably abated,"[49] it was unlikely that Jefferson felt the same way about his adversary's Anglophilia.

Notes

1. "The Stand, No. I," New York *Commercial Advertiser*, March 30, 1798, Syrett and Cooke, 21:382, 386.
2. AH to Pickering, March 17, 1798, ibid., 365–66.
3. Jefferson to Edmund Pendleton, January 29, 1799, in Lipscomb and Bergh, eds., *Writings of Thomas Jefferson*, 10:86.
4. AH to King, June 6, 1798, Syrett and Cooke, 21:490.
5. AH to Pickering, June 7, 1798, ibid., 495.
6. AH to Wolcott, June 29, 1798, ibid., 522.
7. Cooke, *Alexander Hamilton*, 193.
8. AH to King, May 1, 1798, Syrett and Cooke, 21:455.
9. AH to Pickering, June 8, 1798, ibid., 501.
10. "The Stand, No. VI," New York *Commercial Advertiser*, April 19, 1798, ibid., 440.
11. AH to Jay, April 24, 1798, ibid., 447.

12. Richard H. Kohn, *Eagle and Sword: The Federalists and the Creation of the Military Establishment in America, 1783–1802* (New York: The Free Press, 1975), 230.

13. Quoted in Elkins and McKitrick, *Age of Federalism*, 603.

14. AH to Pickering, July 17, 1798, Syrett and Cooke, 22:24.

15. Ibid.

16. AH to Washington, July 29, 1798, ibid., 36–37.

17. Miller, *Alexander Hamilton: Portrait in Paradox*, 480.

18. Washington to AH, October 21, 1798, Syrett and Cooke, 12:210.

19. AH to McHenry, December 16, 1798, ibid., 369.

20. Washington to McHenry, December 13, 1798, ibid., 22:345.

21. AH to Otis, January 26, 1799, ibid., 440–41.

22. King to Pickering, October 20, 1798, ibid., 208.

23. William S. Robertson, *Life of Miranda*, 2 vols. (New York: Cooper Square, 1969), 1:177.

24. AH to King, August 22, 1798, Syrett and Cooke, 22:154–55.

25. AH to McHenry, August 19, 1799, ibid., 23:326.

26. AH to McHenry, September 21, 1799, ibid., 456–57.

27. Herbert Sloan, "Hamilton's Second Thoughts: Federalist Finance Revisited," in *Federalists Reconsidered*, ed. Doron Ben-Atar and Barbara Oberg (Charlottesville: University Press of Virginia, 1998), 74.

28. AH to Jonathan Dayton, October–November 1799, Syrett and Cooke, 23:600.

29. Ibid., 604.

30. AH to Otis, January 26, 1799, ibid., 22:440–41.

31. Cooke, *Alexander Hamilton*, 203.

32. Letter from Alexander Hamilton, Concerning the Public Conduct and Character of John Adams, Esq. President of the United States, October 24, 1800, Syrett and Cooke, 25:213–14.

33. AH to Pinckney, December 22, 1799, ibid., 24:116.

34. AH to King, January 5, 1800, ibid., 169.

35. Quoted in Miller, *Alexander Hamilton: Portrait in Paradox*, 505.

36. McHenry to AH, June 2, 1800, with enclosure, McHenry to Adams, May 31, 1800, Syrett and Cooke, 24:555–56.

37. Quoted in DeConde, *Quasi-War*, 276.

38. Quoted in Cooke, *Alexander Hamilton*, 218.

39. Letter from Alexander Hamilton . . . , Syrett and Cooke, 25:229–30.

40. Ibid., 230.

41. Jefferson to William B. Giles, April 17, 1795, in Lipscomb and Bergh, eds., *Writings of Thomas Jefferson*, 9:305.

42. AH to Jay, May 7, 1800, Syrett and Cooke, 24:465.

43. AH to Sedgwick, May 10, 1800, ibid., 475.

44. McHenry to AH, June 2, 1800, with enclosure . . . , ibid., 557.

45. AH to Wolcott, December 16, 1800, ibid., 25:257; AH to Gouverneur Morris, December 24, 1800, ibid., 273.

46. AH to Gouverneur Morris, December 24, 1800, ibid., 272; AH to Gouverneur Morris, December 26, 1800, ibid., 275.

47. AH to James Ross, December 29, 1800, ibid., 281.

48. Jefferson to Madison, December 19, 1800, in Lipscomb and Bergh, eds., *Writings of Thomas Jefferson*, 10:185.

49. AH to Bayard, March 8, 1801, Syrett and Cooke, 25:320; AH to Bayard, January 16, 1801, ibid., 320.

8

Epilogue

For a man who lived as public a life as Alexander Hamilton, retirement to private life was not possible, whatever his professed intentions. He made a point of writing how harassed he had been "in the base world," so that "it is natural to look forward to complete retirement."[1] It was certainly natural that a sense of rejection on the part of his political allies would have pushed him into this posture, even to despairing about his place in America—and about the fate of America itself. After all his services to the nation, he found himself reviled by Jeffersonians as an enemy of the Republic and ignored by fellow Federalists. Perhaps the constitution he helped to create was nothing more than a "frail and worth less fabric. . . . Every day proves to me more and more, that this American world was not made for me."[2]

Hamilton did retire to cultivate his law practice, with the success he had always seemed to find in the past in his relatively brief periods out of public life. And he enjoyed the role of paterfamilias among his large brood and with his devoted wife. Much of his time was spent building a house suitable for the kin of a Scottish laird, which he named "The Grange" after the ancestral home of his Scottish relatives. He had "purchased [in present-day upper Manhattan] a few acres about 9 Miles from Town," as he wrote Charles C. Pinckney in 1801, and occupied it a year later. He busied himself transplanting fruit trees, repairing fences, and instructing his gardener on the kinds of flowers to be planted. He knew precisely what he wanted from his new property.

But the life of a gentleman farmer sufficed for this man of action no more than the life of a lawyer. He had been at the center of power too long to leave it voluntarily. For a time, he nourished the hope that the people would recognize the errors and dangers of the new administration and turn to the Federalists for salvation. Two weeks after Jefferson's Inaugural Address, he was haranguing his fellow citizens to turn George Clinton out of the governor's office. Although he failed once again to achieve this old objective, he made his speech to New York Federalists an opportunity to parse Jefferson's address and expose the hypocrisies of the anti-Federalists, even if his nominal subject was the election of a New York governor. He saw once again the duplicitous hand of Aaron Burr in determining the election's outcome. But preference for Jefferson over Burr in the presidential contest did not inhibit him from excoriating the opposition in familiar hyperbolic language: "The pernicious spirit which has actuated many of the leaders of the party denominated antifederal, from the moment when our national constitution was first proposed down to the present period, has not ceased to display itself, in a variety of disgusting forms."[3]

The domestic issues of New York State seemed to fall away as he proceeded to lay out the follies of the opposition, beginning with its support of France. He asserted that the spectacle of a dictatorship under Bonaparte should be a warning to all Americans in light of the devotion the Republicans had shown to the French Revolution. With heavy-handed irony, Hamilton asked, "To what end, Fellow-Citizens, has your attention been carried across the Atlantic, to the revolution of France, and to that fatal war of which it has been the source? To what end are you told, that this is the most interesting conflict man ever witnessed, that it is a war of principles—a war between equal and unequal rights, between republicanism and monarchy, between liberty and tyranny?"[4] The retired statesman missed his mark here. He knew that Jefferson's Francophilia had been severely mitigated by the quasi-war and by the responsibilities of his new office. If his tirade had a purpose, it was to rekindle emotions that might have yielded advantages for Federalists in the 1790s but fell on deaf ears in the Jeffersonian era.

What was most revealing in this address to the electors of the state of New York was his personal distress at being charged with such crimes as inaugurating the funding system, providing taxes for public revenue, establishing a "Federal City," securing benefits from a British treaty, and creating "a Standing Army; and they tell us in plain terms that these are 'abuses no longer to be suffered.' " These charges were palpably unfair, he claimed, since many of the actions in his years of influence were shared with the Republicans.

His opponents, indeed, should applaud his fiscal reforms. "It is impossible without them to pay the debt of the nation, to protect it from foreign danger, or to secure individuals from lawless violence and rapine." As for blaming the Federalists for Jay's Treaty, they should have celebrated the preservation of peace, the British surrender of Western posts, and the flourishing of the nation's commerce.[5]

Probably the most controversial of Jefferson's charges was the implication of a military dictatorship in Hamilton's creation of a "standing army." The newly retired general ridiculed this connection: "As to a *Standing Army*—there is none except four small regiments of infantry insufficient for the service of guards in the numerous posts of our immense frontiers . . . and two regiments of artillery which occupy in the same capacity the numerous fortifications along our widely extended sea-coast. What is there in this to affright or disgust?" He went on to observe that if these forces were abolished, the militia would be an unsatisfactory substitute, "not a measure of economy, but a heavy bill of additional cost, and like all other visionary schemes, will be productive only of repentance, and a return to a plan injudiciously renounced."[6] These words were written in March 1801. Hamilton would not live long enough to see his forebodings realized.

Implicit—but uncharacteristically understated—in his criticism of the new administration was a recognition that Jefferson's Inaugural Address was essentially a backhanded tribute to Hamilton's contributions. What other construction could one make of an address that included "THE HONEST PAYMENT OF OUR DEBT, AND SACRED PRESERVATION OF THE PUBLIC FAITH"?[7] In Hamilton's view, Jefferson was taking credit for Hamiltonian accomplishments while calling them crimes when perpetrated by Hamilton. Arguably, the unkindest cut of all was his knowledge that the president's popularity was built on the Federalist infrastructure. The New Yorker's hope that the public would return Federalists to power was shattered by the Virginian's success in adopting Hamiltonian policies. Among them was the Jeffersonian sponsoring of a military academy, an objective Hamilton had failed to achieve in his role as Inspector General.

Jefferson's success as a Hamiltonian extended to foreign relations in particular. As the Louisiana crisis gathered steam over the next two years, Hamilton was repeatedly forced into a situation where he was in substantial agreement with his rival. This concord was rarely acknowledged. Whenever possible, he seized on

perceived weaknesses in the president's foreign policies to drama-
tize the differences between his Federalist position and his rival's.
By the end of 1801—a traumatic year that included the death of his
oldest son, Philip, in a fatal duel on November 24—the bereaved
father was a principal founder of the *New-York Evening Examiner,* a
newspaper intended to expose the follies of the Jefferson administration and raise the morale of dispirited Federalists. Its editor,
William Coleman, Hamilton's acolyte, effectively turned over major editorial decisions to his mentor. Between December 17, 1801,
and April 8, 1802, eighteen essays were published under the pseudonym of "Lucius Crassus," each intended to expose the shortcomings of Jefferson. Although there is no proof that Hamilton was the
author of these broadsides, there were sufficient indications, such
as the resemblance of their style to the "Camillus" letters, to credit
the paper's founder with their authorship.

Certainly the contents of the first "Examination" were demon-
strably Hamiltonian. The subject was Jefferson's first Annual Message to Congress, in which the president opened himself to criticism
for his contradictory stance on Tripoli's attack against American
ships. The Bey of Tripoli had declared war, as Jefferson clearly noted
in his address, but the president deemed that "there was not power,
for want of *sanction of Congress,* to capture and detain her cruisers
with their crews."[8] Hamilton granted that the Constitution had
given Congress the power to declare war, but when war was already in progress, "any declaration on the part of Congress is nuga-
tory: it is at least unnecessary." This was not the only absurdity
Lucius Crassus observed: the message asserts that while the American navy could engage the enemy and take lives, as it did, "it may
not restrain the liberty, or seize the property of the enemy." What a
way to conduct a war! Hamilton exclaimed. "Who could restrain
the laugh of derision at positions so preposterous, were it not for
the reflection that in the first magistrate of our country, they cast a
blemish on our national character? What will the world think of
the fold when such is the shepherd?"[9]

But once again, Jefferson trumped his adversary. What the nation gleaned from Jefferson's war with Tripoli was a Hamiltonian
exercise of executive power that led to Tripoli's suing for peace in
1805. The Federalist leader on the sidelines had seized on a minor
incoherence that was ignored by the public.

The Barbary Wars, however, did not compare in importance
with the threat of France's potential occupation of Louisiana. One
day after the signing of the Convention of Mortefontaine, France

made a secret agreement with Spain, on October 1, 1800, to return Louisiana to France in exchange for Austrian territory in Italy. Secrecy was required, inasmuch as Bonaparte had not yet secured these Italian properties. But the First Consul kept this information from Americans because he knew that even a friendly Republican administration would be unhappy with a powerful neighbor controlling the mouth of the Mississippi River. Bonaparte was right. When Rufus King, still minister to Great Britain, learned of the transfer through British intelligence, the news distressed President Jefferson. The question, then, would be what path would the new administration follow to cope with the danger posed by future French occupation of the Mississippi Valley.

Inevitably, the prospect of a French presence in New Orleans attracted Hamilton's attention and his comments. It was obvious that he would recognize the potential threat. The danger appeared immediate when Spain abruptly terminated the right of deposit of American goods in New Orleans secured under Pinckney's Treaty in 1795. The thought of a powerful neighbor in the West had preoccupied Hamilton in the 1790s. The Directory's imperialistic behavior in Europe disturbed Hamilton when he noted how France treated such smaller neighbors as Genoa. This was in 1797. Five years later, France under an aggressive young leader was an even greater menace. How would Jefferson, the former friend of France, treat its reoccupation of Louisiana?

Hamilton held out few hopes of the decisive action against France that he would have taken had he been in power. Conceivably, the nation would be sufficiently alarmed by the incompetence of the administration to return to the Federalists for aid. There certainly were sufficient grounds for a reversal of public opinion. As he told Rufus King, who first informed the administration of the Louisiana retrocession, "At headquarters a most visionary theory presides. Depend upon it this is the fact to a great extreme. No army, no navy, no *active* commerce—national defence, not by arms but by embargoes, prohibition of trade etc.—and as little government as possible—these are the pernicious dreams which as far and as fast as possible will be attempted to be realized."[10] Yet Hamilton was pessimistic about rallying the party; too many were seduced by Aaron Burr's prospects or by the administration's efforts to adopt some Federalist policies. He advised King to "return home. There is little probability that your continuance in your present station will be productive of much positive good."[11] Although he believed that a change of administration was no reason of itself for quitting public office, King as a Federalist of good character, he thought, should not serve a government that not only persecutes his party but also undermines the security of the nation.

Dispirited as he was by the Federalist failure to respond to his concerns, Hamilton was even more concerned by his party's unwillingness to condemn Jefferson's weak response to the French challenge. He could not understand why "the follies and vices of the Administration have as yet made no material impression to their disadvantage."[12] No folly appeared more pernicious than the president's second Annual Message to Congress in December 1802. Despite the interruption of the deposit of U.S. products at New Orleans two months before, Jefferson ignored this action and made only a mild reference to the Louisiana cession beyond observing that if completed, it will make a change in the aspect of our foreign relations, "which will have just weight in any deliberations of the Legislature connected with that subject."[13] Hamilton was exasperated by the "soft tun" of the message when a strong riposte was called for. But the president had few options given his abandonment of taxes needed to conduct a war. He wondered how Jefferson could preserve his popularity if he sacrificed Western interests. His own solution was clear and direct: "I have always held that the Unity of our empire and the best interests of our Nation require that we should annex to the Ustates all the territory East of the Mississippia [sic], New Orleans included."[14]

Upon learning of Monroe's appointment as Minister Extraordinary and Plenipotentiary to France and Spain, Hamilton elaborated on his concerns about the administration's management of the Louisiana problem. Given the potential dismemberment of the United States by Spain's cession and the direct violation of the Pinckney Treaty by withholding America's right of deposit, war against Spain was justified if it was expedient. Two paths were open. First was the Jeffersonian effort to purchase New Orleans and to go to war if negotiations failed. Second was Hamilton's advice "to seize at once on the floridas and New-Orleans, and then negotiate." Bonaparte's ambitions, he felt, were too grand to be bought off with money, while war after protracted negotiations might leave the French too strongly entrenched in Louisiana. But with France's navy crippled and its treasury empty, obstacles to a coup de main were minimal, particularly since "we might count with certainty on the aid of great Britain with her powerful navy." General Hamilton could not resist adding that the army should be increased to 10,000 men and the militia to 40,000 men. "If the President should adopt this course," he averred, he might yet "retrieve his character ... exalt himself in the eyes of Europe, save the country, and secure a permanent fame. But for this, alas! Jefferson is not destined!"[15]

It is not difficult to perceive in these admonitions, published in the *New-York Evening Post* under the pseudonym of "Pericles," a species of schadenfreude. Ostensibly, Hamilton regretted that Jefferson was unable to meet the challenge that he would have met in the manner of the Athenian hero. More likely, he would have been envious of the president's achievement had Jefferson taken the militant stance he had advocated. But was such a position possible for a leader who lacked the revenue and soldiers to win fame and territory before the French occupied Louisiana? The answer to this question had to be negative.

But Jefferson had confounded him with his purchase of Louisiana in 1803. No army was needed, no new sources of revenue had to be tapped. Bonaparte, short of funds for renewing a war with Britain that would leave French Louisiana defenseless, surprised Monroe and Livingston—as well as his ministers—with an offer to sell not only New Orleans, which the American envoy was sent to buy, but all of Louisiana as well. It was an impressive victory for American diplomacy, the consequence of Jefferson's threat of a British connection should the First Consul refuse to budge.

Hamilton admitted that "the business of New-Orleans has terminated favourably to this country," but this was a grudging concession. "Every man," he claimed, "possessed of the least candour and reflection will readily acknowledge that the acquisition has been solely owing to a fortuitous concurrence of unforeseen and unexpected circumstances, and not to any wise or vigorous measures on the part of the American government." It was sheer good luck that Bonaparte had wasted French resources trying to subjugate Haiti and lost the troops scheduled to occupy Louisiana. The resumption of war between Britain and France then produced "a situation substantially as favourable to our views and interests as those recommended by the federal party here, excepting indeed that we should probably have obtained the same object on better terms."[16]

The retired general had more to say in this commentary on Louisiana for the *New-York Evening Post*. There were unsettled questions about the purchase. Not least among them was the potential consequence of the vast territories west of the Mississippi, which might "hasten the dismemberment of our country, or a dissolution of the Government." Accepting too much territory was an error; it was New Orleans and control of the Mississippi that should have sufficed. Acquisition of Florida from Spain, he asserted, would have been "of far greater value to us than all the immense, undefined region west of the river." Hamilton concluded these reflections with a swipe at Monroe when he noted that the deal was concluded on April 8, 1803, while the envoy extraordinary did not arrive in Paris until April 12. Given Monroe's failed mission to France in 1794, "we really cannot but regard it as fortunate, that the thing was concluded before he reached St. Cloud."[17]

No matter how unwilling Hamilton was to give credit to Jefferson for the acquisition, and no matter how many caveats he made about the implications of the accession of this territory, he was in essential agreement with the president about the necessity of removing Louisiana from French control. In harboring this sentiment, he was out of step with his former followers from New England. Timothy Pickering, for example, was prepared then and later to speak of secession from a union whose center would be both Republican and Western. Dismemberment of the United States was abhorrent to Hamilton; he associated the idea with Aaron Burr's ambition to be the "chief of the Northern portion," when he warned fellow New York Federalists, in February 1804, against supporting Burr for governor.[18] His subsequent death in a duel with Burr less than six months later was a fatal consequence of his successful derailing of the vice president's efforts to take over leadership of the Federalist Party.

Biographers have been tempted to attribute Hamilton's death to a variety of reasons: a personality shaped by the circumstances of his birth, his romantic search for glory, or the memory of his eldest son killed in a duel in 1801 while defending his father's honor. That it was a needless tragedy was obvious. It is almost equally obvious that his political career had ended with Jefferson in power. His adversaries had appropriated much of the economic infrastructure he had put in place in the 1790s, and his allies had abandoned their leader when they rejected his persistent nationalism. Had he lived beyond his forty-ninth year, it is likely that he would have remained on the sidelines as a successful lawyer but also as a carping critic of Jefferson's inadequate embargo in 1807 and Madison's inept conduct of the war in 1812. Based on his record, his opposition rested on the tactics rather than the strategy of the Jeffersonians. American independence from the entangling ties of the Old World was as much a Hamiltonian as a Jeffersonian objective.

The paradigm of Jefferson versus Hamilton will always be a convenient and, for the most part, usable way of distinguishing between the two men, if not always between their differing approaches to government. Hamilton was impetuous where Jefferson was cautious; Hamilton reveled in the excitement of battle where Jefferson avoided conflict whenever possible. It is noteworthy that, at critical moments, Jefferson turned to Madison to respond to Hamilton; the latter never hesitated to speak for himself on any occasion. Jefferson's private life remained closed while Hamilton exposed his own; compare the ambiguities in the Virginian's relations with Maria Cosway and his silence about the place of Sally Hemings in his life with the New Yorker's susceptibilities to the charms of Benedict Arnold's wife and his confessions about his affair with Mrs. Reynolds.

Yet the opposing personalities repeatedly found a consensus in foreign relations. This is not to deny Hamilton's Anglophilia, which led to indiscreet disclosures to British ministers in the Washington administration. Nor can there be any denial of Jefferson's Francophilia, which once led him to welcome a French invasion of Britain in the same period. Each man, with some justice, accused the other of excessive partisanship for one or the other belligerent in the 1790s. But there was always a common ground on which the two statesmen stood at critical moments.

In retrospect, the first crisis over Nootka Sound revealed differences over how to respond to a potential British request for passage through American territory, not whether or not to grant permission. Similarly, the divisive issue of a neutrality proclamation in 1793 was modified by Jefferson's basic acceptance of the principle. In the quasi-war of 1798, Jefferson may have been leery of Hamilton's ambitions, but he had lost whatever illusions he had about France's imperialist ambitions. Throughout the Federalist decade, Hamilton displayed a wariness about the British connection that his rival would have appreciated had he known of those reservations.

Hamilton assumed that Jefferson as president would not tear down the structure he had been instrumental in building, even as he denigrated his abilities and disparaged his old ideological affinities. He was correct in his assumption. The irony of Jefferson's accomplishing through devious and fortuitous means what the Federalist leader failed to do directly was galling. The military academy (West Point) that the Inspector General wanted came into being under Jefferson's auspices; the funds to pay for the Louisiana Purchase were available because of Hamilton's fiscal policies; and the exploitation of Britain in pursuit of American interests had been a Federalist policy. It became apparent, though not credited by either party, that both statesmen intended to use their foreign friends to advance the independence of the United States from the political and economic grip of the two European superpowers. Herein was an unacknowledged consensus over the future of America's relations with Europe.

The Plutarchian image of parallel lives, celebrated by the Jeffersonian diplomat and biographer Claude Bowers, tended to obscure the contributions to the foundations of American foreign relations that Hamilton made prior to Jefferson's arrival on the scene. They were not all positive, and not simply because of a pro-British bias. Hamilton's inclination to elevate executive authority at the expense of the legislative as well as his willingness to use the army as an instrument of first resort offered an uncomfortable model for successors, even if such strategies were rarely exercised. But more essential in the development of foreign relations was the infrastructure he helped to establish—a solid economic foundation that won the respect of creditors, a banking system that provided the means of war, and a national government that had sufficient executive authority to deal with external challenges.

Hamilton was convinced that the fragile new nation could cope with external threats only by creating internal institutions that gave strength to a central government. A voracious reader in his youth, the New Yorker seemed to have assimilated the histories of the world's nations long before he expressed some of these ideas in *The Federalist Papers.* As early as 1780, the lieutenant colonel was advising his seniors that the Continental Congress was fatally flawed, and that the Congress of the Confederation was only marginally less flawed. As he told the New York leader, James Duane, the Confederation "is neither fit for war or peace. The idea of an uncontrollable [sic] sovereignty in each state, over its internal police, will defeat the other powers given to Congress, and make our union feeble and precarious."[19] Before the United States could deal successfully with Britain, France, or Spain, it had to have its house in order. Although Hamilton often emphasized domestic "order" at the expense of other prerequisites for a successful foreign policy, he identified the ways whereby a vulnerable new nation could survive in a hostile world.

Notes

1. Quoted in Cooke, *Alexander Hamilton*, 230.
2. AH to Gouverneur Morris, February 29, 1802, Syrett and Cooke, 25:544.
3. An Address to the Electors of the State of New-York, March 21, 1801, ibid., 352.
4. Ibid., 353.
5. Ibid., 363.
6. Ibid., 364.
7. Ibid., 365.
8. "The Examination, No. 1," December 17, 1801, ibid., 454.
9. Ibid., 456–57.
10. AH to Rufus King, June 3, 1803, ibid., 26:14–15.
11. Ibid., 11–12.
12. AH to C. C. Pinckney, December 29, 1802, ibid., 71.
13. *Annals of Congress*, 12:14.
14. AH to C. C. Pinckney, December 29, 1802, Syrett and Cooke, 26:71–72.
15. *New-York Evening Post*, February 8, 1803, ibid., 84–85.
16. Ibid., July 5, 1803, 129–30.
17. Ibid., 133, 136.
18. Speech at a Meeting of Federalists at Albany, February 10, 1804, ibid., 189.
19. AH to James Duane, September 3, 1780, ibid., 2:402.

Bibliographical Essay

The literature on Hamilton's life and career is vast. Although books concentrating on his influence on American foreign relations are relatively few in number, almost all his biographers touch in one way or another on his views of America's role in the world. Arguably, it was in the post–Civil War United States that Hamilton was hailed as the most important of the Founding Fathers. In the twentieth century, he had to compete with the rising reputation of his rival, Thomas Jefferson, often to his disadvantage. Claude G. Bowers, in *Jefferson and Hamilton: The Struggle for Democracy in America* (Chautauqua, NY: Chautauqua Press, 1927), was an early exemplar of a Jeffersonian bias that would grow stronger in the midtwentieth century. At the beginning of the twenty-first century, Jefferson's aura has dimmed more than Hamilton's, while John Adams has won the favor of popular historians such as David McCullough with *John Adams* (New York: Simon & Schuster, 2001), and academic historians such as Joseph T. Ellis with *Passionate Sage: The Character and Legacy of John Adams* (New York: Norton, 1993).

Given the primary role Hamilton played in the formation of the nation, it is likely that he will continue to attract the attention of scholars. They will have the benefit of the full correspondence of this Founding Father in a magisterial and authoritative edition. *The Papers of Alexander Hamilton*, ed. Harold C. Syrett and Jacob E. Cooke, 27 vols. (New York: Columbia University Press, 1961–1987), represents the most complete collection of his works. Letters written by Hamilton but signed by another (in his capacity as aide to General Washington) are identified. Letters from correspondents are included in this edition. Valuable exegetical commentary accompanies many of the documents. Two important editions preceded the Columbia project: John C. Hamilton, ed., *The Works of Alexander Hamilton*, 7 vols. (New York: D. Appleton, 1840), a reverential treatment by Hamilton's son of his father's writings; and Henry Cabot Lodge, ed., *The Works of Alexander Hamilton*, 12 vols. (New York: Putnam, 1904), an appreciation of Hamilton as the apostle of nationalism and industrialization. The specialized edition of Julius Goebel, *The Law Practice of Alexander Hamilton: Documents and Commentary*, 5 vols. (New York: Columbia University Press, 1964), is particularly useful for the foreign policy implications in his court cases.

Hamilton's prolific correspondence with the leaders of his time makes it worth noting the writings of his contemporaries, even though many of them are included in the Columbia volumes. Of special significance is John C. Fitzpatrick, ed., *The Writings of George Washington*, 39 vols. (Washington, DC: Government Printing Office, 1931–1944). Fitzpatrick identified letters and papers drafted by Hamilton but signed by Washington. Ultimately, the ambitious editorial project of the University Press of Virginia will replace the Fitzpatrick edition. It consists of five series, of which only the Retirement Series has been completed. Among his friends, John Jay, as a fellow New Yorker and early patron, deserves special mention. See Henry P. Johnston, ed., *The Correspondence and Public Papers of John Jay*, 4 vols. (New York: Putnam's, 1890–1893), which should be supplemented by Richard B. Morris et al., eds., *John Jay*, 2 vols. (New York: Harper & Row, 1975–1980). Another confidant was Rufus King, minister to Great Britain from 1796 to 1802, in Charles R. King, ed., *The Life and Correspondence of Rufus King*, 6 vols. (New York: Putnam's, 1894–1900).

Of his adversaries, James Madison is the most ambivalent in light of his collaboration in *The Federalist Papers*. See William T. Hutchinson et al., eds., *The Papers of James Madison*, 17 vols. through 1801 (Chicago: University of Chicago Press and Charlottesville: University Press of Virginia, 1962). There was less ambivalence in Jefferson's writings, in Adams's commentaries on Jefferson, or in the frosty and formal communications between Hamilton and his two rivals. See Julian Boyd et al., eds., *The Papers of Thomas Jefferson* (Princeton: Princeton University Press, 1950–); Charles Francis Adams, *Works of John Adams*, 10 vols. (Boston: Little, Brown, 1850–1856); and Robert J. Taylor et al., eds., *The Papers of John Adams* (Cambridge: Harvard University Press, 1979–).

Hamilton's contributions in legislative records may be seen in New York, *Journal of the Provincial Congress . . . Committee of Public Safety, 1775–77* (Albany: Thurlow Weed, 1942), and in United States Continental Congress, *Journals, 1774–1789*, 34 vols. (Washington, DC: Government Printing Office, 1904–1937). Mary Giunta and J. Dane Hartgrove, eds., *The Emerging Nation: A Documentary History of the Foreign Relations of the United States under the Articles of Con-*

federation, 1780–1789, 3 vols. (Washington, DC: National Historical Publications and Records Commission, 1996), shows Hamilton's relatively minor official roles in these years. U.S. Congress, *The Debates and Proceedings in the Congress of the United States, 1st to 18th Congresses, March 3, 1789–May 16, 1824*, 42 vols. (Washington, DC: Gales & Seaton, 1834–1856), better known as the *Annals of Congress*, displays Hamilton's influence in the early Congresses.

Other important documentary collections in which Hamilton plays major roles include Max Farrand, ed., *Records of the Federal Convention*, 4 vols. (New Haven: Yale University Press, 1911–1937); Carl Van Doren, ed., *The Federalist* (New York: Heritage Press, 1945); Frederick Jackson Turner, ed., *Correspondence of the French Ministers to the United States, 1791–1797*, in the Annual Report of the American Historical Association for 1903 (Washington, DC: Government Printing Office, 1904); and Bernard Mayo, ed., *Instructions to the British Ministers to the United States, 1791–1812*, in the Annual Report of the American Historical Association for 1936 (Washington, DC: Government Printing Office, 1941).

Hamilton's influence was evidenced in major secondary works on the Confederation and Federalist periods that I consulted. The most important recent study displaying Hamiltonian leanings is Stanley Elkins and Eric McKitrick, *The Age of Federalism: The Early American Republic, 1788–1800* (New York: Oxford University Press, 1993). Elkins and McKitrick's work replaces John C. Miller, *The Federalist Era, 1789–1801* (New York: Harper, 1960), which reflects a stronger Hamiltonian bias. Covering both the Revolutionary and Federalist eras is Lawrence S. Kaplan, *Colonies into Nation, 1763–1800* (New York: Macmillan, 1972). Bradford Perkins's first volume in his magisterial trilogy on Anglo-American relations in the early national years, *The First Rapprochement: England and the United States, 1795* (Berkeley: University of California Press, 1961), provides a balanced account of Hamilton's relations with Britain.

The Hamiltonian tilt in the above-listed volumes has not gone unchallenged. Bowers's entry in the 1920s paved the way for the next generation's elevation of Jefferson to the summit. Dumas Malone, *Jefferson and His Times*, 6 vols. (Boston: Little, Brown, 1948–1981), and Julian Boyd et al., eds., *Papers*, set the Jefferson tone in the midtwentieth century that was not modified until the 1990s. From the standpoint of foreign relations, two critical studies—Robert W. Tucker and David C. Hendrickson, *Empire of Liberty: The Statecraft of Thomas Jefferson* (New York: Oxford University Press, 1990), and Doron S. Ben-Atar, *The Origins of Jeffersonian Commercial Policy and Diplomacy* (New York: St. Martin's Press, 1993)—have a revisionist slant in Hamilton's favor.

Implicit rather than explicit in their endorsement of the Jeffersonian vision is Felix Gilbert, *To the Farewell Address: Ideas of Early American Foreign Policy* (Princeton: Princeton University Press, 1961), which finds the origins of American foreign policy more embedded in Jeffersonian idealism than in Hamiltonian realism. And Alexander DeConde's *Entangling Alliance: Politics and Diplomacy under George Washington* (Durham, NC: Duke University Press, 1958), and his *The Quasi-War: The Politics and Diplomacy of the Undeclared War with France, 1797–1801* (New York: Scribner's, 1966), two volumes in an impressive trilogy, place Hamilton at the center of American policy making without a concomitant acceptance of the wisdom of these policies. The most forthright Jeffersonian in this period is Albert H. Bowman, *The Struggle for Neutrality: Franco-American Diplomacy during the Federalist Era* (Knoxville: University of Tennessee Press, 1974), a vigorous argument that the Virginian's policies were more realistic than Hamilton's. More ambivalent on the subject is Lawrence S. Kaplan, *Thomas Jefferson: Westward the Course of Empire* (Wilmington, DE: Scholarly Resources, 1999.)

Hamilton's formative years were affected by senior Revolutionary leaders, most notably General Washington. Douglas S. Freeman, *George Washington: A Biography*, 7 vols. (New York: Scribner's, 1952), particularly volume 4, and James T. Flexner, *George Washington in the American Revolution*, 4 vols. (Boston: Little, Brown, 1968), are the standard works. Frank Monaghan does full justice to Hamilton's early patron in *John Jay, Defender of Liberty* (Indianapolis: Bobbs-Merrill, 1935). Richard B. Morris, *The Peacemakers: The Great Powers and American Independence* (New York: Hoper, 1965), makes Jay the prime mover among the American peacemakers. Louis R. Gottschalk, *Lafayette and the Close of the American Revolution* (Chicago: University of Chicago Press, 1942), examines Lafayette in America at a time when Hamilton was close to the French general. Among Revolutionary leaders, Don Gerlach, *A Proud Patriot: Philip Schuyler and the War of Independence, 1775–1783* (Syracuse: Syracuse University Press, 1987), is an admirer of Hamilton's supportive father-in-law. Biographies of Hamilton's fellow aides-de-camp offer insights into the young officer's life in this period. Among them was his closest friend, John Laurens, who appears in David D. Wallace, *The Life of Henry Laurens, with a Sketch of the Life of Lt. Col. John Laurens* (New York: Putnam's, 1915). Max M. Mintz, *Gouverneur Morris and the American Revolution*

(Norman: University of Oklahoma Press, 1970), offers a different perspective from another member of Washington's "family."

The literature of the Confederation contains at least two classic works: John Fiske, *The Critical Period in American History* (Boston: Houghton Mifflin, 1888), and Merrill Jensen, *The New Nation: A History of the United States during the Confederation, 1781–1789* (New York: Knopf, 1950). The former is an appreciation of the Constitution that saved a divided nation; the latter, a defense of the states' accomplishments under the Confederation. Clarence L. Ver Steeg, *Robert Morris: Revolutionary Financier* (Philadelphia: University of Pennsylvania Press, 1954), deals with Hamilton's financial ideas. A preview of Hamilton's future economic policies may be found in E. James Ferguson, *The Power of the Purse: A History of American Public Finance, 1776–1790* (Chapel Hill: University of North Carolina Press, 1961). The only work concentrating on foreign relations remains Frederick W. Marks III, *Independence on Trial: Foreign Affairs and the Making of the Constitution* (Baton Rouge: Louisiana State University Press, 1973). Hamilton is a marginal figure in all of these volumes despite his influence on such leaders as John Jay.

The Hamiltonian voice, however, is heard clearly in most studies of the Constitution and its ratification. Arguably, the most visible is still Charles A. Beard, *An Economic Interpretation of the Constitution* (New York: Macmillan, 1913), for whom Hamilton was the enemy of an agrarian America. A more traditional picture is presented in Max Farrand, *Framing of the Constitution* (New Haven: Yale University Press, 1921). Robert E. Brown, in *Charles Beard and the Constitution: A Critical Analysis of "An Economic Interpretation of the Constitution"* (Princeton: Princeton University Press, 1958), dissents. Jack Rakove, *James Madison and the Creation of the American Republic* (Glenview, IL: Scott, Foresman, 1990), gives pride of place to Madison, while Clinton Rossiter, *Alexander Hamilton and the Constitution* (New York: Harcourt, Brace & World, 1964), asserts Hamilton's primary role. Carl Van Doren, introduction, *The Federalist* (New York: Heritage Press, 1945), is one of many editions of the nation's most important essays in political philosophy. Frederick Mosteller and David L. Wallace, in *Inference and Disputed Authorship, The Federalist* (Reading, MA: Addison-Wesley, 1964), sort out the respective contributions of Hamilton, Madison, and Jay.

In Washington's first administration, Secretary of the Treasury Hamilton's program is favorably presented in Bray Hammond, *Banks and Politics in America from the Revolution to the Civil War* (Princeton: Princeton University Press, 1958); and in Herbert Sloan,

"Hamilton's Second Thoughts: Federalist Finance Revisited," in Doron Ben-Atar and Barbara Oberg, eds., *Federalists Reconsidered* (Charlottesville: University Press of Virginia, 1998). Ben-Atar's *Orgins of Jeffersonian Commercial Policy and Diplomacy* is, in effect, an endorsement of Hamilton's economic policies. Less favorably inclined is John R. Nelson Jr., *Liberty and Property: Political Economy and Policymaking in the New Republic, 1789–1812* (Baltimore: Johns Hopkins University Press, 1987), who judges that Hamilton's economic policies led the country into a neocolonial dependence on Britain. Thomas P. Slaughter, *The Whiskey Rebellion: Frontier Epilogue to the American Revolution* (New York: Oxford University Press, 1986), presents the aggressive side of Hamilton's persona.

The first serious crisis during Hamilton's tenure as secretary of the treasury, though aborted, was the Nootka Sound controversy in the Pacific Northwest. It has not attracted of itself much scholarly interest, and William R. Manning, ed., "The Nootka Sound Controversy," in the Annual Report of the American Historical Association for 1904 (Washington, DC: Government Printing Office, 1905), 279–478, remains the major resource. Two books on Spain and Britain, respectively, Warren L. Cook, *Flood Tide of Empire: Spain and the Pacific Northwest, 1543–1819* (New Haven: Yale University Press, 1973), and J. Leitch Wright Jr., *Britain and the American Frontier, 1783–1815* (Athens: University of Georgia Press, 1975), pay some attention to the issue. Samuel F. Bemis, *Pinckney's Treaty: America's Advantage from Europe's Distress, 1783–1800* (rev. ed., New Haven: Yale University Press, 1960), touches on the controversy, and his *Jay's Treaty, A Study in Commerce and Diplomacy* (rev. ed., New Haven: Yale University Press, 1962), deals with it more fully. Arthur P. Whitaker, *The Spanish-American Frontier, 1783–1795: The Westward Movement and the Spanish Retreat in the Mississippi Valley* (Lincoln: University of Nebraska Press, 1927), fits the Nootka Sound crisis into his thesis on the decline of Spain in America.

Hamilton was a more central figure in the American response to the French alliance and Anglo–French war. Julian P. Boyd, *Number 7: Alexander Hamilton's Secret Attempts to Control American Foreign Policy* (Princeton: Princeton University Press, 1964), exposes Hamilton as a British agent compromising Jefferson's foreign policies. Charles M. Thomas, *American Neutrality in 1793: A Study in Cabinet Government* (New York: Columbia University Press, 1931), emphasizes the limits of a neutral's freedom of action. Harry Ammon, *The Genet Mission* (New York: Norton, 1973), is the standard work on a mission that strengthened the Hamilton position at

Jefferson's expense. Buxton I. Kaufman, ed., *Washington's Farewell Address: The View from the Twentieth Century* (Chicago: Quadrangle, 1969), contains essays that identify the changing interpretations of the address and its authors.

The two major treaties of the midnineties, Jay's and Pinckney's, have undergone thorough examinations. Samuel F. Bemis, *Jay's Treaty*, with its ambivalent view of Hamilton's role, is still the standard. Jerald A. Combs, *The Jay Treaty: Political Battleground of the Founding Fathers* (Berkeley: University of California Press, 1970), complements the Bemis book with its emphasis on the domestic political scene. Bemis is equally authoritative in his *Pinckney's Treaty* in emphasizing that Europe's, particularly Spain's, distress over the possible implications of the Jay treaty was to America's advantage. Arthur P. Whitaker's *Spanish-American Frontier* explains Spain's concessions in Pinckney's Treaty in terms of American pressures in the West.

The standard work on the XYZ imbroglio that opened the first crisis of the Adams administration is William C. Stinchcombe, *The XYZ Affair* (Westport, CT: Greenwood, 1981). Marvin R. Zahniser, *Charles Cotesworth Pinckney, Founding Father* (Chapel Hill: University of North Carolina Press, 1965); Albert J. Beveridge, *The Life of John Marshall*, 4 vols. (Boston: Houghton Mifflin, 1916–1919); and George A. Billias, *Elbridge Gerry: Founding Father and Elder Statesman* (New York: McGraw-Hill, 1976), cover the ill-fated mission that inspired the XYZ Affair. Peter P. Hill, *William Vans Murray, Federalist Diplomat: The Shaping of Peace with France, 1797–1801* (Syracuse: Syracuse University Press, 1971) illuminates a key figure in moving President Adams toward a new mission to France. Samuel F. Bemis, *John Quincy Adams and the Foundations of American Foreign Policy* (New York: Knopf, 1949), touches on Adams's role in this classic study. James E. Lewis Jr., *John Quincy Adams: Policymaker for the Union* (Wilmington, DE: Scholarly Resources, 2001), is a worthy addition to the list of John Quincy Adams biographies.

The quasi-war was a critical time for Hamilton's ambitions. His military plans are fully described in Richard H. Kohn, *Eagle and Sword: The Federalists and the Creation of the Military Establishment in America* (New York: Free Press, 1975). Hamilton's dalliance with the Venezuelan adventurer Francisco de Miranda is noted in William S. Robertson, *Life of Miranda*, 2 vols. (Chapel Hill: University of North Carolina Press, 1929). James R. Jacobs, *Tarnished Warrior: Major-General James Wilkinson* (New York: Macmillan, 1938), notes the uncomfortable relationship between Hamilton and Wilkinson in 1798. Bernard C. Steiner, ed., *The Life and Correspondence of James McHenry, Secretary of War under Washington and Adams* (Cleveland: Burrows, 1907), and Gerald H. Clarfield, *Timothy Pickering and American Diplomacy, 1795–1800* (Columbia: University Press of Missouri, 1969), present the roles of Hamilton's loyalists in Adams's cabinet.

Much of the literature on Hamilton's conflict with John Adams tilts to the president's position, both with respect to the build-up of an army and the termination of the Franco–American alliance. This interpretation is evident in older biographies such as Stephen G. Kurtz, *The Presidency of John Adams: The Collapse of Federalism, 1795–1800*, and Ralph A. Brown, *The Presidency of John Adams* (Lawrence: University Press of Kansas, 1975). More recent studies at the beginning of the twenty-first century reinforce the revival of Adams's reputation at the expense of both Hamilton and Jefferson. Joseph J. Ellis, *The Founding Brothers: The Revolutionary Generation* (New York: Knopf, 2001), accentuates the esteem he expressed in *Passionate Sage*, while David McCullough's *John Adams* elevates him above the other founding brothers. Much of this attention derives from appreciation of the president's role in achieving the Convention of Mortefontaine. The election of 1800 has attracted Bernard A. Weisberger, *America Afire: Jefferson, Adams, and the Revolutionary Election of 1800* (New York: Morrow, 2000), who celebrates the peaceful transfer of power. Hamilton's name is not in the subtitle, but his positions are visible throughout the book.

Jefferson's foreign policies inspired extensive negative commentaries from Hamilton in his last years. Robert Ernst, *Rufus King: An American Federalist* (Chapel Hill: University of North Carolina Press, 1968), reflects Hamilton's ambivalence as King temporarily remained minister to Britain in 1801. For the Louisiana Purchase, Alexander DeConde, *This Affair of Louisiana* (New York: Scribner's, 1976), suggests an American imperialist motive that Hamilton might have accepted. Not surprisingly, the tragic death of Hamilton at the hands of Aaron Burr has always found commentators. Thomas P. Abernathy, *The Burr Conspiracy* (New York: Oxford University Press, 1954), typifies the interpretation of Burr as villain. More recent interpretations have been more sympathetic to Burr, at least in his relations with Hamilton. Arnold A. Rogow, *A Fatal Friendship: Alexander Hamilton and Aaron Burr* (New York: Hill and Wang, 2000), sees little distinction in virtue between the two statesmen, while Roger G. Kennedy, *Burr, Hamilton, and Jefferson* (New York: Oxford University Press, 2000), provides a title that ranks Burr before Hamilton and Jefferson. Thomas Fleming, *Duel: Alexander Hamilton, Aaron Burr, and the Future of America* (New York: Basic Books, 1999), suggests that the duel cut off opportunities for both men, but particularly Burr, to serve their country as "Republicanism tottered into political futility in the hands of Jefferson's inept successor."

Hamilton's biographers have become more sophisticated since the simplistic tribute of Henry Cabot Lodge, *Alexander Hamilton* (Boston: Houghton Mifflin, 1898). The twentieth century witnessed the appearance of numerous studies, many of them finely nuanced. James T. Flexner, *The Young Hamilton: A Biography* (Boston: Little, Brown, 1978), and Broadus Mitchell, *Alexander Hamilton: Youth to Maturity, 1755–1788* (New York: Macmillan, 1957), are good introductions to the early years. Mitchell has written the most thorough multiple-volume. Useful for the present work has been his *Alexander Hamilton: A Concise Biography* (New York: Oxford University Press, 1976). Nathan Schachner, *Alexander Hamilton* (New York: A. S. Barnes & Co., 1946), provides a lively and sympathetic account of his life. Even more supportive is Forrest McDonald, *Alexander Hamilton* (New York: Oxford University Press, 1958). More critical is John C. Miller, *Alexander Hamilton: Portrait in Paradox* (New York: Harper, 1959). A recent biographical contribution is Richard Brookhiser, *Alexander Hamilton: American* (New York: Free Press, 1999), a well-written, if self-consciously conservative, appreciation. The most useful biography for the purpose of this study is the slim but authoritative volume of Jacob E. Cooke, *Alexander Hamilton* (New York: Scribner's, 1982). Cooke was also co-editor of the comprehensive Columbia University edition of the Hamilton Papers. Two edited books offer insightful commentaries: Milton Cantor, ed., *Hamilton* (Englewood Cliffs, NJ: Prentice-Hall, 1971), and Mary-Jo Kline, ed., *Alexander Hamilton: A Biography in His Own Words* (New York: Harper, 1973).

Studies centering on Hamilton's role in foreign relations include Helen Johnson Looze, *Alexander Hamilton and the British Orientation of American Foreign Policy* (The Hague: Mouton, 1969), an uncritical and unsatisfactory treatment of Hamilton's positions. More satisfactory and more thorough, but still too partisan, is Gilbert L. Lycan, *Alexander Hamilton and American Foreign Policy: A Design for Greatness* (Norman: University of Oklahoma Press, 1970). The most perceptive analyses of Hamilton's conceptions of foreign relations were the products of two political scientists. Gerald Stourzh, *Alexander Hamilton and the Idea of Representative*

Government (Stanford: Stanford University Press, 1970), is a paean to Hamilton's realism in fabricating a powerful state based on a Hobbesian Weltanschauung. A new entry with a similarly appreciative evaluation of Hamilton's contributions to America's security is Karl-Friedrich Walling, *Republican Empire: Alexander Hamilton on War and Free Government* (Lawrence: University Press of Kansas, 1999), in which Walling notes that the reality of the French menace in the 1790s did not undermine Hamilton's attachment to republican institutions.

Index